ODYSSEY

OF AN ARTIST

FOR SANDY

ISBN 13: 978-1-4621-3575-2

Published by Plain Sight Publishing, an imprint of Cedar Fort, Inc.
2373 W. 700 S., Springville, UT 84663
Distributed by Cedar Fort, Inc., www.cedarfort.com

Library of Congress Control Number: 2020931141

Cover design by Shawnda T. Craig
Interior Design by Shawnda T. Craig

Printed in the United States of America

10 9 8 7 6 5 4 3 2 1

Printed on acid-free paper

ODYSSEY
OF AN ARTIST

THE ART AND LIFE OF
KARL MOMEN

Silent Witness to Political Turmoil in the Middle East

HERMAN DU TOIT, PhD

PLAIN SIGHT PUBLISHING
AN IMPRINT OF CEDAR FORT, INC.
SPRINGVILLE, UTAH

PRAISE FOR ODYSSEY OF AN ARTIST

"Herman du Toit has wonderfully told this story of a singular life, wholly dedicated to art, in a riveting manner that makes this well-researched study engrossing reading. It is a truism that every eminent artist must have a quintessential piece d'resistance that epitomizes his or her entire oeuvre. Examples may be seen in Michelangelo's Sistine Chapel, Frederic Auguste Bartholdi's Statue of Liberty, or Pablo Picasso's *Guernica*. Such was the case with Momen's 87-foot-high *Tree of Utah* on the Salt Flats in north-western Utah."

"Momen, while crossing the Salt Flats, had a numinous experience. Such transformative encounters come rarely, but always with a mandate to action, and so one of Utah's most significant works of art came about—through the prescience, tremendous energy, and enthusiasm of one man. Momen's altruistic nature and the spiritual resonance of this work of art struck a cord with those associated with the Art and Belief Movement and helped make the *Tree* a reality. Du Toit has perceptively understood that Karl Momen's art was not abstractly isolated from life, but touched on the greatest issues of our day and perhaps of all time."

—Vern G. Swanson (PhD, Courtauld Institute of Art, University of London) former director of the Springville Museum of Art in Utah.

CONTENTS

CONTENTS

ACKNOWLEDGMENTS

I express my profound gratitude to my former colleagues at the Brigham Young University Museum of Art, especially Virgie Day and the late James Mason, who originally granted me the opportunity to curate an early exhibition of Karl Momen's work at the museum in the summer of 1995. This exhibition introduced me to this remarkable artist and the creation of his enigmatic sculpture, the *Tree of Utah*, in the Great Western Desert.

I thank Karl Momen for the many hours of interviews he granted me as I prepared this account of his remarkable life, his prodigious oeuvre, his engagement with Middle Eastern powers and of his dealings with Utah's art establishment in building his iconic *Tree of Utah*.

I am grateful for the support I received from local conservationists, environmental educators, legislators, public officials, entrepreneurs, and arts administrators, for Karl Momen's vision for a Visitor and Environmental Interpretive Center at the site of the *Tree of Utah*. The Center would showcase the history, conservation, and future of the Great Salt Lake and the Bonneville Salt Flats and tell the story of the Tree, its creator, and its architectural significance as the only Bauhaus structure of its kind in the Western United States. Specifically I would like to thank Rep. Merrill Nelson, Rep. Norman Thurston, and Rep. Timothy Hawks, of the Utah House of Representatives; Carlos Braceras, executive director of Utah Department of Transportation; Lynn de Freitas, executive director of Friends of the Great Salt Lake; Jim Russell, director of Utah's Division of Facilities and Construction Management; Kent Singleton, past president of Bonneville Salt Flats Racing Association; Patti White, curriculum specialist with Granite School District; Alex Porpora, executive director: Utah Society for Environmental Education; Shawn Milne, Tooele County Commissioner; Paul Monson, president of Institute of Classical Architecture and Art; Garth Norman, director, Archeological Research Consultants; Crystal Young-Otterstrom, executive director Utah Cultural Alliance; Chris Layton of Layton Davis Architects; Donna Neri-Wells, coordinator Utah's Business Enterprise Program; Steve and Tonia Grogan of Grogan Vending, and Kevin Hunt CEO of New Concepts Construction, to name but a few.

And most auspiciously, to Sandy my wife, for her gentle sustaining influence throughout this project.

FOREWORD

This account reflects more than the life an individual artist. Rather, it defines the trajectory of events and circumstances that coalesce around the artistry that is the focus of a life. This study encompasses a journey through both time and place, as it outlines how today's world was shaped by war and peace, by statecraft and democratic elections, and through petty disputes between individuals, corporations, and principalities. It seems as though Karl Momen often sits in the eye of the storm. However, not content with waiting in the lull, he carefully records all that swirls in the violent turbulence that surrounds him.

Born and raised in Northern Iran, which at the time had a porous border with the Soviet Union, he had early exposure to the contemporary art that was part of the Russian revolution. In his home city of Mashhad, he was not only exposed to such avant-garde artworks, but he also met several of the Russian artists who had found refuge in Momen's homeland, away from the turmoil of the civil war that raged in the Soviet Union. Another source of inspiration came in the form of the American movies that reached his city, and for which he was often commissioned to paint promotional billboards. This experience in all likelihood contributed to the cosmopolitan worldview that became his—with Iran, Germany, Sweden, the oil states in the Persian Gulf, California, Florida, and Utah becoming a few of his places of activity.

Although art posed a strong attraction for him, he realized, partly because of a push from his family, that training in architecture would open doors to a more secure livelihood. The account of how he arrived in Stuttgart with little money, but through the confluence of a set of fortuitous circumstances found himself in the right company with access to professional training and quick employment, is akin to reading a modern version of *The Boy with the Golden Pants*—Max Lundgren's classic adventure story of a boy who stumbles upon a pair of pants containing an unlimited amount of money.

Training at architecture school in Stuttgart also meant that he had close contact with the modern art world—a world that was working hard to regain its footing in a postwar Europe. The new Germany took up traditions from the Bauhaus. Oskar Schlemmer (1888–1943), who was born in Stuttgart, had a retrospective exhibition in Stuttgart in 1959, which made a strong impression on Karl Momen. Max Ernst was a close friend of his teacher at the art academy and often visited the school. These visits led to Ernst becoming a friend and mentor to Karl Momen. It was through Ernst that Momen was introduced simultaneously to both prewar art and modernism.

The Germany he encountered when he arrived from Iran consisted largely of piles of ruble and bombed-out ruins. He unwittingly became a cog in the activity that transformed this broken country into a prosperous federal republic with such speed and alacrity. Karl Momen's contribution to the process centered on his designing of modern hospitals. This was the specialty that quite quickly landed him a position at an architect's office in Stockholm, and he became a Swedish citizen. Sweden also found itself at the beginning of the 1960s in an expansive phase of social development toward a welfare state where job opportunities were abundant. However, even though employment as an architect provided a good and stable income, the lure of painting and sculpture did not cease, and this would, as the 1960s progressed, take up an ever-increasing part of his life.

Karl Momen once received advice from Max Ernst to go his own way and to give no heed to what the world expected of the contemporary artist. The fact that his skill as an architect influenced his paintings is undeniable. The images of rooms and buildings are depicted with spatial clarity in his scrupulous compositions. For a person with his humanistic predisposition, the exposure to European theater and classical music became a crucial influence in his life. In a series of paintings, he explored both Richard Wagner's music and William Shakespeare's theater. These suites resulted in graphic interpretations with iconic overtones.

THE *TREE OF UTAH*

The focal point of Karl Momen's life's work, and that which in recent years has taken a great deal of his attention and energy, is the *Tree of Utah*, dedicated in 1986. This sculpture is eighty-seven feet high, built of steel reinforced concrete, and is the only vertical element in a desolate landscape where practically nothing grows for many miles around. Utah's Great Salt Lake is an attraction in itself, although a rather barren one.

At the time of writing, Karl Momen, the artist, architect, and entrepreneur, has been meeting with both federal and local government officials to create a museum and interpretive center at his *Tree*, which is already a popular destination despite the fact that traffic is forbidden to stop along the federal highway that passes by the sculpture. That will now be changed.

FOREWORD

The sculpture is a manifesto, with Constructivist antecedents, and with an unwillingness to be constrained by any form of restriction on the expression of essential human spirit. The *Tree of Utah* is a synopsis of what Karl Momen did in painting and sculpture over more than half a century as an artist. It is also a quiet tribute to the Russian artists he met in his youth who came to his country to gain energy and resolve to continue their missions.

Special meaning arises for the *Tree* through its relative proximity to Robert Smithson's *Spiral Jetty* that lies in the Great Salt Lake. Starting points and expressions for both works are far apart from each other. However, Smithson spoke for them both when he wrote, "The desert is less 'nature' than a concept, a place that swallows up boundaries. When the artist goes to the desert, he enriches his absence and burns off the water (paint) on his brain. The slush of the city evaporates from the artist's mind as he installs his art . . . a consciousness of the desert operates between craving and satiety."[1]

In this case, the same desert has challenged two temperaments with completely different life experiences. A large part of Smithson's work was based on the concept of entropy. He sought out and constructed at places where energies were leveled against a zero point, and where he witnessed how the earth, in the broadest sense, took back the material it made available to humanity. His *Spiral Jetty* disappears occasionally under the Great Salt Lake's surface and during some seasons can only be seen from a bird's eye view. With time, erosion will complete the entropic process and the work will disappear completely. Nothing says a "tree" constructed in concrete in this desolate and salty environment has an eternal life. However, its defiant verticality brings with it a legacy of the early twentieth century belief that circumstances can be overcome, that one can build oneself up from what appears to be an infertile or barren situation. In the tension between *Spiral Jetty* and *The Tree of Utah,* the world becomes greater. It also becomes more expansive when one follows the journey of Karl Momen's life through war and reconstruction, through despair and democracy, and across continents with completely different cultural orientations.

—Olle Granath
Former Permanent Secretary of the Royal Academy of Fine Arts, Stockholm

Pastel rendering of the Tree of Utah *during its early planning stages,* 1982

INTRODUCTION

Karl Momen traveled from Iran and enrolled as an impressionable nineteen-year-old student at the Kunstakademie in Stuttgart, Germany, in 1953. He quickly adopted a European lifestyle and worldview. Upon graduating as an architect, he moved to Stockholm, Sweden, where he practiced as a successful designer of hospitals in the Middle East. However, he soon relinquished his architectural profession to embark on his true vocation as an artist, working in the United States. As an Iranian-born, Swedish-American artist with an oeuvre spanning five decades, his paintings and sculptures have been exhibited at museums and galleries on three continents. His life experience in negotiating contrasting cultures and political systems in one of the most strife-torn regions of the world and his Bauhaus-inspired training in art and architecture became the underlying scaffolding for his Constructivist aesthetic.

A confirmed bachelor, he never married. Working as an artist became his all consuming passion. His critics have referred to him as the "vagabond" of the contemporary art world. He never employed an agent to promote his art, nor been much concerned with the ephemeral stylistic shifts of the contemporary art market. He remained true to the initiation he received early in his career into the modernist paradigm that still informs his distinctive style to the present day.

At the time of writing, Momen is one of the most long-lived exponents of early twentieth-century Geometric Abstraction, a movement that typified the work of artists such as Kasimir Malevich (1879–1935), Vladimir Tatlin (1885–1953), and El Lissitzky (1890–1941) during the heydays of the Suprematist and Constructivist art movements. The work of these artists and their compatriots was widely influential throughout Europe and led to the establishment of the Bauhaus in Germany and the DeStijl group in Holland. These groups also ushered in the International Style in architecture—a style that spread throughout the world, becoming the dominant architectural style until the 1970s. As a student, Momen had also worked as an intern with Le Corbusier, the father of the International Style, at his studio in the south of France.

These artists, and the art movements they initiated, became the motivating catalyst for the young Momen when, shortly after World War II, he enrolled for art and architecture studies in Germany. It was within this cultural milieu that the young Karl Momen gained his first impressions of the most significant avant-garde art of his day. In time, his art would become the product of a unique synthesis of these cosmopolitan influences. He would produce paintings, buildings, and sculptures that exemplified the most enduring characteristics of these modern art movements in their most iconic forms.

Karl's life is significant also for the range and extent of his socio-political experience. He was born into a large extended family and raised by Persian parents, with a father of Russian descent, near the Russian border in Iran. He experienced, first hand, the effects of political intrigue and economic strife at a pivotal period during this region's history. Throughout his career he often had to negotiate the troubled waters of political and financial self-interest. Notwithstanding the cultural ethos into which he was born, he quickly transcended the turmoil of a strife-torn society, and he was readily assimilated into the western world of sophisticated professionalism. Although his art became his first love, he developed an abiding passion for the opera that sustained him throughout his life.

The geometric abstraction of Karl's work operated as a welding link between western and occidental cultural forces at a time when there was little else that served to mitigate the political divisiveness in this region. However, his art rises above the soullessness of pure formalism. In spite of its abstraction, his art engages us because of the constant tension we find between the cool, rationally conceived compositions and the dynamic use of color and texture that enliven familiar shapes with the passion of a warm and sensitive human spirit. He is ever cognizant of the viewer as a sentient being. His emphasis on balance, control, composition, and craft is counterbalanced by the spontaneity and freshness of scintillating color and texture.

Just as Paul Cézanne maintained "art is a harmony parallel to nature," so has Momen created his own universe of balanced forces held in perfect equilibrium, a tribute to his Bauhaus-inspired training—in a world that is not far removed from our own. His bright compositions and Utopian vision continue to impress with amazing resilience and inviting familiarity.

Chapter 1

AT ORIGIN

Karl Momen was born to Persian parents in Mashhad, Iran, in 1934, the son of a famous rug designer and producer. Although named Karim at birth and raised by that name, he later changed his first name to Karl when he moved to Europe as a young adult. Iran stands at the crossroads of East and West, with a rich cultural heritage that extends back to the dawn of civilization. Formerly known as Persia, its territory stretched from India to the Mediterranean Sea. For centuries the Persian Empire greatly influenced both Asian and European civilizations. Most Iranians are descendants of people who originally came from the vicinity of the Aral Sea in Central Asia. The most important of these peoples were the Medes and the Persians, who settled in this region over four thousand years ago and later established the Persian Empire that flourished until the third century AD.

Under the rule of Cyrus the Great, Persia was the first country that succeeded in unifying all of what is known today as the Middle East and became one of the world's first highly organized states. In the seventh century, Arab Muslims took control of Persia, bringing an end to its Golden Age, and introduced Islam to the Persian people. Between the tenth and sixteenth centuries, Persian writers such as Firdausi, Saadi, Jami, Rumi, and Omar Khayyàm contributed some of the world's finest literature. During the Qajar dynasty of the nineteenth century, Persia grew weaker, suffering economic failure as well as losses of large areas of territory in the north to Russia. In 1907, Russia and Britain created zones of influence in Persia, with Britain in the south, Russia in the north, and a neutral area between the two. Later during World War I, the country was further weakened when it was used as a battleground by the warring powers.

The stormy history of this embattled nation continued into the twentieth century when, under the rule of Reza Khan, the name of the country was changed to Iran. Kahn's son, Mohammed Reza, became Shah in 1941 and tried to advance the industrialization and modernization of the country begun by his father. Sweeping reforms were financed by the large income Iran received from its oil reserves. But the Shah moved too quickly for some, and in 1979 he was deposed. Students rejected the Shah's absolute rule, and Muslim leaders feared that he was undermining traditional religious values. The Ayatohla Khomeni, who had long been in exile in France, became the leading figure of the revolution that returned the country to fundamentalist Muslim rule.

Modern-day Iran is located on a high plateau in southwestern Asia encircled by high, rugged mountains. Situated between the Caspian Sea and the Persian Gulf, the country is bordered by Iraq and Turkey to the east, Russia to the north, and Afghanistan and Pakistan to the west. Iranians have had a strong artistic tradition that has manifest itself in book illustrations and in painted miniatures on ivory and bone. The Persian craft of rug weaving is world renowned, as is the quality of the intricately designed silverware, jewelry, and brass artifacts that have been made in this region for many centuries.

Momen was raised in Mashhad, a city of 1.5 million inhabitants, situated in the northeastern corner of Iran not far from the Russian border. Mashhad is one of the oldest known cities and the most important holy city of Islam in Iran. It is reputed that Alexander the Great passed through the city on his travels to the north. Every year hundreds of thousands of Muslim pilgrims visit its famous Imam Reza shrine and the ruins of Haroun Al Rashid's summer palace. Central to this pilgrimage is the tomb of the eighth Imam Reza, who died here in AD 818. The city is also the commercial and agricultural hub of this region, producing wheat and traditional rugs from local wool. The city has the largest sugar refinery in the country and is situated in the major wheat-producing region of Iran. This region is also renowned for its fruit production and has become a major exporter of dried fruit to Europe.

Karl's paternal great-grandfather was Russian and moved to Persia from Georgia, Ukraine, at the end of the eighteenth century. Like many Russians and Jews at that time, he passed around the Caspian Sea, traveling through Urzibakistan, Turkmenistan, and Bokkara, to eventually settle in Mashhad. His grandfather was a fine shawl manufacturer and spent much of his time traveling in order to market his products. Karl's father, Hadjiabdul, grew up in Mashhad and often traveled with his father on excursions to the Baku, Tbilisi, and Bokkara regions. Hadjiabdul started producing Persian rugs early in his life, and by the beginning of the twentieth century was one of the major producers of Persian rugs in Mashhad. Although his professional name was Hadjabdol Momen, he became known as "Hadjagha," a name reserved for venerated and respected members of the community. He specialized in large rugs for the Persian aristocracy and for export to the courts of Europe, Russia, and Austria. During the early 1900s, before the First World War, one of his most prominent customers was Calouste Gulbenkian, the foremost oil magnate of the day. A large number of fine rugs were produced for his European courts. Some of these rugs have been well preserved and can be seen in the Gulbenkian Museum in Lisbon to this day. Hadjagha was married twice and had several children by each of his successive wives. Karl's mother was of an old and aristocratic Persian family in Mashhad. Together she and Hadjagha established an enduring marriage. Karl was born on April 3, 1934, just one year before the ruler Reza Khan changed the name of the country to Iran. He was the youngest of fourteen children, born after his father's eightieth birthday.

When Karl was four years old, his father sold the rug factory to the Iranian Rug Company, with an agreement that his services would be retained as a paid consultant for the remainder of his life—he died twenty years later at the age of 104 years! During these early years, Karl believed that his mother was his grandmother and his father was his grandfather because of their advanced age. Throughout their lives he would refer to them as "grandpa" and "grandma." Most of his nephews and nieces were older than he was. His parental home was comfortable but never ostentatious. The family had moved into a large converted mansion before Karl was born as a result of his father's financial hardship. Hadjagha had suffered a financial reversal due to his support of Colonel Mohammad-Khan Persian, one of the founders of Iranian democracy. Pessian was murdered when Reza Shah came to power, and many of Hadjagha's carpets were confiscated as retribution for his support of Pessian.

Although reduced in size, the home was large and commodious enough to accommodate Karl's extended family in several buildings surrounding a large stone-lined pool that provided welcome relief from the debilitating summer heat. Situated in the northeastern part of the town, on a wide birch-lined boulevard, the home was adjacent to Hadjagh's rug factory and even comprised a row of street-front shops on the main boulevard. Being raised in a large extended family provided a secure, happy, and gregarious environment for Karl's childhood years.

The only artworks that were displayed in his parental home were a few small copies of traditional Persian miniature paintings and two or three icon-like depictions: one of the prophet Daniel in the lion's den, and another of the Virgin Mary with the infant Jesus on her lap. Karl always found it curious that his home contained Christian images instead of the customary depictions of Mohammed that were found in other Muslim homes. Nearby were a teachers' training college and the American Hospital that was staffed and operated by Americans. His neighbors were merchants, bankers, and bazaar keepers. Most were Russian immigrants who had fled the Bolshevik Revolution. Many had migrated from Caucasia and Armenia. Some were Orthodox Christian, others Jewish. All contributed to the rich worshipful life of this community. Hadjagha could speak both Russian and Turkish and would often have long conversations with his multi-cultural neighbors. Karl's home language was Farsi, the official Iranian language. Significantly, his family was not overtly religious and did not align with the prevailing Islamic faith. Rather, Hadjaga would immerse himself in the classical literature of the Persian writers and the prophets of the Old Testament, particularly the book of Kings, or Shahname, since this text is known in the Persian culture. As a child, Karl would often sit at his father's side as he worked at intricate rug designs or decorative wall patterns with the aid of an eyeglass. He would marvel at the stories he heard his father tell on these occasions. Hadjagha had a remarkable memory and would spend hours reciting the poetry of Ferdowsi and whole chapters from the book of Kings.

On winter evenings when it was cold and the nights were long and dark, the family would sit around the warming heat of a samovar in the absence of modern distractions. Hadjaga would smoke his pipe and recite from the Persian poets for several hours on end. He would often recite a few hundred verses without a break. These were memorable days for Karl although he was no more than six or seven years old at the time.

Karl considered himself favored because his father had never spent so much time with his other children, and he had never told the others so many stories of his own youth. In earlier years Hadjaga had been more active with his rug factory, and he had not granted himself much time at home with his children. The old patriarch had a lucid and perceptive mind, and he would often engage Karl in long discussions as he taught him of his past. Karl felt especially privileged since he came to know more about his family's history than his older brothers and sisters. His siblings considered their father old, and they were not prepared to take the time to sit with him and listen to the wonderful tales of their family history.

However, Karl was different. He was in awe of his father's striking appearance. He had piercing blue eyes and close-cropped white hair. He regularly dyed his beard a rich chestnut red with the juice of henna leaves to remove any trace of gray. Karl noticed that some of his nieces and nephews had the same striking blue eyes.

Some were blonde, and some had chestnut red hair, just like his father's beard.

The day after Karl was born, his father sat in the local teahouse, listening to a recitation from the book of the Kings, as was his custom. It was then that the thought came to him that he should name his newborn son "Korosh" after Cyrus the Great, the first king of the ancient Persian Empire. However, when Karl's aged mother went to register her newborn son, she had forgotten the name, and the baby was given instead the more common name "Karim," a popular Persian name. Karl never liked this name, especially after his father told him in later years that he should have received the name of a Persian king. Eventually, when he was old enough, he changed his given name to Karl. His father died in 1958 at the advanced age of 104 years.

Karl's first recollection of seeing an oil painting was when he was only four years old. It was a hot summer's day, and his mother had taken him along with her to visit his eldest sister. She was married to a prominent regional politician who lived in one of the largest houses in the city and drove one of the few automobiles. Although it was customary to take a nap after lunch, especially in the summer, Karl's mother and sister continued to chat quietly while his brother-in-law rested in the bedroom. Karl's mother had put down a blanket in one of the adjoining reception halls, anticipating that he too would take a nap. It was the biggest room that he had ever seen at his tender age. The room had many Persian rugs and sumptuous furnishings that he came to know in later years to be of art deco in style. The ceiling was covered in stucco leaves and flowers in various colors above the hanging chandeliers. Karl's attention was drawn to the radiance of the multifaceted crystal ball suspended beneath one of the chandeliers. This house was a world removed from his own home, which was built in the traditional Persian manner with plain ceilings supported by rustic wooden beams that were carved and painted with geometric motifs. Karl's home was illuminated by simple kerosene lamps. This was not an uncommon condition, and in later life, Karl often pointed out that former President Jimmy Carter also grew up without electricity in his hometown in the United States during these years.

He lay quietly looking up at the ceiling, his eyes moving slowly back and forth over the ornate ceiling in wonderment. When his eyes fell on one of the walls, the first thing he saw was a huge gilt-framed painting. The young boy was awestruck. This painting would leave an indelible impression on his young mind. He would always remember the impressive old man with white hair and a white beard depicted in the painting. The man wore a blue jacket and purple-red boots. He stood in an upright position, holding the head of a partly clothed young boy with curly black hair, with his left hand. In the man's right hand was a dagger, poised above the boy, as if he was about to stab the boy. Karl then noticed another little boy, with blond hair and blue eyes, floating in the background. This angelic figure was restraining the man's arm with one hand while gesturing toward a goat in the background.

CHAPTER 1

He would never come to know the origin of this splendid depiction of Abraham and Isaac. At that moment his enraptured gaze would not leave the painting's surface, and he lay motionless. Not a sound escaped his lips. He lay transfixed on the floor, observing every detail of the scene depicted before him. It was the most marvelous vision he had ever seen. He was so amazed and absorbed that he became oblivious to the passage of time. Karl had always been an active child from an early age, and he consistently avoided taking afternoon naps by humming or singing as he whiled away the time. Now his mother and sister, who had been conversing quietly in the adjoining room for over an hour, became concerned with Karl's silence and, suspecting that something was amiss, rushed to the room where they found him lying on his back, motionlessly staring at the painting on the wall.

Concerned with this uncharacteristic behavior, the women moved the boy from the large hall to the adjoining dining room, close to where they were sitting, and laid him down again. This room was equally well appointed, but the curtains were open before the large windows, allowing the light to stream in. Here Karl became aware of yet two more paintings. One was a dark painting of an early ocean schooner tossed on a stormy sea. The sails of the ship were torn, and he glimpsed a lighthouse in one corner of the painting. The severity of the storm and the perilous state of the ship evoked emotions of fear and terror in the boy's impressionable young mind. The scene was completely believable to him and became etched in his memory. The other painting was of a winter landscape with a team of horses pulling two men and two women on a sleigh. He could see the powder snow billowing up behind the sleigh as it coursed across the winter terrain. With his gaze he explored the vista of snow-tipped birches in the background. The experience of seeing these paintings had totally entranced Karl, and the memory of this hot summer afternoon would always remain with him.

Many years later he would discover that Aivazovsky, a popular nineteenth-century Russian marine painter, had painted the picture of the schooner in distress. The painting of the winter sleigh scene was by Ilja Repin and was sold some years later for a handsome sum when Karl's brother-in-law moved to Tehran to take up a parliamentary position. A few days after this seminal experience, Mahmud, Karl's adult brother took him to the Kohsangi city public park to see the gardens and fountains in the center of the city. Surrounding the large ornate pool were a series of nude and partially clothed figures in Neoclassical style. This was his first encounter with sculpture, and this experience left an equally indelible impression on his young mind. These marvelous figures were destroyed some years later with the rise of the Ayatollah Khomeini's fundamentalism. In the same area was another large sculpture that captured his attention like a magnet. This was a larger-than-life depiction of a man of godlike proportions wrestling with a crocodile. The muscular man was depicted wrenching the jaws of the reptile wide open. Again the boy's mind was totally transfixed by this spectacle.

Later that afternoon, one of Karl's brothers took him to the festivities in the Baghe-Melli Park where a garden party had been hosted in honor of the wedding of the crown prince Mohammed Reza to Princess Fowzia, sister of Egypt's King Farouk. That day several orchestras performed in the grounds. Karl was enchanted and delighted with what he beheld. At the entrance to the park was a man with large round glasses, dressed in a series of inner tubes, advertising Michelin tires. Then came the fireworks—again the first such display that he had ever seen. To top off the evening, Karl's brother bought him the most delicious ice cream sundae that he had ever tasted. The festive atmosphere and the fireworks display overwhelmed him, and he marveled at everything he had seen.

This memorable event occurred during the rule of Reza Shah, when traditional chadors for women and turbans for men were forbidden. All the men wore Pahlavi hats. The pageantry was all so different to what he had been used to at home. This festival was an unusual occasion in the civic life of this region since public events of this nature were few and far between. However, as a sensitive and impressionable young boy, Karl never forgot the wonders of that afternoon. Little did his brother realize that he had provided a seminal experience that would initiate his younger brother into a lifelong love for the arts.

Several years later, when Karl was seven years old, he noticed posters in his eldest brother's home. These posters were of paintings by Vladimir Tatlin (1895–1956), the father of the Russian Constructivist movement, and were later bought by Russian officers who in turn sold them to other Allied officers and art collectors. This was at a time when the works of the avant-garde artists were not understood or accepted in the Soviet Union. It is highly likely that Karl's brother had no idea of the true value of these paintings.

Another significant exposure to works of fine art occurred at his uncle's house. Mirza Kazem Khan was an eccentric and highly individualistic man who had been well educated in France at the end of the nineteenth century. In later years, he reminded Karl of Agatha Christie's Inspector Hercule Poirot in his meticulous dress and pedantic mannerisms. He even sported a mustache similar to that of the famous detective. It was in Mirza's house that Karl saw paintings that in later years he attributed to Kasimer Malevich (1878–

1935). When he first saw these paintings of faceless Russian farmers, he realized that they were almost identical to the paintings in his uncle's house, and that the same artist must have painted them. These paintings were later sold through a middleman to an English diplomat.

Early exposure to these examples of avant-garde art sensitized Karl's young mind to a range of pictorial representation that extended beyond traditional figurative painting and confirmed to him that artists were also capable of working with abstracted forms and nonobjective subject matter. Although he was unable to articulate these thoughts in these early years, the latent power of these images, with their strong colors and geometric designs, would later become the touchstone for his artist development.

Chapter 2

PORTENTOUS AWAKENINGS

Karl's first noteworthy drawing was made when he was only five years old. One evening he was playing with his ten-year-old nephew. He watched while his nephew drew a duck with a few deft lines on a piece of paper with a fountain pen. Karl found the experience mesmerizing, even though it was not a particularly talented drawing. The pen was then passed to Karl with the challenge that if he could draw the cherry on the plate in front of him, he could have the pen. Karl was given a sheet of paper, and he set about drawing the cherry on the plate exactly as he saw it. Somehow he managed to draw the cherry so accurately with its little leaves, shadows, and reflections that his cousin ran from the room calling to Karl's mother and older brother, "Come and see! Karl has just made the most precise drawing of a cherry! I can't believe it!"

They were all amazed. Not many days later, Karl's cousin brought him a pad of paper and a box with six colored pencils, and Karl started drawing in earnest. He drew whatever he saw—trees, houses with smoke billowing from their chimneys—anything and everything.

A couple of months later, Yuri Popov, a local painter, came to visit Karl's brother-in-law. Popov was known affectionately by his nickname "Aedris." When Aedris saw what Karl had been doing, he exclaimed, "This boy is really talented. Give him more paper and more colored pencils, or chalk, or whatever!"

When Karl's brother-in-law, Lieutenant Governor Mokarram Sultan, asked Aedris if he would be prepared to teach Karl, he replied, "No, no, it is not necessary. He is too young. Let him play, let him to do exactly what he wants to do."

Thereafter Karl became a veritable monster with a voracious appetite for drawing all his waking hours. He would draw on anything he found. This was rather disturbing for the family. When he ran out of pencils, he would use charcoal, and when he ran out of paper, he would use the white painted walls of his home.

Yuri Popov had been one of the avant-garde artists in the early 1900s. He was a cousin of the more famous Liubov Popova (1889–1924), the short-lived Russian avant-garde painter. Uri was a royalist, and when the Bolsheviks came to power in Russia after the Revolution, he was forced to flee, as many did in those years. He decided to settle in Mashhad. However, he soon found that he could not sell his own abstract avant-garde paintings. No one understood what he was painting, and he was forced to occupy himself with portraiture and decorative murals. There was a demand in the city for mural paintings since there was no wallpaper in those early days. Aedris completed a fine mural at Karl's sister's mansion in the city. The remembrance of geometric patterns, interlocking squares, rectangles, and "U" shapes remained with Karl. Aedris had made stucco ceilings and painted wall patterns for a living as a young man in Russia. Then, from time to time, he painted abstract works for himself that no one would buy. As a boy, Karl would often visit his studio and watch him put a new ground over an old painting so that he could paint a new painting over the old one. In this way he used his canvases over and over again since he could not afford new canvasses for all his experimental work.

As time passed, Karl busied himself with lots of Russian art books and catalogs. Some of these publications had pictures of paintings from the nineteenth century that reminded him of similar ones he had seen in his sister's home of seascapes, schooners, and portraits. However, Karl also came across pictures of abstracted geometrical figures that looked remarkably like the patterns that Aedris had applied to the walls and ceilings of the houses he had decorated. Aedris told him that these were the same motifs and patterns that his father Hadjaga had regularly used to simplify his depictions of flowers, leaves, trees, horses, or people as he worked out the designs for his rugs. Aedris called this "abstraction," a word young Karl had never heard before. Aedris saw Karl staring in wonder and told him with a smile, "You are too young to understand." However, the young artist internalized these experiences and tried to paint squares, circles, and other geometrical shapes with different colors at home. Later, when Karl was older and could read, he would come to know the full implications of this shift in the art world to geometric abstraction.

As a six-year-old boy, Karl would play with other children around the neighborhood, ever ready to sketch and make a quick drawing. One day he found himself outside the American Hospital where he busied himself with a sketch of an ambulance. He had just completed the drawing when a doctor and a nurse came out of the building. The nurse saw the boy sketching and asked if she could have it for herself. Karl precociously responded, "Of course you can have the sketch, but what can I have from you?"

The nurse went back into the hospital and returned with a chocolate éclair. This was his first business transaction involving an artwork.

It was during these early carefree years of childhood that he discovered the studio of an accomplished painter by the name of Piraste who had emigrated from Baku in Russia. Piraste operated an art studio and shop just two blocks from Karl's parents' home. Here Piraste made his living painting landscapes and the portraits of local doctors, officers, and businessmen and their wives. Most of his portraits were executed in charcoal on large sheets of paper, but from time to time, he would complete a portrait in oil paints. Most of his landscapes were painted from small post cards. He would paint in his street-level shop with his easel backed up to the street window so that passersby could not see what he was painting. Karl would sneak down the side of the artist's shop where he found a small hole in the back wall through which he could watch Piraste working on his canvasses. He would often spend several hours watching at his spy hole, absorbing every action of the artist as he worked at his easel with his paints and brushes.

Piraste knew that he was being watched, but he ignored the boy. Later he and Karl would become good friends, spending much time chatting about painting techniques. Piraste painted in the conventional realist style common to nineteenth-century Russia. He was a devotee of such painters as Ilya Rapin (1844–1930) and Viktor Vasnetsov (1848–1926), who were acclaimed academic painters of this period. Piraste was quite content with this style and never wavered from it. Four decades later, when Karl revisited his hometown, he had lunch with the aged artist and found that he was still painting in exactly the same manner. It was through his friendship with Piraste that Karl learned invaluable lessons in academic painting techniques that would stand him in good stead later in life.

Chapter 3

THE RUSSIANS ARE COMING!

When Karl was old enough, he started attending a local coed primary school in Mashhad. In the fall of 1941, his father was out of town on an assignment from the government to set up a new factory for the Iranian Rug Company in Birdjand, a city to the south. Karl was seven years old at the time, and his father had left Karl's twenty-two-year-old brother in charge while he was away. His brother was attending an officers' training course at the local military college. He was tall and handsome. The weather was still hot after a long summer, and the family often slept on their bedding under mosquito nets on the veranda of the house. Before dawn on the morning of the tenth of September, Karl was awakened by a series of loud explosions. He heard his six-year-old sister shout, "The Russians are coming! The Russians are coming!"

He was shocked to see his mother leap into action. She quickly gathered his brother's military uniform and everything that might have associated him with the army and poured kerosene over the bundle on the mosaic floor of the balcony. She set fire to his belongings, and Karl watched as flames reduced the bundle to ashes in the early morning light. Iran was being invaded. Karl's ten-year-old brother was tall for his age and well developed physically. Confused about the events unfolding around him, he dashed about in a valiant attempt to defend his family.

Elsewhere in the city people were caught up in the mad fervor of panic. Karl ran to the rear of the house and opened the door to the alley. There was total confusion throughout the neighborhood. Then at the height of the tumult, horse-drawn wagons pulled up along the streets in front of the houses. As if from nowhere, people began piling their blankets, clothing, and essential provisions onto the waiting wagons. Karl's family bundled what they could grab in their haste and left their home without even locking the front door. Soon they had joined over three hundred thousand inhabitants fleeing the city. Like an endless caravan, the wagons weaved their way out of the city toward the countryside. Huddled together in the early morning light, they heard the dull thud of mortars and the crack of gunfire in the distance.

The Russians had not bombed any civilian targets but had concentrated their efforts on military installations such as the airport and military buildings. Warplanes crisscrossed the sky overhead as Karl's family made their way toward the country home of Abas, one of Karl's older brothers. Abas was an economist in the agricultural cooperative of the area and lived in Samasghand, a hamlet twenty miles south of the city. Soon his office and administration buildings were filled to capacity, with twenty or thirty family members and friends to a room.

Karl and his brothers were not unduly concerned and treated the entire episode as an exciting adventure. The family stayed four days with Karl's older brother, and then, when it was confirmed that it was safe to do so, they made their way back to the city. On the return journey they saw Russian tanks on every street corner, and the city appeared to be overrun with Russian troops. The Iranian police were conspicuously absent from the scene. Along with the troops came Russian women in various capacities, such as drivers and traffic police officers. Karl marveled at their skirts and blouses and blonde hair. He was amazed at how young they looked.

As they neared their home they were confronted with yet another spectacle. Loudspeakers, like large trumpets, had been fixed in the trees along the main boulevard. The streets rang with strident marching music and every half hour announcements were made in both Russian and Persian. These were propaganda broadcasts by the Russians. Statements such as "We are here to help you!" and "Nobody should feel scared!" reverberated throughout the city. On reaching their home, the Momens were relieved to find everything intact, and nothing had been disturbed.

The Russian troops were, by and large, quite disciplined. A few days after the occupation, a soldier was executed in the town square for allegedly raping a Persian woman. However, the invaders had no qualms about helping themselves to the city's natural resources. Within a few days every wheat silo had been emptied and all the sugar supplies at the major sugar refinery in Mashhad had been transported to Russia. Supplies of fabrics and leather also vanished overnight. A major food shortage followed, and the Momens were forced to rely for their survival on the rice, flour, and other staples that they had stored in large barrels in the cellar of their home. The schools were closed, and the children spent their days watching the comings and goings of the Russian troops. Soon the town was witness to endless convoys of supply trucks. German U-boats had disrupted the shipping lanes across the Atlantic, and the Russians were forced to move raw materials, food, clothing, and weaponry by road from India through Mashhad and then on to Ashekabad, which was in Russian territory, sixty miles to the north.

Four weeks after the Russian invasion, life in the city seemed to return to normal, and Karl returned to his coed elementary school. Food remained in short supply, and the city streets still crawled with Russian soldiers. Every evening in the town squares there were screenings of Movietone News documentaries from the war front and propaganda films extolling the virtues of the socialist way of life in Russia. In 1942, a year after the occupation started, Karl was in his second year of schooling when Hoseinejad, one of his teachers, organized an after-school art group. Hoseinejad was a young man with a keen interest in arts and handcrafts. With permission of their parents, students could stay after school two or three times a week to sketch and paint. Hoseinejad became Karl's first art teacher, providing his first lessons in sketching and painting.

Karl's first completed drawing in Hoseinejad's class was of a bird sitting on the branch of a pine tree. He sketched exactly what he saw with remarkable verisimilitude, first using a lead pencil to sketch the form and then colored pencils to complete every fine detail. It took the boy several weeks to finish the work. These after-school classes became his preoccupation, and his family was happy that he was productively occupied out of the house. Karl continued attending these after school classes for two years. Hoseinejad had also shown him how to enlarge his portraits on large sheets of German watercolor paper. His favorite subject was Shirley Temple, who was wildly popular at the time. She was constantly depicted in the media—playing tennis, dancing, skating, and doing a host of exciting activities. His second most loved model at the time was Napoleon Bonaparte. Karl sought out every depiction of the emperor that he could find and then produced his own images in charcoal. This practice also started his early career as a portraitist.

By the time Karl was ten years old he was trading portraits for pastries at the local teahouse and haircuts from the local barber. He would also sell his portraits for pocket money. He also started visiting Yuri Popov at his studio. He would often accompany Popov on his stucco and interior decorating jobs. He would help Popov apply the colors to the walls in multiple layers until the result was quite spectacular. Popov had contemporary art books, with many illustrations that he shared with Karl. Many of the works depicted in these books were completely abstract, and this

Chapter 4

FREEDOM TO THINK AND LEARN

The Russians had no intention of leaving Iran. The influence of the occupation permeated the lives of Karl and his friends in Mashhad. The Russians were quick to establish cultural centers in the cities as venues for pushing their brand of socialism to the local populace, particularly the youth. Karl made friends with the Russians and became a member of their cultural center in the city. He was also beginning to make an income from his artwork. At thirteen years of age, he made portraits of Uri Popov and some of his relatives who were on good terms with the occupying Russians.

Karl and his friends were members of Vox, a cultural center where young people could go to play pool, billiards, snooker, chess, table tennis, and to read books. He was an avid reader and it was here that he discovered Victor Hugo, Charles Dickens, Mark Twain, Maxim Gorky, and the Russian revolutionary writers. Karl's favorite novel at that time was Alexander Dumas's *The Three Musketeers*. He became a friend of the officer in charge of the library, and when the officer found out about his artistic skills through Uri Popov, he was commissioned to make ten large copies of famous Russian paintings of the period. In exchange, Karl and his friends were granted unlimited access to the facilities of Vox. This meant a lot to Karl since he loved to play billiards at the time.

Consequently, he painted fine reproductions of Ilja Repin's Cossack scenes, as well as copies of Vasnetsov's painting of the Russian folk tale *Aljonushka and Ivanushka*. He also reproduced several paintings that resembled the work of Tatlin. These paintings were about four feet by five feet in size. Karl had a long discussion with the director of the local Vox during which the director, a Russian Major, tried to explain to Karl that the only paintings he would be allowed to copy would be mainly from the nineteenth century. He gave Karl a long article that had been translated from Russian into Farsi that spoke of the need for the art of the socialistic soviet republic to mirror the life of the working class—most of whom were employed on the farm cooperatives and in factories. Therefore Karl was forbidden to depict the lives of the rich bourgeois capitalists. Instead, he was specifically asked to paint a picture of a poor Persian rug merchant on his dilapidated cart on a muddy road. He was allowed to paint still life as long as his paintings exemplified proletarian values. When Karl mentioned the books he had seen in Aedris's workshop, the Major responded that most of these artists were reactionaries who had immigrated to the "vulgar bourgeois capitalist" parts of Europe.

Karl was deeply influenced by his observation of Aedris's painting of the Ferdowsi movie theater that had been one of the finest art deco buildings when it was constructed for Herand Mangasarian fifteen years previously. This time Aedris did not use his familiar technique of flower motifs in the stucco as he had done so many times with the family homes he had decorated in the past. Instead, he painted the entire oval ceiling white and then drew a series of lines forming circles, squares, and other geometric shapes in the dome, which he then painstakingly filled in with bright colors. When the scaffolding was removed six months later, Karl saw that the overall design looked like the avant-garde depictions he had become so familiar with from the books in Aedris's workshop. To Karl the wild composition looked like a combination of stylistic elements that ranged from Kandinski to Malevich.

Mangasarian wished to celebrate the restoration, so he invited all the Russian military personnel to a special screening of Stalin's favorite movie "Alexander Nevsky" by Sergei Dissentient, with music by Sergei Prokofiev. The rumor was that Stalin saw in this portrayal his own self-portrait.

After Karl's commission for the Major was successfully completed, he was asked to paint a large portrait of Stalin on canvas. As a reference, he was able to obtain a portrait photograph of Stalin. The final portrait was six feet tall and five feet wide and was hung at Vox until 1953, when Mossadegh became Prime Minister and the Shah fled to Rome.

Most of the teenagers in Mashhad had become sympathetic to the Communist cause. Karl attended several Communist Tudeh Party meetings but adopted a passive stance to political involvement, choosing instead to remain on the sidelines to watch the unfolding spectacle. The Party's concern with social issues did not interest him.

There was a large community of Armenians in Karl's hometown who had lived there for several generations. Many were good craftspeople. Some were technicians, mechanics, engineers, and doctors. The Armenians also ran all the liquor bars and delicatessens. When he was fourteen years old, he had several good school friends who were Armenian. One young girl in this group was the same age as Karl, and he thought she was one the most beautiful girls in the city. Her older brother, Herand Mangasarian, owned several movie theaters in the city. These theaters were housed in beautiful old-fashioned Art Deco buildings. Herand had been impressed with Karl's paintings at the Vox Cultural Center, and it did not take him long to seek him out to paint the giant billboards that were hung above the entrances of his theaters to advertise the films that were being screened there. These billboards usually featured the popular American film stars of the day. In this way Karl gained further experience at painting on such a large scale. The first image he painted was for the 1946 Columbia Pictures feature film *Gilda*, starring Rita Hayworth and Glenn Ford. More than twenty posters for American westerns and musicals that were popular with the Iranians followed posters for *Ivanhoe* and *For Whom the Bell Tolls*. Of special appeal to local audiences were paintings of the "pinup" girls Betty Grabble, Dorothy Lamoure, and Ester Williams. Karl also completes billboards for Sergei Eisenstein's films *Alexander Nevsky* and *Ivan the Terrible*.

During this period Karl assisted the director of cultural department of Vox with the stage setting for the Bertold Brecht play *Mother Courage*. The director for this production was a striking Russian woman who always wore a military uniform and spoke fluent Azerbaijani Turkish, which Karl could understand fluently at the time. Bertold Brecht's books were the most popular books at the Vox lending library. The works of Maxim Gorky and Lenin's Manifesto were obligatory reading for the students to become members of Vox. Karl complied so that he could play billiards, table tennis, and chess.

At this time, 20 percent of the Mashhad population could speak Turkish, as could the Momen family. Karl's father and older brothers were fluent in the Turkish dialects. His father and older brother also spoke Russian. Karl's portraits were in high demand, and he was fully occupied on Saturdays and Sundays, taking no summer vacation since he received so many commissions to paint the portraits of businessmen and their wives. He also painted a large religious painting of the Islamic Imam Ali that still hangs in Mashhad in Karl's great nephew's home.

After Khomeni came to power, it was forbidden to paint images of the prophet or of an Imam. Illustrations of literary works were also forbidden. Ironically, pictures and statues of Khomeni and the current despot Khameni flooded the country. Large, six- to eight-foot paintings supporting religious groups were seen throughout the town. As a counter balance to this religious fervor, Karl delighted in painting copies of old masters and pin-up girls for the doctors, officers, teachers, and young state employees. These activities kept Karl busy from 1949 to 1955.

When Karl turned sixteen years of age he was employed by Herand as a projectionist in one of his theaters in addition to producing the publicity billboards. He worked four hours each night after school, running the projector in the theater. During this time he would also paint the large paintings. Once he took a partially completed poster home. One night Karl was working on a painting advertising the 1949 Italian realist film *The Bitter Rice*, starring Silvana Mangano, in his makeshift studio at home that he often used for his painting. His father, who was then ninety-six years old, came to watch him paint. The old man had a special glint in his eye as he sat at the window seat, lit his pipe, and silently watched his son complete his painting of the statuesque Silvana Mangano.

During these teenage years, Karl became businesslike about his art. In addition to the public portraits, he also painted many copies of the 1940s and 50s pin-up girls for young professional men. He worked from popular prints produced by Wargash, a Hungarian illustrator working in the USA. It was also during this time that Herand brought him several Russian icons to copy. He did not realize that the correct method of painting these icons was to first lay down a thin layer of plaster on a cloth membrane that would serve as the ground for the tempera paint. In his naïveté, he simply ordered some wood paneling, varnished the surface, and then applied the tempera in the traditional manner of Persian miniature painting. He painted a number of these icons with subjects ranging from Jesus rescuing Adam from hell and the Resurrection, to numerous depictions of Mary and the infant Jesus. Among these works were copies of Madonna and Child paintings by Kazanskya and Dimitrie, two significant seventeenth-century icon painters. Although some of these works were quite large, Karl painstakingly rendered the subjects in the Persian miniature technique in which he had been well schooled. A recurring motif from these early days was a golden cross that often formed part of the icons. The cross was usually rendered in gold within a dark umber frame. He put his heart and soul into these simple depictions, because he knew they would be used in a religious setting. Because he did not know enough about painting on wood to ensure their permanence at the time, they deteriorated over the years and some of the paint eventually flaked off; however, the icons in the Armenian Church in Masshad were still intact fifty years later when he visited the city.

By the time he was sixteen years old, he was fully occupied with his school studies, portraits, film posters, and projectionist work. Karl actually felt like a little businessman in high school. It was in these years that a new era dawned in Iran.

Dr. Mossadegh was elected Prime Minister of Iran in the first free election held in that country. With Mossadegh came complete intellectual and press freedom. At his instigation, the oil contract with Britain was revoked and the Iranian oil fields were nationalized. This signaled the beginning of the oil crises that reverberated around the world and resulted in the blockade of the Persian Gulf in 1951. Ironically, Iran entered a new era of democracy at this time. The socialists became more vocal with the liberal-minded attitudes of the government, and the Vox Cultural Center in Mashhad reverberated with the propaganda of socialism. During these years, Karl's painting and portraiture business flourished. However, as a teenager he would spend the money as fast as he earned it. He would spend his earnings by taking his nephews and all his friends on outings to the bakery, the movies, the restaurant, or on picnics.

This was a time of great intellectual freedom in Iran. Previously forbidden literature was unbanned. Books could be bought freely, and there were no restrictions on what one could read. In this liberal climate, Karl indulged his passion for reading and attended numerous political meetings. Although this was a difficult time economically for the country, the people felt as though the shackles had been removed from the country's intellectual life. Political and religious meetings were held everywhere. In this new democratic spirit, education flourished, and new ideas abounded; however, new economic woes set in, and eventually the people grew weary of economic hardships under the rule of the Shah. The resulting revolution led to the Shah fleeing to Italy in 1953. Then a couple of months later, the Shah was reinstated with the aid of powerful American influences. In the reactionary period that followed, rigorous social and political restrictions were imposed. The press was muzzled, the Socialist Tudeh party was banned, and the Vox Cultural Centers were all but destroyed.

The portrait of Stalin that Karl had painted as a young boy was taken down and thrown out into the street, where passersby trod it underfoot and used it symbolically as a mat to wipe their shoes. Karl stood across the street at the time and watched, helpless to intervene in any way. His friends who stood with him sarcastically joked that his "prophet" was gone and that the people were cleaning their shoes on his face.

However, life continued, and during the last year of Karl's high schooling in 1952, he opened a public art school with the help of Mr. Medi, his former teacher. The school was called "Honarsara," which translated means "house of art." Three nights of the week were for ladies, and three nights were for men. People came to learn to paint and to make velvet flowers. The ladies were particularly interested in this skill and ended up producing flowers that were almost indistinguishable from real ones. Classes were popular and soon he and Mr. Medi were teaching local doctors, officers, and their wives. Karl then decided to go it alone, and soon he had a lively following, including some teachers from his own high school who attended his classes. The political situation stabilized, the economy started to improve, and life became tolerable again for Karl and his artist colleagues.

First Stop, 1986

Chapter 5

THE RISE AND FALL OF DEMOCRACY IN IRAN

Karl had lived through some of the most radical political changes in the Middle East, particularly in Iran, or Persia, as this country was formerly known. His extended family was a micro society comprising those that were rich and famous, middle class, politicians, doctors, military offices, clergymen, businessmen, factory workers, bureaucrats, and those less fortunate. There were also diametrically opposed political views within this community.

Karl's bother-in-law Mokarram Sultan was a member of Parliament at the time and the right-hand man of Reza Shah. As a dedicated and loyal subject, Mokarram was instrumental in building the city of Freiman in less than a year—complete with silos, a sugar refinery, and a brick factory. Mokarram's son-in-law was a medical doctor, a professor at the local university, and a liberal socialist. Another brother-in-law of Karl was an electrical technician at a textile factory and a Tudeh socialist party member. Yet another brother-in-law was a highly ranked clergyman whose son was an extremely conservative captain in the military. Karl's oldest brother, Sherkate, was a highly ranked official in the largest farmers' corporative in northeastern Iran. He was a chain smoker and a good listener who never expressed his own opinions about anything. He presented the best poker face that Karl had ever seen.

Karl's father always talked of his rug-producing workshop—of both the good and the bad times. As an avowed fatalist he never took the blame for any personal misfortune, believing the good and the bad were part of his destiny. He admired German workmanship and would often reminisce for hours of the good times when Bismarck was Chancellor of Germany. He was ninety years old when the British sank the German battleship Bismarck during World War II. He was unhappy when he saw pictures of the sinking in the newspapers and on posters at his regular teahouse. He believed that the Bismarck was the most beautiful battleship imaginable. When Karl's brothers laughingly asked him if he had ever seen a battleship in real life, he retaliated by asking them if they had ever seen Istanbul before 1910.

During the Reza Shah period, and until the allied occupation of Iran, most of Iranian industry, including railways and armament factories, was built with German help and expertise. Until the allied occupation, there were many German engineers and technicians in Iran. Karl did not recollect ever seeing men with turbans and women with chadors on the street or in public places when he was a boy in elementary school. These items of apparel were only allowed in mosques and shrines. Karl's brother-in-law, who was a mullah, carried his turban under his arm, and he only put it on when he entered their home.

When the Russians invaded Iran, Reza Shah was forced into exile, and Mohammad Reza Shah became the young king. The Germans fled the country, and the Mullahs gained ascendancy. Boys and girls attended separate schools, and on occasion, one could see wailing women wearing chadors who had lost family members on the street. The city was almost divided in two. The old town that surrounded the Shrine became active with a high concentration of mullahs. The South and Northwest regions remained unchanged as they were before the occupation, with women's clothing and hairstyles aligned with western styles of the 1940s. The wearing of chadors and turbans was not allowed in schools, hospitals, banks, and in government or private corporation offices until the Islamic revolution of 1979.

By the end of the 1940s, the Tudeh democratic (Communist) party tried to partition Iranian Azerbaijan and create a Communist satellite state by means of a military coup. The coup was led by Pishevari and was supported by the Soviet Union. However, the Iranian army under the leadership of the Shah, and backed by President Harry Truman's administration, defeated the Pishewari force on December 1, 1946. This day was declared a national holiday known as Azar Mah in commemoration of the event. When Karl was an elementary school student, he and his classmates were dressed in uniforms of gray pants and white shirts, and they marched in formation before the Shah, with the army parade of tanks and armored vehicles at the football stadium on this day in 1949.

It was in August 1946 that Karl first heard the name Mohammad Mossadegh. He was at his sister's home, and it was school summer vacation. His brother-in-law Mokarram was also on summer vacation in Mashhad and was visiting. Before lunch he engaged his son-in-law Nasiri in a discussion about the possibility of Mossadegh nationalizing the Iranian oil industry. This was nothing new, since people discussed the oil situation on almost every occasion. It was talked about at every social gathering, and all the newspapers carried headlines about recent developments concerning the oil industry. Karl was sitting on the opposite side of the room sketching a flower in a vase. Mokarram was of the opinion that Mossadegh was an ambitious man who was a stranger to reality for wanting to nationalize Iranian oil. He gave two clear reasons for his opinion: first, the English would never allow it, and second, it would ruin the country. Nasiri responded that he didn't believe that Mossadegh was such a stupid man and a traitor to his country. In fact, he thought he was a real patriot. Karl remembered that their discussion was polite but not accompanied with the laughing or joking that was customary in his family.

This was the first serious discussion that Karl had witnessed between his relatives, and he realized then that politics had as much to do with governing as with dividing people's attitudes toward each other, even between close relatives. After this experience, he started reading the political pages of the newspaper and listening to political debates on the radio. He realized that people really did discuss these matters seriously and that their feelings and perceptions of how to live their lives often differed greatly. He also realized that they were not solely concerned with fine clothing, houses, and material wealth. They were also concerned with the direction the government should take and how the country should be organized and governed.

A few weeks later, Mokarram returned to Tehran. All the newspapers were in great anticipation of what Mossadegh would say in his opening speech to Parliament. In his speech that was broadcast on the radio, he condemned Britain for robbing the poor people of Iran and announced that British ownership of Iranian oil fields would come to an immediate end.

AWAKENING POLITICAL INTEREST AMONG STUDENTS AND YOUTH

In 1949, immediately after Mossadegh proclaimed that Iranian oil fields would be nationalized, the British imposed economic sanctions on Iran, effectively curtailing any export income. There was a noticeable shortage of necessary goods, and the minority opposition group in Parliament demanded Mossadegh's resignation. Reading the uncensored newspaper became a major attraction for the boys of all the high schools. Every afternoon after school, Karl and his friends would gather in front of the local newsstand where the owner would staple the pages of the latest newspaper to long plywood boards and hang them on the trees on the roadside so that passersby could read the latest developments. This bookstore owner gave away ten copies of each issue of the newspaper to the girl students who did not dare stand on the side of the street among the boys to read the latest news. It was a contagious preoccupation. The owner of Bromand, one of the largest bookshops in the city, would spend hours discussing politics with the boys. He was a Tudeh Party member, and he would mention to them in private that he thought that if Mossadegh would go to Moscow, then Stalin would give him all the support he needed. Eventually the lack of income from the oilfields brought the economy to a standstill. Mossadegh was under pressure from both the right and the left.

In 1951, Mossadegh went to New York to attend a meeting of the United Nations General Assembly. He delivered a tearful and dramatic speech accusing Britain of imposing unjust sanctions on poor countries and stealing their only source of revenue. He pleaded for help from the other countries. The British vigorously opposed a resolution by the Security Council to prevent Britain from imposing sanctions. Mossadegh met with President Harry Truman and Dean Acheson in Washington. During this tumultuous period, Mossadegh fell ill, and the Shah demanded that he return to Tehran for treatment. Truman dismissed this idea, stating that the United States was entirely capable of taking care of Mossadegh and had him hospitalized in New York.

It was at that time that a rumor began circulating that Churchill had asked the US to help in arranging a people's coup against Mossadegh. Truman, who was known for not having had any sympathy for Churchill, opposed such an act. For Truman the Cold War and the aggressive behavior of Stalin were of more strategic importance than England's economic interests. Mossadegh appeared on the cover of Time Magazine as "Man of the Year." He was a master speaker and one of the most intellectual politicians in Iran, having been educated in international law in Switzerland. The Iranian youth, including Karl, relished these events and read all of Mossadegh's speeches. They held him in high regard, and it made them proud to see him standing up against such intense international pressure in behalf of his people. They saw him as an Iranian Gandhi.

Chapter 6

THE WINDS OF CHANGE

In the three years from 1950 to 1953, a new political mood swept through Iran. Media censorship disappeared, and political meetings promoting diverse ideologies were allowed. Many political meetings were held in the high schools and at the university. Some of these meetings supported Mossadegh, the prime minister, and some were opposed to him. The high schools and the university became the incubator for sympathizers of an entirely different political system. Pishevari first started the Tudeh Party during the Russian occupation in the 1940s in Tabriz. It was here that the Tudeh Party found its main supporters.

The Tudeh party was a hybrid of socialism (Communism) and nationalism. Years later, Karl would recall this movement as similar to the 1968 student uprisings in Europe. There were numerous small cells that met secretly until Mossadegh's government came to power. These cells were typically comprised of a teacher, a young doctor, a civil servant, an industrial worker, a student, and sometimes a merchant from a bazaar, but seldom a farmer. During this time, Karl was preoccupied with his schoolwork and with painting billboards and portraits. However, he read voraciously and never missed the many public political meetings that were held.

Stalin died on March 1, 1953, leaving a political vacuum in Iran. A rift appeared, creating a division between the religious nationalist group and the Tudeh Socialistic Communist party that demanded the abolition of the monarchy. Mossadegh was convinced that a parliamentary system was the only model for Iran after more than a two-thousand-year history of Shahs or kings. Consequently, Mossadegh proposed that the Shah's role should be purely ceremonial, with him having no political influence over the Parliament.

Clergymen such as the Ayatollah Kashani delivered speeches at mosques in various cities. Although some of the Ayotollah's speeches supported Mossadegh, he was opposed to a free press and radio from mid-1950 to 1953. TV had yet to be introduced in Iran. In the summer of 1952, the Ayatollah Kashani, the most vocal clergyman who supported Mossadegh in his reforms, came to a meeting in Mashhad that was hosted by Ahmad Khyami, the founder of a political group named Sadate Husseini (the descendants of Imam Hussein). Khyami was a good friend to Karl, and he and his brother Shahidi ran a small workshop for servicing cars and the few taxis in Mashhad. After school Karl helped Khyami with their logo and wrote their political posters for them in fine calligraphy. Ahmad Khayami and his supporters, including a large group of student teachers and a few hundred Bazaris welcomed the Ayatollah Kashani the day he arrived at Mashhad airport. There were no industrial workers among them, because most were sympathetic to the Socialist Tudeh party.

The Ayatollah Kashani and his entourage of Bazaaris left the airport in a convoy of cars, buses, and taxis, all headed for the shrine of Imam Reza. The Bazaaris were small shopkeepers and merchants who comprised the traditional middle class of Iran. The Ayatollah Kashani and some of the clerics who were traveling with Kashani went directly to the Imam Reza shrine. Most of the other supporters who had turned out to meet the Ayatollah returned to work. Karl traveled in a car with Khayami and Shahidi as they followed the Ayatollah to Husseinieh, a religious center connected to the Moghbel Mosque. They arrived at 1:00 p.m., together with over a hundred supporters, many of whom were known to Karl. As they entered the Husseinieh center, they found the walls lined with cushions and an elegant sofreh extended down the main hall. A "sofreh" is a cotton runner that is placed on the floor to serve as a table for guests sitting on cushions on either side. Many delectable Persian dishes, fruits, pastries, and rice were placed on the sofreh. A plate was provided for each guest who was seated along both sides of the sofreh. Before the food was served, the Ayatollah Kashani began with a long prayer in which he spoke about the value of Islam in society and the dangerous appearance of the "Godless Bolsheviks" in Iran, since this would bring about a terrible catastrophe for Muslims. He then pointed to a large portrait of Imam Hazrate Ali on the wall and assured everyone that as long as they were all under the protection of Ali, no communist evil would harm them.

After lunch Khayami introduced Karl to the Ayatollah as the artist who painted the Imam Ali portrait on the wall. The Ayatollah gave Karl his blessing and told him,

"I hope every time you start to work on a holy image you don't forget your Woozo." The Woozo is the ritual washing and purification that all devout Muslims undertake before daily prayer. On the next day, the Ayatollah addressed over a thousand people at Goharshad Mosque. He spoke of the risks of collaborating with the dangerous Tudeh Party. He said that it was sinful and against God to do so. On that occasion, Dr. Khorshid, one of the most influential lawyers and the city prosecutor, whom Karl also knew well as an artist and talented watercolorist, told Shahidi and Karl that Mossadegh was going to experience grave problems with Ayatollah Kashani.

Karl had always been liberal-minded, but he never took sides, remaining neutral in his allegiance to political, social, and religious matters. Throughout their thousand-year tradition, the Iranian people had a special respect for artists, poets, and master builders, as well as rug and handicraft producers. They were welcomed into any group or public meeting without having to be dedicated to their cause. Since his early childhood years, Karl had been totally free and independent in choosing a school and a line of study without any pressure from his parents and family. This was also the brief period of freedom of thought, uncensored publications, and open expressions of political and social points of view in Iran. It was during this period that he chose to go his own way in becoming a liberal but neutral person, respecting all the different viewpoints but not following any of them. It became his habit not to argue at a political discussion but rather to ask for a book or pamphlet to better understand the point of view being expressed, remaining neutral all the while. He believed he exemplified the Persian anecdote: "To be a pea in any kind of soup without losing one's individuality."

The Ayatollah started openly criticizing Mossadegh for his tolerant attitude toward the Tudeh party, which he saw as a godless group of intellectuals who were supported directly from Moscow by the troika of Malenkov, Beria, and Kagnowich, who came to power two months after Stalin's death. Beria was the head of the Soviet secret police, as were many of the Tudeh leadership. Beria radicalized the Iranian Tudeh party and demanded a ministerial position for the party in the cabinet. The pressure on the Shah mounted for him to give up his veto right in Iran's Majles Parliament. The Majles Parliament was reduced to turmoil at the hands of a minority group headed by Malekmadani, the Speaker of the House, followed by Mokarram and Gharai who were opposed to the Majles Parliament. In mid-July the Shah left Iran for Italy. An unsettled atmosphere prevailed in the country. There was a distinct absence of military personnel or police on the streets. It appeared as if the powers-that-be were ignoring what was happening.

CHAPTER 6

Karl frequented a local teashop in the afternoons after school during this unsettled time. One Friday in May 1953, it was the turn of Professor Ghawam Nasiri from the university to host his faculty colleagues at lunch, followed by bridge and a game of gin rummy at the teashop. Karl was on hand to keep their score and bring them tea, hoping to get a tip from the winner. His income as a painter was not yet much, and he was considered a poor high school student. The doctors in this group were known for their sympathy for the Tudeh party, particularly doctors Shafigh and Shahidi. Karl's host at the teashop was more liberal. Doctors Ziaie, Assadi, and Samirad were royalist and became members of Parliament after the coup d'état. Doctors Shafigh, Shahidi, and Ghawam Nasiri were arrested a few weeks after the return of the Shah and served three to six months in jail.

On this particular afternoon there was not much joking and laughter at their card game. A more somber mood prevailed as Dr. Shafigh described the current political situation. He was of the mind that with Stalin gone, and a power struggle in Moscow, and with Eisenhower the new US President, Churchill would not allow Russia to take over Iran. In the following month of June, people became increasingly nervous. Workers went on strike, there was a run on the banks, and, finally, the Shah left for Rome. Members of the Tudeh party demanded to be part of the government. The Mullah's prediction was being realized.

Karl spent June 19, 1953, with his sister and her family in Wkilabad, a large wooded park on a high plateau on the Golestan River that flowed into Golestan Dam. The thousand-acre park was heavily wooded with hundred-year-old maple and birch trees. The park had three Olympic-size pools, and it was the most popular recreational park, situated twenty kilometers west of Mashhad. Hadji Hosein Agha, a noted philanthropist and one of the richest tycoons in Iran, had donated the park. He had also donated Baghe Melli City Park in central Mashhad to avoid confiscation by Reza Shah. Wkilabad was a picturesque wooded park where hundreds of families spent time camping for weeks on end to escape the forty-degree heat in the summer.

Hadji Hosein Agha visited Mashhad for a few days every year. Khaledy, one of the finest violinists in Iran, accompanied him. Also with the group were a few famous vocalists. Hadji Hosein was about eighty-five years old at the time, and he was accompanied by a few good-looking nurses. He enjoyed art and music and was one of the best literary experts on Persian poetry. He had established Ketabkhane Melli, one of the finest libraries in Tehran, that remains open to the public to this day. A spectacular six- by four-meter Mashhad rug that Karl's father had designed and produced is still on display at this library.

Hassan Mokarram, Karl's brother-in-law, was Hadji Hosein Agha's trusted friend and overseer of all his properties in Iran.

He was also the leader of the opposition in Parliament and spent over a month on strike with Malak Madani, the Speaker of the House, after the Shah fled to Rome. On the Shah's return to power, Mokarram went back to Parliament in Tehran.

Karl's family would often use Hajj Hussein Agha's vacation house in Wakilabad for family get-togethers and celebrations. On one particular sunny afternoon, there were about twenty of Karl's family gathered at the vacation house. At about two o'clock, Karl noticed Mokarram's driver come across and talk quietly with Makarram. Karl saw a smile creep across the old fox's face as he took in what the driver had to say. Makarram turned to the assembled party and announced that the Shah was returning and continued his conversation with Dr. Gghawam as if nothing had happened. Makarram was a highly ranked member of the Dervish sect of the Mullah Sultan lodge, as well as an officiator of the Iranian Freemason society. He would be pleased with the Shah's return since just a few months previously he was in the minority group that rose against Mossadegh in Parliament. But the Shah's return would be less fortuitous for his son-in-law, who was a liberal socialist, who would be sent to jail for a month, and also for his brother Professor Ghawan Nisiri, the dean of the medical faculty in Mashhad, who would lose his job and be sent to jail for a year.

With the news of the Shah's return, Karl's nephew Mammal suggested that they go to the city. He was a devoted Shah supporter. So together with Captain Mehdi and Ghawam Nasiri, the police chief for the Arg district, they drove into the city with Karl's nephew at the wheel of their 1951 maroon Pontiac. The driver remained in Wakilabad. Entering the city they found themselves in the midst of a sea of flags waving and cars with their horns blaring. Chants of "the Shah is back," "death to Mossadegh" and "long live the Shah" could be heard above the clamor. As they reached Mashhed's fashionable main street, they stopped in front of Baghe Melli, the public park. Karl saw that the Vox Soviet Cultural Center was being looted, and the Stalin portrait that he had painted five years previously was lying on the sidewalk on the other side of the street. The mob was ceremoniously wiping their shoes on the painting where it lay. The table tennis and billiards tables on which he had played so frequently as a youth were being loaded onto small trucks. Then he noticed that the books were being thrown out and burned. He could guess that among them were Lenin's *Manifesto*, Maxim Gorky's *The Mother*, and Marx's *Das Kapital*, which he had read in the many hours he had spent at Vox.

Karl first read the complete account of the CIA-staged coup against the legally elected government of Mohammad Mossadegh in 1989 in *The Shah's Last Ride* by William Shawcross. He bought

CHAPTER 6

numerous copies of this book when it was published to send as gifts to relatives and friends and as party gifts. In his book, Shawcross accurately describes the scenario of how Kermit Roosevelt, the grandson of the late President Roosevelt, staged the CIA-led coup, and how on August 19, 1953, at 5:00 a.m., Kermit Roosevelt sent a bribe of ten thousand US dollars to the Ayatollah Kashani in the Holy City of Ghoum.

It has been said that a sharp sword kills the enemy no matter who he might be. With the Shah gone, the Iranian army was in unknown territory. Many of the top American-trained generals and commanders were executed. The Iranian army was taken over by revolutionaries with no real military training. Saddam Hussein, who had respected the Iranian military during the Shah's rule, seized the opportunity to establish himself as the strong man in the Persian Gulf. He acted to prevent Iraq from falling under the domination of the mullahs. He subsequently invaded Iran to take possession of two of the country's most important cities and their oil fields.

A month after the Iraqi invasion, the Iranians conceded that their young and inexperienced revolutionary guards could not stop the Iraqis' progress, so the Ayatollah gave the order that all Iranian generals and top commanders who had not been executed or forced to retire should join the fighting force. General Ali Dadpanah, who was one of the most experienced Special Force commanders in the Iranian army, was ordered to report for duty as a strategic planner at the Iranian Army command center in Tehran. After the war, Ali wrote to Karl that he had worked at the command center because it was his duty as an Iranian, but after the Iraqis and the Iranians agreed to a cease fire, he wrote that he had to stay on at the command center because he was told that the regime could not guarantee his teenage son's safety if he declined to serve his new masters. Like many young men during the Shah's rule, he was not a practicing Muslim, but he respected the mullahs, his father being a clergyman. The last time Karl heard from him, he said he attributed all of Iran's misery to their religion.

Chapter 7

A PORTRAIT OF STALIN AND AN EXHIBITION AT THE AMERICAN CONSULATE

After the violent CIA coup d'état of 28 Mordad (the second month of summer), and the arrest of Prime Minister Mossadegh, the leader of the Tudeh party, and his supporters, the Shah was returned to power in August 1953. Life in Iran started to return to normal as personal hardships and food shortages became a thing of the past. New school and university principals, with views critical of Mossadegh's rule, were appointed. People looked to a better future under the guidance of the more realistic leadership of the Shah. Mainly people were hoping for protection from Russia and feared the threat of becoming lost behind the Iron Curtain. The name of SAWAK, the secret military police, became synonymous with fear. Censorship of the media was complete, and there was no longer a free press.

Many educated young people became interested in the American lifestyle. There also seemed to be a growing interest in paintings and art. This movement favored Karl since he was receiving more commissions and honoraria for his portraits. Even the evening painting classes that he had started with Medi, his former teacher, were being well attended. Karl received more orders for billboard paintings from Herand Mangasarian, the local movie theater owner. He thoroughly enjoyed painting his favorite Hollywood femme-fatales and the latest silver screen beauties such as Rita Hayworth, Lana Turner, Gene Tierney, Lauren Bacall, and Barbara Stanwyck. He painted a twelve-foot-high billboard of Hedy Lamarr for *Samson and Delilah*. Many of his posters remained on the walls of these theaters long after the films had completed their run and he had left Mashhad. He painted a billboard of Ester Williams, the swimming icon, and enjoyed illustrating the Italian New Realism films. He remembers painting the voluptuous Silvana Mangano, and also Gina Lollobrigida as Esmeralda in *The Hunchback of Notre Dame.* He came to know every visible detail of these actresses as he painted them with the passion they demanded.

Then one day, in the fall of 1954, all the well-known artists, including Karl, received an invitation from Donald E. Webster, the American Consul General in Mashhad, to attend a preview of twentieth-century American and European paintings. These works were to be exhibited for the first time at Baghe Melli, the central city park. When Karl arrived at the Consulate some of the artists were already leaving. He was late since he had been detained at his high school to complete a test. Like all the other artists who had been invited, he could not speak English, but there was an official translator from the consulate on hand. Karl happened to know this young man as his nephew's teacher before he left for Cambridge, England, to continue his education. He was kind enough to explain the reason for Karl's late arrival to Mr. Webster. He also mentioned that Karl had worked in the studio of Yuri Popov, the Russian avant-garde artist who had left Russia during the revolution.

Mr. and Mrs. Webster welcomed Karl and invited him to the buffet table. Through the translator, Mrs. Webster asked if Karl had some pictures of Popov's work. He said that he did not but that he could oblige them if they pleased. She was the first American woman that he had met in person. She looked like the typical American housewife that he had imagined from the movies, with long blond hair, a blouse, a knee-length skirt, short white socks, a bright smile, and a cool manner. Images of Dona Reed, Eva Marie Saint, and Tippy Hedren came to mind. For these Iranian high school teenagers, Hollywood was their second home. They knew everything about the actors but especially the actresses and saw their movies over and over. In this way teenagers of Karl's generation in Iran were completely socialized into the values, norms, and cultural perspectives of Western society. The power of this socialization cannot be underestimated. American movies became the lens through which this generation came to see the world. These recreational experiences formed a critical component of Karl's informal education that enabled him to meld into Western culture in a seamless fashion in later years.

The translator then said to Karl that he should wait until the other guests had left. At that point, Mr. Webster joined Karl, who was with the translator, and together they looked at all the original paintings and lithographs. Through the translator, Webster asked Karl if he knew any of them, and Karl proceeded to point out some Picasso lithographs and paintings by Vasarely, Miro, Delaunay, and Dali. He also identified a few original nineteenth century American landscape and portrait paintings, as well as two paintings by Kokoschka. Webster was surprised that he had pointed out Vasarely and Delaunay. He said that none of Karl's artist colleagues had paid any attention to these paintings. Karl mentioned that he had seen these works in the Russian and European avant-garde books at Edris Popov's studio and at the home of his teacher Herr Steinbeck at the technical high school, who had a few posters of Oskar Kokoschka's paintings. Webster put his hand on Karl's shoulder and exclaimed "Very good!" and started to talk with his wife. They laughed and turned to Karl as the translator explained to him in Farsi that they would like to invite him to be the host of the art show at the pavilion at Baghe Melli, the folk park. Karl accepted willingly. Then, as if all this had been the buildup to a grand finale, Webster asked Karl if he could arrange for him to meet Popov.

The show started after a month's preparation. The day before the show opened, Edris guided Karl through the exhibition halls and explained the catalog inscriptions for each of the works. There were 140 works in total, most from Webster's own collection. It was one of Karl's proudest moments to stand at the side of the American Consul General and his wife to greet the governor, the mayor, and numerous other dignitaries. But most of all, Karl's greatest pleasure was greeting the dean of his technical high school, Engineer Tabrizi. This was a significant event in his life and demonstrated to him the importance of art and the effect that it could have on people. Subsequent visits to the Consul resulted in Karl's first exposure to western European culture. The Consul was a collector himself and knowledgeable about contemporary art and artists. It was in the company of Webster that Karl was later introduced to additional lithographs by Piet Mondrian, Pablo Picasso, and Sonia Delaunay.

Chapter 8

BECOMING A STUDENT OF LIFE

Karl graduated from the technical high school in Mashhad in 1954. As a nineteen-year-old, he was still uncertain about what direction his career should take. He wanted to paint, but his family and peers did not consider this a "real" occupation. He also felt the urge to go to Europe to educate himself. After much soul searching, he decided to pursue a career in architecture as a reasonable compromise between his need for artistic expression and his family's expectations of a sound profession. He had always been interested in buildings and had excelled in drawing at high school.

A career in architecture would allow him the opportunity to develop his talents in a productive and socially acceptable manner. However, it was extremely difficult for an Iranian national to study outside the borders of the country at the time. The first requirement was prior admission to a college or university in the foreign country. It was then necessary for the student's family to pledge real estate as collateral security to the government and provide a regular living allowance of two hundred dollars per month for the student for the entire period of the student's study abroad. Because Karl's father was already over a hundred years old, he felt he could not ask him to commit himself in this way. Karl's brothers were trying to raise their own families, and he did not want to burden them either.

Things were made even more difficult by the fact that he could not even leave the country to commence his studies until he had completed his compulsory military service with the Iranian government. So at the beginning of 1955, Karl went to Tehran, the capital of Iran, and enrolled at the military academy. After nine months he was promoted to the rank of lieutenant. During the period of his training, he became a good friend of the commander of the school, who was also the Commander of the Sixth Army. When the commander found out about his artistic talent, he commissioned Karl to paint a portrait of him. He was so impressed with Karl's painting that he arranged for Karl to teach his wife to paint. Karl rented a room at the officers' club where he gave art lessons to the sons of generals and other military commanders. Soon he was painting portraits of these high-ranking military personnel. Karl saved the money he earned through these activities for his future trip to Europe. He was also granted privileges that the other cadets did not receive. He did not have to do menial tasks and was allowed time off for his painting. He received a commission from General Afsharpoor, the commander of the military academy, to paint a portrait of the Shah of Iran in marine uniform. Karl excelled himself, and the fine portrait was later presented to the Shah. This commission led to other well-paid commissions, and he was able to improve his financial situation significantly. During this period, he painted a Russian copy of a work by Repin for General Sepahdoust, the commander of the Military Academy. Sepahdoust would be executed on the first day of the revolution.

After receiving his commission, he was sent to Sanandadg for the remainder of his military duty, where he was able to continue his portrait painting. He even opened a portrait painting school at the officers' club for some of the young officers and the children of high-ranking military personnel. In this way he was able to save enough money to make going to Europe a possibility. He applied to several universities in Germany and received four acceptances. He also completed additional courses in algebra and trigonometry to gain higher grades. Karl was now ready to apply for his student passport.

First, he had to undergo a rigorous interrogation by SAWAC—the notorious Iranian intelligence service. They asked questions such as "Why did you paint Stalin?" and "Why did you paint certain Russian artists who disappeared after the Shah's return in 1953?" Then he had to tell them why he had frequented Vox, the Russian cultural center in Mashhad. He tried to explain that he was one of a local group of students who all attended Vox for the free billiards, chess, and table tennis facilities that were provided there. They also wanted to know what books he had been reading. He explained that he had been reading from a young age and had read books by Emile Zola, Victor Hugo, Alexander Dumas, Mark Twain, Dostoyevsky, Tjechov, Tolstoy, Balzac, and Dickens. He decided it was in his own interests not to tell them about Maxim Gorky and Lenin or Marx's manifestos. He wryly told the officers that he had found reading to be the most inexpensive pastime during Mossadegh's rule.

During the months that he had to wait for his passport to be approved, he exhausted his savings and had to complete several portraits and landscape paintings to bring in some money again. Then he was informed that he would have to furnish proof of employment in Germany. Consequently he went to the offices of the Bosch electrical company in Tehran to seek employment. He was accepted as a draftsman to work in the company's offices in Stuttgart. Karl was now free to make his way to Germany via the Turkish border; however, the exorbitant cost of obtaining the passport had used up all his remaining funds again. In the end, he had to turn to his brothers-in-law Mokarram and Ghwam Nasiri, who was then dean of the medical school at Mashhad University, for loans to help him leave the country. They had always encouraged Karl and helped him in the past. They complied, and he gratefully accepted their assistance.

Karl caught a bus to the Turkish border where he bought a train ticket to Istanbul. He spent four days in Istanbul in the company of another Iranian student who was in the same predicament. He finally obtained visas to travel through Greece, Bulgaria, Yugoslavia, Austria, Munich, and then on to Stuttgart. He departed for Germany. When he disembarked at Stuttgart's Grand Central Station, he was awestruck by the immensity of the heavy granite building. Immediately beyond the station was the imperious Hotel Graf Zeppelin that was equally impressive. He soon arrived at the Königstrasse, the main boulevard of the city, and Karl was shocked to see that all the buildings had been demolished. In the place of attractive shops and buildings were hastily erected wooden barracks and sheds. He would soon learn that most of Stuttgart lay in ruins—the awful consequence of war.

With less than one hundred marks in his pocket, Karl went to register at the architecture and art academy at Kielesberg, a suburb of Stuttgart. From here he proceeded to the Bosch Company offices in the city to sign on at his new job. He could not speak German very well but was happy to be assigned to the mechanical engineering drafting department. The weekly pay was welcome, and he was able to find rented accommodation at a local bed-and-breakfast. Karl spent his days in the drafting office and his nights reading German in order to master the language. Although he was employed as a draftsman, he soon discovered that he could make more money in the machine shop. Karl's supervisor was a kindly man, and he could see that the young man was a struggling student, unlike many other foreign students from wealthy families who flaunted their money. Soon Karl was transferred to the machine shop, where he spent the next three months working double shifts of sixteen hours a day manufacturing mechanical parts. He was able to save most of the money he earned in preparation for college. After his classes started at the college, he was able to supplement his income through part-time work at a local architectural office.

Stuttgart was undergoing intensive rebuilding as a result of war damage, and there was an abundance of work to be had in the construction industry. Construction was going on around the clock, seven days a week in the city. A good Iranian friend of Karl's was stationed at the American Air Force base in Stuttgart, and before long, he was being introduced to the American officers at the base. Karl's portraiture skills soon became known, and shortly he was receiving commissions to paint officers' wives. This practice developed into a lucrative business for Karl, and he was soon making more money than his fellow Iranian students who were supported from home. This practice also provided him with sufficient free time for his studies. Professor Gutbier, one of Karl's architecture teachers, also employed him to do part time architectural drafting during his second year of study. Karl was good at perspectival drawing and could render elevations of buildings better than many architects at the time. He was paid commensurately.

Tanhauser, 1999

Chapter 9

A STAR-STRUCK RELATIONSHIP

After two weeks of traveling by train from Tehran to Stuttgart, Karl spent the first few days finding a room to rent. He booked in at a bed and breakfast for five marks a night, with only fifty marks in his pocket. He needed to start his new job as a draftsman at the Bosch design offices as soon as possible. On his second day in Stuttgart, he went to the Bosch office in Degerloch. When he explained to the engineer that he had only fifty marks to his name, the engineer said that Karl could start work the next day. He continued on to the Hochschule student advice bureau. Here he was given the address of a room that he could rent in a family home in Sonnenberg, a suburb forty-five minutes away by streetcar. It was in the opposite direction from the Bosch offices and meant that he would be traveling half an hour each way on a daily basis. The rent was forty marks a month, and the owner was a retired engineer.

Sonnenberg was a small suburb but with upscale homes. Karl had no time for any recreation or entertainment since he was attending evening classes to learn the German language. He was also waiting to start his architectural studies in two months and had little money.

Mrs. Hadele was wheelchair bound, but Karl could see that this couple was well cultivated because they listened to classical music on the radio all day long. He lived in their rental accommodation for six months, and throughout this period he never saw Mr. Hadele without a tie. One Saturday afternoon in mid-September, Mr. and Mrs. Hadele invited him for "Kaffe und Kuchen." Mrs. Hadele asked if he preferred tea, and he said that the coffee aroma he smelled every day from her kitchen was so good that he would rather have coffee. He was served a steaming cup of coffee and a slice of the most delectable apple tart. Mr. and Mrs. Hadele spoke slowly and clearly for Karl's benefit and corrected him when he mispronounced a word or used incorrect grammar.

They asked him about his schooling and said that they had noticed that he had brought some paintings with him. Karl immediately went to his room and chose a copy that he had made of an original painting. When Mrs. Hadele saw the painting, she began to cry. She said that she had always loved this painting and that her parents owned it along with a few other original paintings by this artist. In fact, the original of this painting had hung in her parental home in Russia before the Communist takeover. Her parents lost their home and most of their possessions when they immigrated to Germany. She asked Karl if he knew the name of the painter. He replied that it was by the Russian painter Viktor Vasnetsov (1848–1926) and that it depicted Aljonushka and Ivanushka, two famous Russian folktale characters. Mrs. Hadele began to cry again. Even though she was wheelchair bound, he could see that she had an aristocratic bearing and that she must have been a beautiful woman in her youth.

"You should go to the Volkfest in Bad Cannstatt. It is a harvest festival—you should go there and enjoy yourself," she insisted.

"My finances do not allow me to spend money," he replied.

"With your looks," she laughed, "you are sure to be invited by the girls. You should eat more—you are too thin!"

Karl thanked them for the coffee and said that he would buy his monthly streetcar ticket and then he would attend the Volkfest.

Bad Cannsatt is a district of Stuttgart where the Mercedes Benz headquarters and factories were located. The Volkfest was set in a large area with many tents and carousels. It was crawling with people. After walking around and taking in the sights for more than an hour, Karl finally sat down on a bench. Suddenly someone put their hands over his eyes from behind. When he turned around he saw two laughing girls. One of the girls spoke in a Schwabisch dialect and asked if he had come from a funeral. Karl asked them to speak slowly. The other girl had a beautiful smile and asked if he was Italian. He said no and that he was Persian. She ran her fingers through his hair and loudly proclaimed,

"You are going to be my very own Shah!"

At that time the most popular German magazine story was *Shah and Soraya,* and everyone was familiar with it. Then amidst gales of laughter, they lifted him up on both sides and dragged him toward the Hofbrau beer tent. It was a huge area with more than five hundred people eating at tables and benches. An orchestra played in the background as people noisily enjoyed themselves, eating and quaffing beer.

The girls found some empty seating and placed Karl in the middle. While giggling and ruffling his hair, they told people on either side, "He is OUR Shah!"

The girls asked Karl if he would like a beer and a bratwurst. When he asked how much that would cost, the tall blonde girl said, "My name is Barbelle, and my friend is Elizabeth, and you are my guest."

That was the second time he had tasted beer. The first time was just few months before his trip to Germany. Karl's brother-in-law had offered him a glass of beer in Tehran. At that time, most of the old Iranians took their beer with a pinch of salt. This time the beer tasted much sweeter and better. The enormous tankard held a liter of beer. Throughout the night, the girls became increasingly friendly and playful, most likely a little drunk. Barbelle asked Karl to meet her the following day at the Marquart coffee bar. When they met again, she looked much more attractive than the previous evening. This time he asked to be allowed to pay for the coffee. Barbelle invited him to a dance that afternoon. Karl asked to be excused since he could not dance. Then she told him quite decisively that he would be going to evening ballroom classes. The next week he enrolled in the cheapest dance program. Instantly Barbelle became his girlfriend, and he became attracted to her. When she asked if he loved her, he told her that he liked her very much but he was not sure about loving her. Karl was not sure if he indeed had fallen in love with her. One evening she came to the cantina of the dormitory Karl was staying at to pay him a visit. Karl was sitting in a corner, arm-in-arm and laughing with another academy student. Then, as if from nowhere, Barbelle was standing in front of them. She looked at the two and exclaimed,

"This is how you love me!"

She was instantly annoyed.

"I can change a shoe but not a man!"

With this exclamation, she stormed out of the building. Later she sent Karl a letter telling him that he had made the biggest mistake of his life and that maybe after ten or twenty years he would realize his loss. The letter said that he would never know what he had missed out on and that he should never call her ever again. Karl had really liked her and missed her for a long time. He often reflected on this chance meeting and hoped that if she was to be his eternal companion that she would be waiting for him at the pearly gates.

Karl was progressing with his studies and would go dancing every weekend, sometimes with a lady friend, sometimes with a group of friends, and sometimes on his own. This pattern became a ritual for him that continued even when he went to Sweden. He was never of a jealous or possessive nature and always had congenial relations with members of the opposite sex, treating them with due respect. A few of these liaisons blossomed into lifelong friendships that became like family to him.

From time to time, as he reflected on his life as a confirmed bachelor, he never regretted the life he enjoyed. He did not think that he would have been a good husband or a long-time partner. Years later he realized that no woman of a sound mind would allow a husband, or partner, to pursue such a crazy life, allowing him unlimited freedom to crisscross the world the way he had, while squandering his fortune as a compulsive spender, as he had unfortunately done.

One thing he was deeply grateful for was having many kind and loyal relatives, friends, colleagues, gallery owners, and journalists. Proof of this occurred when he fell ill with a deadly form of lymphoma. He received hundreds of emails, phone calls, and letters. He also received flowers from around the world, with sincere prayers for his recovery. He regarded these well wishes as a heavenly blessing, for which he was eternally grateful. He envied Pygmalion, who created his own ideal woman as a sculpture and named her Galatea. The sculpture was so perfect that the gods gave her life and awarded her to Pygmalion as his ideal wife. Karl would complete his Odyssey of world travels, but there would be no Penelope waiting for him on the shore when he returned.

Siegfried, 1990–1994

Chapter 10

ONE GERMAN MARK BUYS A LIFETIME OF CULTURAL ENJOYMENT

During the fifties and sixties, students at the Academy of Art and other technical colleges in Stuttgart had their lunches and dinners at their student canteens close to their dormitories. For just ninety pfennig—approximately one US dollar—one could get a decent meal. Every month Karl paid his rent, bought a monthly streetcar pass, and fifty canteen coupons. The canteens served lunch and dinner Mondays to Friday's and lunch only on Saturdays.

One pleasant Saturday afternoon, Karl had his last meal for the weekend at the canteen. He had just one German mark left in his pocket. That weekend he thought he would be doomed to promenade in the parks and sightsee in the city with its ruined World War II buildings. He lived in a one-room apartment rented out by a family on Breitsheid Strasse, just five hundred yards from the canteen. The concert hall was also nearby. He had passed the hall every day on his way to and from college for the past six months. He had once had a class visit to the concert hall with the professor who had designed it. It never occurred to Karl to go to a concert there. At that time, all he knew of classical music were the names Beethoven and Mozart. The only piece of music he recognized was Straus's Blue Danube.

As he approached the concert hall, a poster caught his attention. It announced that there would be a rehearsal of Beethoven's symphony number 3 at 2:00 p.m., admission 1 mark. While he watched he saw some students and elderly people going into the hall. Thinking that he could do very little with the mark in his pocket, he decided to spend it on a ticket for this Beethoven concert that he had seen advertised. He bought the ticket, went in, and sat down in the auditorium. One of his student colleagues took the seat at his side and began explaining to him about the conductor Rudolf Kempe, who later became one of Karl's favorite conductors of Wagner and Anton Brukner. Karl became good friends with this young student and they met together again on many occasions in the city.

Before he started conducting, Kempe explained a little about the second movement that was to be performed without costumes since this was a rehearsal. Those in the audience were student intellectuals and retirees, most of whom had little money. Karl read the introduction, but it was like giving a poetry book to a toddler. The musical vocabulary was too advanced for him. His student friend gave him a short explanation of what he should expect. The conductor stepped onto the podium, and immediately the audience applauded. He did not know why they were applauding since he did not know the relationship between the conductor and the orchestra.

Karl had never known what the role of the conductor was. His student friend explained to him that the conductor stands before the orchestra and makes them play the notes the way he wants them to. He gives each instrument its tempo and volume. After listening to the first and then the second movements, the music held Karl's attention. On leaving the concert hall, he concluded that this was an engaging way to spend a Saturday afternoon. It was a dramatic change from attending the weekly dances at the Kilesberg Schloss Gardens ballroom and was the catalyst for a lifetime of music connoisseurship.

Chapter 11

PATRONS APPEAR

Karl was a registered student at the Stuttgart Kunstakademie supporting himself, so like many other students, he took part-time employment with local architectural firms to provide much-needed financial support. In November 1958, the architectural office of Herman Reiser, a highly acclaimed architect and designer of luxury mansions for the rich and famous, hired him. Reiser had seen some of Karl's elevation and perspective drawings at the Academy and had been impressed with his skill and precision. He asked Karl if he could work for him at his office in the late afternoons after his classes. Karl accepted.

Reiser's office was located under his large villa, just a ten-minute walk from the Art Academy's architecture school situated in the Old Castle on a hill in Kilesberg overlooking Stuttgart. It was located in one of the most fashionable areas of the city. As a working student, Karl took every opportunity to earn some extra money. It was for this reason that he also often accepted commissions to paint portraits of the wives of American Air Force officers.

He started working for Reiser at the beginning of November 1958 and was immediately assigned to complete the drawings for a large villa. A previous architect had drawn the plan for this villa but had resigned before finishing the work, and Reiser now needed Karl to complete the project. Reiser was so impressed with Karl's work that he immediately gave him a raise after he had completed only the first elevation. Reiser then asked Karl to accompany him to the house of Helga Heinkel, who had commissioned Reiser's firm to draw up the plans for the villa. When Helga Heinkel discovered that Karl was a work-release student from Iran, she specified that she wanted Karl to do all the elevation drawings for her new luxury villa. It turned out that Helga Heinkel was the daughter of Ernest Heinkel, whose company, Heinkel Flugzeugwerke, produced the Heinkel He 178, the world's first turbojet aircraft, and the Heinkel He 176, the first rocket-propelled aircraft. It was Heinkel's bombers that assaulted London during the Blitz of WWII when more than two hundred of these planes were shot down. Ernest Heinkel had died in January of that year.

Reiser asked Karl not to discuss this new project and the identity of the client with any of his friends, and Karl understood that this was a private operation.

Karl visited Helga Heinkel on several more occasions to obtain her approval for his elevation and three-dimensional perspective drawings of the new villa. When the villa was completed, Karl was invited to the exclusive opening party, organized by Helga Heinkel for a few close friends. After some research of the Heinkel family's history, Karl realized how blessed he was to be a self-supporting student with empty pockets, who had been availed with such choice once-in-a-lifetime experiences.

During the late spring of 1959, Karl started an internship at Gerhard Holtzwart's architect's office in Stuttgart. Holtzwart was a distinguish man, active in society, with good relationships with the leading industrialists of his day. Holtzwart was awarded the design for the personal mansion of Dr. Eiselman, the Daimler Benz CEO, and Karl was assigned as his assistant and began immediate work on the three-dimensional perspective projections. Here his painting knowledge was very useful. When the design reached a recognizable stage, Frau Eiselman, the lady of the house, took complete oversight in dealing with the architects of her new mansion. Her husband was a high-powered CEO and had no time to spend on the house designs. That was the duty of the lady of the house.

At the start of the project Karl would go to the Eiselman's home and spread his drawings out on the kitchen table. He would explain the details of the plans and then ask Frau Eiselman her opinion. He would note the changes she wanted and return to his office to make the corrections. The next week he would return with the latest draft of the drawings for her approval. Frau Eiselman was a good-looking, middle-aged woman, very aware of her social status but also very kind to Karl. She knew he was an Iranian student working his way through college. She insisted that he arrive at around 11:00 a.m., and at noon she would announce, "Lunch time!"

Her maid prepared the lunch, and he was invited to join the lady of the house for a sumptuous spread. Karl soon got the impression that Frau Eiselman's sole intention was to support a poor starving student with a good meal once a week.

The design for the mansion progressed well, and after a while, Karl became Frau Eiselman's trusted adviser. Holtzwart was pleased with him and gave him a key to the office, something that was previously unheard of for a student employee. When his lectures started, he was allowed to work at the office at times convenient for his schedule and for his meetings with Frau Eiselman. Karl's meetings with her now moved to late afternoons, after which he was served dinner. This routine continued for three months. When the mansion was completed, Karl was on hand to provide Frau Eiselman with a range of interior design journals to assist her in her selection of furnishings. The house was already partially furnished with high quality furnishings, and she made a thoughtful combination of new pieces.

When the mansion was completed, the night came for this lady of substance to show off her yearlong planning and decision-making activities to the crème de la crème of Stuttgart's high society. The house warming was a sumptuous affair, designed to elicit the stunned admiration and bravos of her guests and the approbation of her proud husband. In other cases, Karl would have been concerned about the husband's reaction to the final cost of the contract, but in this case, he need not to have been concerned.

As a reward for his labors, Frau Eiselman's generosity toward Karl was limited to a good lunch and a good dinner for a poor student. However, Karl's association with her also helped cultivate his love for good music, the theater, and the opera. The Eiselman's had reserved seats or owned loges in concert halls. When Frau Eiselman found out that Karl had an interest in music and theater and that he was attending the general rehearsals on Saturday afternoons, she invited him to accompany her one evening to a concert. After that, Karl was invited to use the Eiselman's assigned seating whenever they did not attend or were out of town.

Karl's association with the Eiselmans had long-term benefits. Some years later, in 1979, Karl attended a performance of Parsifal at Bayreuth Opera, directed by Wolfgang Wagner, a grandson of Richard Wagner. On this occasion, Karl was introduced to the younger Wagner after the performance by Rudolf Kempe, general conductor at the Stuttgart Concert Hall, who in turn had been introduced to Karl by Dr. and Mrs. Eiselman.

On another occasion in October 1959, Karl accompanied Gerhart Holtzwart to Sulz in Wildberg, Bavaria, to meet the owner of the Steeb AB Corporation. Holtzwart had completed Mr. Steeb's palatial mansion the previous year and wanted to introduce Karl to Mr. and Mrs. Steeb. Karl brought along a fine portrait of a young princess in the court of Khaliph of Baghdad. He had depicted her from the 1954 Hollywood production of *1001 Arabian Nights*. Holzwart was keen to have the Steebs take a look at Karl's portrait. Upon seeing the painting, Mr. and Mrs. Steeb were immediately astonished by its almost photographic acuity and said it would be ideal for the wall above their fireplace in the main hall of their residence. When they asked how much they could buy it for, Holzwart said that it was an expensive artwork, but because Karl was a student, he would be happy to part with it for four hundred marks. This was equivalent to three months' salary at his job in Holzwart's architectural office.

The Roof, 1974

Chapter 12

PFENNINGER'S JUDGMENT

By the end of 1959, Karl was progressing so well in his architectural studies that he decided to seek admission to the art program at adjoining Kunstakademie in Stuttgart in addition to his architectural studies. The Academy allowed part-time registration for students who needed to work full time. These were hard times economically and few students could pursue a full-time program for three or four years on a continuous basis. At the admission interview, Karl presented one of his portraits, a landscape, and some sketches. Professor Pfenninger, a serious man in his early sixties, interviewed him. After reviewing Karl's portfolio, he was ushered into the dean's office. Here Pfenninger and the dean poured over his work and appeared to be impressed.

Pfenninger exclaimed, "Why do you want to come to the Academy? You can sketch and paint in various media like a fully trained artist! I don't think you can learn anything more from us!"

Karl explained to the two men that he had realized, since coming to Germany, that art was more than simply rendering a portrait, landscape, or a still life in a photographically accurate manner. He wanted to learn more about the stylistic development of art and of the contemporary movements in art, such as Expressionism and surrealism. He knew that Professor Pfenninger had produced new expressionistic work himself. Karl was duly registered and became the only student at the Academy from east of the Bosphorous. He immediately started attending Pfenninger's afternoon life-drawing classes. Karl was quick and competent in his work. He found that he could draw the model from several different angles before the other students in the class could complete just one pose. He was interested in Salvador Dali at the time, and after two weeks in Pfenninger's class, he produced a painting in Dali's surrealistic manner. Pfenninger was so taken aback that he took Karl into his private office where he was given an easel and invited to work without interruption. From here on, Pfenninger would give Karl private lessons. Pfenninger explained that he did not want Karl working in the same studio as the other art students, because they were still striving to learn the basic techniques and they might become demoralized by Karl's proficiency. He also recommended that Karl work at home as much as possible and bring him his work for review. He offered to guide Karl wherever he could. Karl got the impression that Pfenninger was gently telling him that he would be wasting his time in the class with the other students and that he was accomplished enough to work independently. Pfenninger and Karl became good friends and spent many hours in discussion about their work.

One day Professor Pfenninger asked Karl to show him how traditional Persian miniatures were painted. Karl demonstrated the technique to him, starting with the background and building up the entire picture with minute stipples with the point of a fine brush. This technique was similar to the work of the Pointillists but on a much finer and minute scale. Pfenninger was also interested in the work of Yuri Popov and the techniques of his mural decoration. Karl explained how together they would make paper stencils and spray paint over them to create repeat patterns on the walls. The motifs that Popov used were often identical to the simple geometric symbols used by the early Constructivists, symbolists, and the Russian avant-garde painters that he studied. Abstract geometric shapes based on squares, circles, and semicircles recurred frequently, often painted in primary colors with touches of black and white. Interestingly, the people who commissioned these patterns for the murals in their houses in Mashhad had no idea of their Russian avant-garde origin but considered them beautiful in their own right.

In September 1958, Karl received an invitation from the new Hilton Hotel in Tehran to complete a large portrait of the Shah of Iran for the lobby of the hotel. He was given private accommodation and all his expenses were paid at the hotel for three weeks while he worked on the twelve-foot portrait painting. He was paid handsomely for this commission. Strangely, history repeated itself some years later when in 1979 the Shah was deposed. Members of the Islamic revolutionary guard stripped the portrait from the hotel wall and threw it into the street for revolutionary troops to march over.

Upon his return to Stuttgart, Karl received a commission to paint a portrait of Mrs. Eiselman, wife of the president of the Mercedes Benz car company. He painted several portraits of lawyers and famous industrialists in Stuttgart, their wives, and their children. From these contacts, he developed a circle of professional friends and associates that was a world removed from the poor working class of his fellow students. He gained confidence in himself and learned from the cultural life that he enjoyed. It was also at this time that Karl's interest in classical music, the theater, and the opera grew. Many of his newfound friends would invite him to their cabins in the Bavarian Alps or in the Schwarzwald. As he became familiar with European etiquette, good wine, music, and conversation, he was assimilated into this new culture. As he acquired these new social graces, he no longer felt intimidated by high society.

In Stuttgart, students at the architecture school had to complete a total of twelve months working in different areas of the construction industry as part of their course requirements. Consequently, in the summer of 1959, Karl took a three-month internship at a construction site in Berlin. While Karl was in Berlin, he took full advantage of his student status. Together with other foreign student friends, he soon discovered that he did not need a passport or visa to pass through Checkpoint Charlie to East Berlin. He and his friends made this trip several times a week and also on weekends, because they discovered that they could exchange their West German marks for four times as many East German marks on the black market. For the cost of one West German mark, they could go to an East German restaurant, have a good meal, and meet interesting people. Many East German intellectuals would gather at these cafés, and he had the pleasure of meeting several of them. It was at one of these informal gatherings that Karl met Lota Lene, Bertold Brecht's consort. Conversations often erupted into heated debates about the virtues of a particular artist's work or the finer points of socialist ideology. Although he was not very politicized at the time, Karl leaned toward the ideas of the social democrats. He favored the Swedish form of government above all others. He was a little "pinkish" in his political alignment, as most students were at time.

On several occasions he ran into Günther Grass, a man who would later become one of his favorite writers and the author of *The Tin Drum*. Grass was interested in the political situation in Iran and stated that although he was not in favor of the Shah, he would think twice before replacing him. Karl was definitely in favor of the liberal reforms of Dr. Mossadegh and would choose him to lead Iran over all others. This was a country in which 70 percent of the population was illiterate at the time. Karl did not think it possible that a largely illiterate population could adopt the high-minded ideals of European socialism. What the people needed first was a democracy that could be built with the help of a common citizenry of people who could at least read and write. If people lacked this fundamental level of education, it would be difficult to lead them toward the ideals of a democratic society. He thought that western democracy could not be easily transplanted into this situation. However, when he saw the misery of life in East Berlin and the extreme levels of control that were imposed on the people, he became less convinced about the socialist system.

In Berlin Karl joined other Iranian students who were anti-Shah and who were opposed to the persecution of leftists in Iran. They petitioned the office of Willie Brandt, who was mayor of Berlin at the time. Karl and his friends met Brandt on two occasions in his office to petition their cause. At this time, Karl received a request to paint a portrait of Brandt, but the Berlin authorities never followed through with it.

Karl also became increasingly aligned with the philosophical viewpoint of the Constructivists and their rationalist ideals. From this time forward, he found naturalistic and representational painting inadequate in providing the means for addressing the unanswered questions that loomed over his society. This self-realization came about as a direct result of his studies at the Kunstakademie. Consequently, he stopped signing his commissioned works. He did not want to be identified with a style that he now considered to be passé and perhaps even non-art. Above all, he wanted to embrace the new modernism that he had been exposed to; however, he continued to gain commissions and painted many portraits of the rich and famous as well as American colonels and their wives while working in Stuttgart. In 1959 he completed a fine portrait of Ludwig Erhard, who was the minister of finance in Stuttgart at the time—all these later works were unsigned.

Chapter 13

LESSONS FROM MODERN MASTERS

THE INFLUENCE OF OSKAR SCHLEMMER

Soon after Karl's arrival in Stuttgart, he discovered the works of Oskar Schlemmer (1888–1943), and he was deeply moved. Karl responded to the strength and conviction he saw in this Bauhaus artist's work. In addition to his painting, Schlemmer was an innovative theater and costume designer who had also experimented with cinematic media. Karl attended a large exhibition of his work in Stuttgart in the fall of 1959, and he was profoundly influenced by this experience. He found such a strong accord with Schlemmer's painting that in later years he would often pay homage to Schlemmer through oblique references in his own paintings.

Karl acknowledged Schlemmer as one of the finest Bauhaus artists and considered it unfortunate that he did not receive as much acclaim for his work as his colleagues. The artistic climate fostered by the Bauhaus permeated all levels of the European art world during the 1940s, 50s and 60s, providing a counterfoil for the American pop art that became increasingly popular during the 1960s. Karl became so interested in the work of the Bauhaus that he avidly read all he could find about this unique school and its exponents.

The architect Walter Gropius founded the Bauhaus School of Art, Craft, and Design in 1919 in Weimar Germany on principles of socialist thinking. The precepts of this school found easy and ready acceptance in Karl's mind at the time. Some of the most celebrated names in the modernist movement of the twentieth century were associated with the Bauhaus, mainly artists and designers from northern Europe and Russia, including Joseph Albers, Theo van Doesberg, Wassily Kandinsky, Paul Klee, László Moholy-Nagy, and Oskar Schlemmer among others. The movement courted industrial technology and offered its students an anti-academic curriculum that embraced architecture and sculpture as an indivisible entity. It was here that Karl found the roots of his architectonic sculptural style, particularly in the work of El Lissitzky and Oskar Schlemmer. These like-minded artists had also received architectural training as the basis for their artistic expression.

When László Moholy-Nagy joined the Bauhaus, he brought with him the latest Russian Constructivist thinking which was imported, in part, from the Vkhutemas (Higher Technical and Artistic Studios) of the Soviet Union. The emphasis of the Bauhaus also shifted from its original handcraft orientation toward industrial production and functionalism. Significantly, Mies van der Rohe, who was the last director of the Bauhaus before its termination by the Nazis in 1933, was also a highly respected architect. Bauhaus designs became widely known through the school's aggressive publishing program and were responsible for influencing design, graphics, and architecture throughout the Western world before Hitler forced out its chief proponents. The powerful climate of artistic foment that prevailed in Germany during these early years provided the ethos within which Karl gained his formative exposure to contemporary western art. He easily accepted the objectivism and abstraction of the Bauhaus, having already been exposed to the avant-garde work of the early Russian Constructivists in his hometown, Mashhad. He had also been predisposed to the forms of abstraction and the use of strong color through his early exposure to the geometric motifs in the mural decorations that he helped Yuri Popow create in his hometown. Moreover, the powerful childhood memories that Karl had of his father's two-dimensional rug design motifs had left an enduring impression on him.

MAX ERNST'S ADVICE

At the Art Academy in Stuttgart, Karl was pleasantly surprised to discover that Professor Pfenninger was a childhood friend of Max Ernst (1891–1976) and that Ernst would often visit the professor when he was in Stuttgart. Ernst traveled to Stuttgart on the occasion of Schlemmer's 1959 exhibition to view his work. Pfenninger used this opportunity to introduce Karl to Ernst as the only Middle Eastern student at the academy. He also told Ernst of Karl's facility with the techniques of Persian miniature painting. Ernst was intrigued and invited Karl to show him his work. Karl complied and spent several hours discussing Persian miniatures and mural ornamentation with Ernst. When

CHAPTER 13

Karl told him that his father was a designer and manufacturer of Persian rugs, Ernst became even more interested. Students and faculty at the academy held Ernst in high regard, and a few months later, Ernst returned to the Academy at the invitation of Professor Pfenninger, who was due for a sabbatical. On a later occasion when Karl was showing his recent work to Ernst, he was confronted with the same question that Professor Pfenninger had put to him at the time of his enrollment:

"What do you hope to learn here at the Academy? Your work is already accomplished, and you are a proficient artist."

Karl replied that he would like to participate in Ernst's class for one week. He was even willing to travel to France to Ernst's studio. He expressed the hope that Ernst would guide him from time-to-time. When Karl showed him a few of his paintings that he had done after Salvador Dali, Ernst's response was quick and definitive:

"Why did you paint this?"

"Well it is surrealistic, and it is very good. Salvador Dali is a brilliant painter, and I am impressed with his technique," Momen replied defensively.

"Maybe you could try something else?" Speaking even more assertively, Ernst drove his point home. "Mr. Momen, we don't need two Salvador Dali's. Do something else!"

Karl immediately realized that he should establish his own style, independent of the artists he had been looking at. He almost lost the desire to paint at all and did not lift a brush for ten weeks, because he thought it would be a waste of time. Ernst was right. He did not want to become a second Salvador Dali. Salvador Dali was an established artist with a very particular character. There was no need for him to mimic his style. Karl got over his despondency and visited Ernst at his studio in France on several occasions.

In 1960, Max Ernst introduced Karl to the work of Jean Arp and Vassily Kandinsky during a visit to their homes in Strasbourg. Both artists had been strongly influenced by the theories of Rudolph Steiner at the time. Ernst referred to their style as "theosophical." He said that this form of art making had evolved from their desire to express pure emotion in their painting. These artists felt that art should portray not merely the objective reality but also the spiritual turbulence of the soul.

Later Karl also met and became good friends with Yves Klein. He liked Klein and considered him to be a thorough gentleman. Through his association with Klein, he lost his anxiety about his own painting. He was inspired by what he saw Klein do with monochromatic techniques and began experimenting with a limited palette. However, these paintings did not satisfy him. Klein struck Karl as one of the most elegantly dressed artists he had ever met. He always wore a suit and tie, even while spray-painting or producing body prints on canvas with blue painted models—even while making enamels with a welding torch.

The way an artist should dress was put into perspective for Karl one day when Max Ernst arrived at class to find one of the students looking very "artily" dressed in leather jacket and pants. Ernst asked the student, "Are you going to a masked ball or a carnival?"

The student replied that it was not carnival time, whereupon Ernst retorted, "Exactly so! An artist should be recognized by his art, not by what he wears!"

Ernst always wore a tweed jacket and looked the epitome of an English country gentleman. Karl reflected that he had likewise never seen Henry Moore without his tweed jacket and tartan tie. Most significant artists of the day were always conservatively dressed. There was never any great difference in the way that Henry Moore, Max Ernst, or Jean Arp dressed. Fontana and Salvador Dali were the exceptions. Dali preferred to dress like the most affected dandy of the day. Fontana was usually overdressed and would often wear an immaculate suit with hat, necktie, and black and tan shoes. Karl had the pleasure of meeting Fontana several times and even bought one of his works. These were hard years for Karl since he still had to complete his architecture studies. Things were made even more difficult by the fact that his heart was not entirely set on an architecture career. The desire to create art that would touch people's sensibilities more immediately and perhaps more profoundly than his utilitarian architectural commissions became a constant concern to him.

In 1965, on the occasion of the Moderne Museet's exhibition of Peggy Guggenheim's collection of Ernst's work, Ernst and Karl had lunch together. Karl showed him some of his own work, which had by this time moved beyond surrealism to a more architectonic style. His advice to Karl on that occasion was again simple and to the point:

"Keep it your way and don't look at anything else. Just keep it your way—do it the way you feel. You have an advantage in that you have good technique. It is also to your advantage that you are an architect with cosmopolitan views, but don't look at anyone else's work. Do it your own way!"[2]

Karl would always remember Ernst's advice. At the time, he was not impressed with the technical quality of Ernst's oil painting, although he thought he had a fine etching technique. Years later, when they met again, Karl confessed that he had never really understood Ernst's art in those early years and that he had judged him purely on technical grounds. Ernst was moved by Karl's simple confession and said that he appreciated his honesty.

LE CORBUSIER AS MENTOR

Ernst had given Karl an introduction to Le Corbusier's architecture studio in Nice. Le Corbusier's designs and writings had a revolutionary influence on the development of modern architecture with his introduction of the international style. Karl traveled to France at the commencement of the summer vacation in 1960 and was offered an internship working as a draftsman for Le Corbusier. On his arrival in Nice, he was immediately impressed with Le Corbusier's beautiful office and its custom-designed furniture. He also noticed that Le Corbusier had a beautiful nomadic Luristan Persian rug on the floor of his office. Karl was confused and exclaimed:

"Le Corbusier, the great architect of this century, and he has a nomadic Persian rug on the floor?"

"They were before everyone. They discovered form long before we did. Your great ancestors have been the precursors to all abstract art," responded Le Corbusier.

Le Corbusier looked favorably on Karl and referred to him as "Monsieur le patron," a term he reserved for his closest associates. Karl's first assignment was to translate Persian texts and to find pictures of historic buildings in Uzbakistan and Afghanistan for a project Le Corbusier was working on in India. Karl provided a wealth of material and also became Le Corbusier's favorite coffee boy. Fortunately, Le Corbusier was multi-lingual, and he could converse with Karl in German since Karl could speak little French. Karl would often work at his side, helping him with his collages. This was a great and memorable experience for him. Le Corbusier was often tough on his architects and studio workers, but he was always relaxed and talkative to Karl.

Le Corbusier expressed a compelling interest in Persian rug design, and Karl obliged by explaining how the idea for the pattern was developed and how the design was transferred from the color chart to the loom. Karl was fortunate in that he had spent two summers working as a pattern draftsman at the Iranian Carpet Company in Mashhad when he was a teenager. Consequently, he could inform Le Corbusier on how a design pattern was conceived and how the design was transferred from a color chart to the loom. Le Corbusier was fascinated by the way the colors were organized and worked into the design. Karl explained how each color was numbered on a chart and how his father would often work with two hundred different types of colored wool, each indicated on his design by a corresponding number. Le Corbusier was intrigued by the fact that someone could work with such a complex pattern and with so many different colors committed to memory. Karl told him of the enormous carpet at the Gulbenkian Museum in Lisbon that his father had designed. Le Corbusier remembered a large Khorisan rug from Masshad that he had once seen, and he marveled that anyone could produce such a complex and beautiful design by simply visualizing the colors in their mind.

Karl's experience with Le Corbusier was positive, and he returned the following two years to the studio in Nice to complete his internship. Le Corbusier gave him one of his collages in appreciation for his assistance. Karl sold the collage on his return to Stuttgart for a few thousand marks, not realizing that it would one day be worth many hundred times that amount. Karl would often sell works from famous artists that he was given, not realizing their future value. It was only when he had become an established architect in Sweden that he realized what opportunities he had enjoyed with important artists of his day, particularly Max Ernst and Le Corbusier.

It came as a welcome release some years later in 1978 when he eventually gave up his highly successful architectural practice in order to devote himself entirely to his art. He remembered that the only reason he had originally gone into the architectural field was that his family, who wanted him to have the security of a well-paid profession, was pressuring him to do so. They had never considered art as a viable occupation that could in any way provide for his financial welfare.

San Francisco, 1991

Chapter 14

WORKING IN SWEDEN

In the fall of 1961, Karl was in the final year of his architectural studies at the Art Academy in Stuttgart under the tutelage of Professor Gutbier. One morning Professor Gutbier asked him if he would mind having lunch, at his expense, with one of his Swedish colleagues. Unfortunately, Gutbier had a prior commitment and would not be able to keep the lunch appointment with the visitor. As a student accustomed to eating military rations in the students' canteen, Karl jumped at the opportunity. Gutbier gave him a couple of hundred marks, approximately half an architect's monthly salary at the time, and sent him on his way.

When Karl met Sergei Merilius, he soon discovered that the Swedish architect, who had been born in Lithuania, had come to Sweden as an immigrant with his parents before the war. Merilius found it interesting that Karl was from Persia and that his father was rooted in the Russian culture. The two men enjoyed an engaging conversation over an excellent lunch. Before they parted company, Merilius invited Karl to come and work in Sweden after his graduation. Karl knew little about Sweden, other than that he believed it to be a model of democratic governance. He had heard that the King and Queen of Sweden often walked the streets unaccompanied by bodyguards and that the Queen went grocery shopping on her bicycle. This seemed an idyllic social system. He remembered studying the Forot system of urban planning, which involved satellite suburbs that had been designed by Sven Markelius, a Swedish architect. Several weeks later he received a formal invitation to work at Merilius's Swedish office as an architect. Karl's mouth fell open when he read that he would be appointed at a salary of fifteen hundred Swedish crowns per month. This was three times as much as a qualified architect could earn in Germany. He left for Sweden at the end of September 1961 to investigate the proposal. He moved to Sweden in February of the following year for what was to have been a six-month trial period, but he ended up staying permanently. He would later become a Swedish citizen.

In February 1962, Karl took a second-class train ticket to Stockholm. He arrived in a bitterly cold blizzard and immediately went to the information desk to ask about an inexpensive hotel where he could stay the night. He was well dressed in a suit, tie, and expensive overcoat and was soon traveling by taxi to the recommended hotel. Upon his arrival, the hotel concierge helped him with his bags. Karl insisted on carrying his most prized possession, a Blaupunkt Model 57 radio that he had bought in Stuttgart with his Bosch Company discount. He paid the taxi-driver and approached the main reception desk in the lobby to check in. A blond and very beautiful young Swedish desk clerk confronted him. After a polite greeting, she disappeared into a back office. After what seemed an eternity, she returned with her supervisor, who politely inform Karl that his reservation was actually at the hotel down the road! It turned out that he had been given incorrect directions at the station and that he had arrived at Stockholm's Grand Hotel, the most ostentatious hotel in the city, when he should have been directed to the local YMCA. The Grand Hotel was a landmark in Stockholm and was patronized by aristocracy and Nobel Prize winners. Karl was embarrassed and turned to walk away. This time the concierge did not offer to help him with his bags, and he left on foot with all his belongings and his Blaupunkt radio under his arm.

He trudged through the cold, wet snow in the general direction indicated by the wave of the bellboy's hand. When he arrived in the vicinity indicated, there was no sign of the YMCA or of a hostel of any kind. All Karl could see was the dark silhouette of the National Museum against the stormy sky. He continued on and eventually ended up at the waterfront. Here he came upon a large three-masted schooner docked at the quayside. He saw a young man approaching on the road and asked him directions to the YMCA. The young man pointed to the nineteenth-century schooner. Karl thanked the young man and boarded the *Af Chapman*, a floating YMCA. He spent a memorable two weeks living onboard. The ship had been divided in half, with men on the one side and women on the other. There were four bunks per cabin. It was aboard this floating hostel that he befriended many young intellectuals who were equally out of pocket but who soon became fine companions and conversationalists. This unlikely "hotel" held such fond memories for Karl that three years later, after he had established himself in the city, he paid the schooner a nostalgic visit. He even stayed overnight to rekindle the memories of many memorable conversations with friends who had since moved on with their lives.

The next day, he took a taxi to Gamla Stan, a carefully preserved historic town situated on an island near the center of Stockholm. The town dated from the sixteenth century, and every detail had been carefully and authentically preserved and restored to its original condition. It was here that Sergei Merilius had his architectural office. Karl had been used to strict punctuality on the job during his stay in Germany. He remembered his first architects' office in Stuttgart, where he started work at six in the morning. It was here that Herman Reiser, the boss, had once reprimanded Karl in no uncertain manner:

"Mr. Momen, six o'clock doesn't mean that you arrive at the office at six o'clock. Six o'clock means that you are sitting behind your desk, you have your white coat on, and you have sharpened your pencil. Then when six o'clock strikes, you draw your first line!"

Germany was poor after the war, and office frugalities were carried to extremes. The draftsmen could only request new lead for their propelling pencils from the office clerk on presentation of their used fragments. They continued to reuse their sketch paper by erasing previous sketches until the paper disintegrated. Office dress was strict and severe. Everyone wore jackets with long dustcoats, even in the summer. Upon arrival before six o'clock in the morning, one would shake hands with everyone in the office and wish them all a good morning. It was obligatory to address everyone in the most formal manner. Draftsmen were not expected to have original ideas of their own.

In his new Swedish office the employees were all on first-name terms with each other. They were all dressed casually, some in turtleneck sweaters, others in ski clothing. Each architect had his own radio at his side. There were some Germans in the group who had graduated the year before Karl. They were still formal and wore ties to work; however, the atmosphere was free and easy. Karl was shown to his office: "Here is your room. Here is a dictionary . . . and here is your first project."

Then he was shown the materials storeroom. It was laden with rolls of paper and boxes of pens that he could help himself to as needed. And, of course, everyone had his or her own roll of sketch paper. Karl was given a key to the building and told that he could work his eight hours per day as he pleased. If he did not have an early morning meeting, he could come late to work or stay late at night as it suited him! He was only responsible for his own project. At nine-thirty that morning, he received yet another shock when Mariane, the office secretary, announced,

"Please come and have coffee" in perfect German.

In the break room Karl soon discovered that his new colleagues were from Austria, Germany, Finland, and Norway and that there were only two Swedes in this company. Sweden had a severe shortage of architects and engineers during these years. A dozen employees enjoyed casual conversation as they drank their beverages and ate large loaves of wiener bread. Karl was under the mistaken impression that this gathering was in his honor and that this special break would give him an opportunity to meet everyone. Later that day he had lunch with Hans Schreier, whom he had known previously in Germany. Then at 2:30 in the afternoon, Mariane again called everyone for coffee. This time Karl declined, because he had not received his first paycheck and had little money to see out the month. Then Hans Schreier, one of the Germans, knowingly approached him and pointedly declared, "You domkopf! The coffee is free!"

Karl soon discovered that in Sweden it was legislated that employees could not work without a break for more than three hours at a stretch. This was so different to his previous work experience in Germany. Sweden had never suffered the hardships that had wracked other European countries during World War II. To the contrary, Sweden had actually benefited economically as its industries sold equipment to the opposing sides throughout the war. The country's economy had never been disrupted and had continued to grow, making Sweden one of the richest countries in Europe at the time.

Three months into his new position, Karl found that he had an aptitude for hospital design. Not much later he gained employment with Pütsep International, an architectural firm that specialized in building hospitals. Karl was soon on good terms with Ervin Pütsep, his new boss. Pütsep was the leading authority in this field, adopting a rigorous scientific approach to his work. He was particularly skilled at designing surgical and operating theater departments. Karl contributed to various seminars on hospital planning and became totally immersed in his work. He was also beginning to earn good money for the first time in his life. The architects in this new company were cosmopolitan and came from Egypt, Yugoslavia, Hungary, Estonia, England, Ireland, Peru, Germany, Japan, and Finland. Karl referred to them as the "International Architectural Society." Ervin Pütsep was one of the most interesting and intellectually stimulating people he had ever met. He was well informed on the latest developments in contemporary art and was a connoisseur of good music and literature. He would often give Karl the benefit of his expert opinion and encouraged him in his artistic endeavors. Although they often clashed in their business relationship, they remained good friends.

Chapter 15

BECOMING SOCIALLY MOBILE

Karl's hometown of Mashhad had a unique religious atmosphere with pilgrims continually arriving from all over the Middle East. This resulted in a conservative culture with little opportunity for any form of sophisticated social life. Tehran on the other hand was home to the private officers' club with its tennis courts and social activities. The club had a small dance orchestra. Karl attended activities there in the company of his nephew, who was an officer in the army. In this manner, Karl gained his first taste of the social graces that accompanied gentile western high society.

As a result of his former student job as a movie projectionist, Karl had become familiar with hundreds of American musicals that were all the rage during his early years. He could name all the dances but unfortunately could not dance himself. All he could do was a kind of fast-moving Russian and Azerbaijani dance for couples that was often seen at festivities such as weddings and parties.

Later, after settling into his apartment in Stuttgart, he befriended another Iranian student, who invited him to a popular coffee shop that hosted dances on the weekends. On one such occasion, he was invited to dance by a young woman but had to decline since he could not dance. Later he recounted this embarrassing experience to a colleague at the Bosch drafting office where he worked. His colleague mentioned that his girlfriend also could not dance but soon learned at a dance studio in the city. Karl started lessons at the dance school his friend had referred him to and, after three months, became proficient in foxtrot, waltz, tango, and the most popular Latin American dances.

Berns Restaurant

During his first years in Stockholm, Karl often socialized with colleagues and other professionals in the city. As an architect, he enjoyed the respect and compliments he received from other professionals. July was summer vacation time in Sweden, and people poured out of the city into the countryside. To avoid feeling bored and alone when everyone was out of town, Karl decided to work that month. He reasoned that he would be receiving a paycheck anyway, so he might as well work!

Then, on the first day back at the office after their summer vacation in September 1962, Ervin Pütsep, the owner of the architectural company, announced that their office party would be held at Berns Restaurant. All the employees applauded the news with great enthusiasm. When Karl asked Elizabeth, the company secretary, what all the fuss was about, she explained that every year Pütsep invited all the employees to a top restaurant or club for dinner—once in September and once in December before Christmas. She then explained to Karl that Berns was the number one restaurant and casino in Sweden and that it also catered to the top musical performers in the world.

Karl knew exactly how to dress for such a formal occasion. He had seen hundreds of American movies as a projectionist in his youth. He remembered that it was considered appropriate and fashionable to wear a black tuxedo in the winter and a white jacket in the summer. So he found a gentleman's outfitter in Drottninggatan, an old part of the city, and asked for a white jacket. The owner respectfully obliged with a jacket that was the perfect size for Karl. Karl then asked if he could have white silk applied to the collar. The tailor gave Karl a quizzical look and replied,

"Why not! But you will have to pay me first!"

Karl complied, and he soon became the owner of a dashing new white coat. The first week of October arrived, and Karl became increasingly nervous. He compared his anxiety to that of Othello about to be deceived by Iago. The night of the dinner arrived, and Karl had a fearful notion that this auspicious event would be of great significance to him. In fact, he thought it would either make or break him socially!

A party of eighteen people arrived at the exclusive restaurant, and Pütsep courteously welcomed all the guests as they entered and directed them to the main table. Karl was impressed with how efficiently Chris Folker, the celebrated restaurant manager, seated the guests at their designated seating on both sides of the long table. This would indeed be a very formal occasion! After a short welcoming address by Pütsep and the introduction of the guests, drinks were served. Although there was an abundance of wine and other alcoholic beverages, Karl drank only mineral water and light beer at this time. Consequently, he had become

CHAPTER 15

the favorite colleague to sit beside. Anyone who sat next to Karl at such occasions could count on also receiving his share of the alcoholic drinks that were served! The dinner commenced with each course accompanied by a generous serving of the appropriate wine. Then, when all the guests had enjoyed the ample dinner and were being served coffee, the lights dimmed and the orchestra started playing the familiar strains of "If I Was a Millionaire." Then Eartha Kit appeared, right on cue as if from nowhere, and started singing on the small stage. She stepped down from the stage and walked across to Karl's table. She continued singing and stood directly behind Karl's chair.

His embarrassment was complete when he noticed that he was the only one with a white dinner jacket at the table. Karl surmised it was the jacket that had attracted Eartha. He turned to face her, smiled his best Bogart smile, and they briefly embraced. The next day Karl donated the white jacket to the Salvation Army.

THE GAMLINGEN KEY CLUB

In Stockholm there were distinct advantages to becoming a member of the prestigious Key Club. By virtue of his familial connections, Karl would soon enter a new stage in his life. When Karl went to the Iranian Embassy in 1962 to renew his passport, he was attended to by Mr. H. Bozorgnia, who turned out to be the son of a member of the Iranian Parliament who was well known to Karl. Bozorgnia had received a British Etonian education and was well spoken. The two men struck up an immediate friendship when Karl mentioned that his brother-in-law, Mokarram, was also a member of Parliament. That afternoon, Karl and Bozorgnia met at the cafe Bäckahästen to reminisce about mutual friends in Mashhad. They discovered that their sisters were also best friends back in Tehran. From that time onward, the two men often had dinner together. As a result of his friendship with Bozorgnia, Karl was introduced to the ambassador and other embassy employees, including Malkmadani, the Charge-d-faire, who was the son of the Speaker of the House during Mosadigh's presidency before the coup d'état of August 1953. Throughout his life, Karl would blame this coup entirely on Kermit Roosevelt Jr. of the United States. All these aforementioned Iranian parliamentarians had been loyal supporters of the deposed Shah. Bozorgnia also introduced Karl to Lars Amble, a celebrated Swedish actor and director, at one of their cafe Bäckahästen dinners. Karl and Lars subsequently became life-long friends.

One evening Lars invited Karl to join him at the prestigious Gamlingen Key Club in Gamlstan on the island of Stadsholmen. The Key Club was situated in a spacious and well-appointed cellar on the corner of Stora and Gråmunkegränd streets in the Old Town of Stockholm. The owner also operated a bar called Stampen on the ground floor with a dance floor and orchestra. Here Karl was presented to Sten Holmquist, the owner of several of these exclusive clubs. During the course of the evening, Holmquist presented Karl with a gold membership key. Hereafter Karl became a regular figure at club events on weekends, especially after opera and concert performances, often in the company of Borzorgnia, Lars Amble, and other theater celebrities. He would often meet clients and engineers he was working with at the club, and later he would attend dances at the club at least two evenings a week.

Karl was introduced to Chris Folker, the owner of Berns, by Chris Seaton, a Scottish architect and mutual friend. Folker was a talented man with interests in art, the theater, and antique collecting, especially old Persian rugs. They soon became best friends. Hereafter Karl could book a table at short notice at a preferential rate. Berns also sported one of the finest Chinese restaurants in Scandinavia. Karl and Pütsep would often entertain their international clients at this restaurant.

Anthony and Cleopatra, 1997

CHAPTER 16

Chapter 16

A SMALL PERSIAN RUG

In February 1963, Karl found himself in Lidingö, a suburb of Stockholm. He had rented a small studio apartment of no more than twelve square meters. He had some money in a savings account that was not enough to buy anything of any real value, but he also did not trust himself from spending it frivolously. So he sent the equivalent of four hundred US dollars to Dr. Ghawam Nasiri, his most trusted relative, to buy a Persian rug in Mashhad. The small rug of two by three meters was to be sent to him.

In mid-March, Karl received a letter from the Nazarian Export & Import Company in Hamburg, informing him that they had received a rug for him, and would he please arrange to pick it up. That Friday afternoon he took the five o'clock train to Hamburg, arriving the next morning at ten o'clock. He walked the block from the Central Station to Nazarian's office, which was on the third floor. He entered an elegant room with a secretary behind a fine desk and an antique silk rug on the wall. He told the young lady his name and she briefly disappeared into another room.

"Please wait. Mr. Nazarian will be with you momentarily," she announced on her return.

While sitting on the black leather sofa, Karl paged through a brochure with the name Nazarian Export & Import emblazoned in red and green ink on the front cover. On the first page was the index of articles: Persian Rugs, Caviar, Saffron, and so on. After a few minutes, Mr. Nazarian, a tall and distinguished gentleman, came out of the adjoining room and welcomed Karl to his office with a firm handshake. The young lady brought them tea and a plate of cookies.

Mr. Nazarian told Karl that they would be leaving for the customs bureau in ten minutes. He asked Karl if he was living permanently in Sweden and what he did for a living. Karl mentioned that he was an architect and that he had lived in Stockholm for over a year. The secretary opened the door and announced that the car was ready. It was a large American limousine, an important status symbol in Germany at the time, and it was parked right in front of the office building.

At the customs bureau the two men entered a large warehouse where two of Nazarian's employees were waiting. They showed Karl a wrapped bundle and told him it was his rug that had arrived from Mashhad. The warehouse was filled with exotic wares, including piles of Persian rugs. Karl could not resist the temptation and asked Nazarian if he could buy another small rug for his hall. Karl selected a forty-by fifty-four-inch Turkmen for eighty US dollars. While one of the employees was wrapping the rug, Nazarian asked Karl what kind of architecture he practiced. Karl told him that he specialized in hospital design. At that moment his tone became more pleasant. "There must be lots of rich doctors in Sweden," he said.

Sweden was at that time the most modern and socially well-developed country in Europe. Most European countries at that time were undergoing reconstruction after World War II.

One of Nazarian's employees gave Karl a ride to the train station, and he caught the six o'clock train back to Stockholm. He remembered thinking that this brief episode had been an interesting diversion. He arrived in Stockholm the next morning with his rugs, which represented the first and most valuable investments he had ever made to date. It was also the Persian New Year. When Karl reached his apartment and excitedly unwrapped his parcels, he found that the larger rug was three feet longer than his room. He sat down on the floor, somewhat bewildered, not knowing what to do.

On Monday morning, Karl's colleagues at the office asked him how his trip had gone and if the rug was up to his expectations. Karl told them that his relative had sent him a much larger rug for the same price. One of his colleagues said that he and his brother might be interested in buying an Oriental rug. The next morning Karl brought the rugs to work by taxi. When they asked Karl how much he would sell them for, he told them that the best way to determine their value was to have them appraised. Karl knew their price in Iran would be much less than in Sweden. One of the engineers knew a salesman at a rug dealer nearby and he was invited to come over to their office after five o'clock that afternoon. They would pay him for his time and expertise.

The appraiser arrived, and after examining the rug told the assembled group that the market price for a similar rug

CHAPTER 16

would be around ten to twelve thousand Swedish crowns. The dollar exchange rate at that time was one US dollar to five Swedish crowns. Afterward, they all went to a bar Bistro near the office, and during dinner, Karl's colleagues agreed to buy the large rug for seven thousand Swedish crowns and the small one for eight hundred crowns. The next day Karl called Mr. Nazarian and arranged to buy an additional three 3- by 2-meter rugs. He would pick them up the following Friday on his way to Hamburg.

Karl knew the taste of architects, engineers, and doctors. He found it easy to sell them rugs during the week, and then on Fridays, he would travel to Hamburg. This time Mr. Nazarian picked him up at the station and invited him to lunch at an expensive restaurant. Karl bought two expensive silk Keshan rugs and brought them back to Stockholm. He paid the duty at the border and sold them to two doctors he knew. By the end of 1963, his savings totaled more than fifty thousand US dollars.

This pattern was repeated on weekends until Christmas, when Karl bought his first car—a Ford Taunus. In October 1964, he rented a street-level showroom with an office at the rear of the premises. The facility had a show window in the front. He hung a few expensive rugs in the larger front room and worked on his architecture projects in the back office. He continued working for Pütsep International on hospital designs and also on small projects such as villas and vacation homes.

Nazarian provided Karl with rugs until 1968, when he convinced Karl to take average quality rugs and to try to sell them in higher volumes. Unfortunately, this scheme did not work out, and Nazarian died of cancer soon afterward. Most of Nazarian's rugs went back to his father-in-law in Hamburg, and Karl's rug business was a thing of the past; however, from time-to-time he would still buy a top quality rug if he found one that was unique. He would later sell it at a profit. This was the case with the rugs that influential people brought with them when they fled Iran at the time of the revolution. By buying their rugs, Karl thought he could also benefit his countrymen. This extra income helped him buy an apartment and also provided the means for him to travel the Middle East on the lookout for large architectural projects. By this time, he had become financially independent.

Chapter 17

RETURN TO THE NEST

Karl had left Mashhad in the fall of 1956 to study architecture, arriving in Stuttgart with only fifty marks in his pocket for five years of studies. He had survived, completing his studies in 1961. After graduation he traveled to Sweden, where he took up residency in Stockholm. Here he worked for an architectural firm for the first five years before branching out as a freelance architect. Karl worked hard those years doing overtime and working on weekends and during vacations. He also started finding Persian rugs for doctors and architects as a lucrative sideline. He moved into a nice apartment in Täby and upgraded his Ford Taunus to a new Mercedes 250 Sedan.

Karl started receiving letters of admiration and offers of support from friends and relatives. There were also letters introducing others who wanted to meet him and purported to hold the keys to his success in Iran—each with their own schemes and stratagems. Karl was heralded as the personification of success; the one who knew everyone of any importance, especially the famous physicians in Sweden. Friends and family tried to introduce other friends and friends of friends to him, hoping to secure referrals to top physicians for medical treatments. They even specified that they wished to visit during his vacation time so they would not interfere with his work schedule at his office.

The flood of visitors started in the summer of 1964. Karl received visits from family members and numerous influential friends and acquaintances. He guided them to tourist places, took them to doctors for checkups, and entertained them at his home and expensive restaurants. He even drove them to Copenhagen and Hamburg, all at his own expense. He had become a "wunderkind" for all his friends and family in Iran.

In 1966, after ten years in Europe, Karl decided to return to his roots and visit Mashhad. The news that he would be returning to Iran spread like wildfire in his hometown and also to his relatives in Teheran. He wanted to arrive without announcement as a surprise to his family and friends. He took the flight to Teheran and stayed overnight at a hotel on Shah Rea Avenue. He arrived without the knowledge of his sister, brother, and his two nephews, all of whom lived in up-scale homes in Tehran. Before the next morning's flight to Mashhad, it occurred to him that after ten years of absence he could not turn up at the front door of his mother's house unannounced. The mixture of surprise and shock could kill her, so he asked the telephonist at the airport to call ahead to tell his family of his imminent arrival.

KARL'S BACK IN TOWN!

As the Iran Air DC3 taxied up to the terminal, Karl looked through the window and saw many family members on the airport veranda and balcony. He immediately recognized his brother-in-law among the many faces. He was a tall and handsome seventy-year-old statesman and had been one of Mashhad's most influential politicians. He stood in front of the rest of the family. Karl's mother was not with them. His brothers and sisters were likewise at home preparing for his arrival. He was first taken to his sister's home where, as a teenager, he had spent more time than at any other place. On his arrival at the house, a concerted cry went up: "The lost Joseph is back! Be happy!"

The house was bustling with activity as lunch was being prepared for the large group of family and visitors. A large number of extended family members always required a lot of work, especially for those who had no servants. It was also costly.

Beside the adult relatives, the house was crawling with a number of teenage boys and girls that Karl had never seen or heard of. They referred to him as "Uncle," but he did not know them. The babies and small children were reserved for the following greeting session with their fathers and mothers.

Now came the moment when it was to be decided with whom, and on which evening, Karl would attend the welcoming parties at each family member's house. It was obligatory that these visits be made in the order of the social status, age, wealth, and rank of each family to be visited. This was an important tradition and caused constant burdens on families with less money and social status, since they too had to participate in this tradition. Karl had already become accustomed to the Swedish tradition, which meant that it was enough to have a cup of tea or a drink at such gatherings. He thanked the assembled party, and then, to their amazement, he informed each one individually that he would not be participating in their reception parties. This came as a terrible shock to them, but they knew that he meant it. Karl believed it was also a welcome relief for many of them. The tradition of having such big dinners still prevails in Iran to this day. In the end they were not angry with Karl. Rather, they saw him as an oddball and loved him all the more for it.

The happiness and relief of getting rid of family obligations dissipated momentarily, however, when Karl's brother asked, "What about all these important people who visited you in Stockholm. You cannot reject their invitations to stay?"

The news of his return to the city spread quickly, and the next day, as tradition dictated, Karl had a reception in the large salon-like room of his family home and listened to their thanks and appreciation for his time and kindness in hosting their visits to his home in Stockholm, for showing them around, and for arranging their visits to various top physicians. Karl sat all day and welcomed old and new friends who had visited him in Stockholm.

Although he had rather abruptly declined to take part in the special homecoming celebration that his family had planned for him in his honor, his brothers told him that while they understood that he did not want to be fêted in this manner, it was scandalous to reject the attentions of people he had hosted in Stockholm. He should present himself in order to be acknowledged and thanked by them. Consequently, he found himself compelled to host a reception for distinguished friends and acquaintances.

Members of his family were invited, as well as many famous personalities. At that time, people of rank and education had large mansions that were tastefully furnished with both traditional and modern furnishings. It was summertime, and the party was held outdoors in a sumptuous garden setting with an overlooking veranda. Each member of this group of well-dressed socialites was welcomed with an obligatory drink, and Karl was formally thanked for being such a wonderful host. The dinner provided a large selection of dishes, including a Swedish smorgasbord, with Persian foods and one or two French dishes. Beverages included wine, beer, and soft drinks. Deserts were served afterward, while the men and women danced Foxtrots and Rumbas together. No traditional Persian dancing took place, since most of the guests were European-educated professionals. This was before the Islamic Revolution, after which such behavior would be punished with severe fines or even lashes.

At such parties one could always find young women who had recently graduated from high school or who were university students. They were often quite beautiful and elegantly dressed. They were educated with interests in the arts and in world travel.

CHAPTER 17

They were smart and vivacious. Some were more reserved, but they were all delightful, and Karl thought it a pleasure to host them. At the end of the evening, his praises as host were roundly celebrated again.

Karl's relatives asked him which of these young ladies he found most interesting. They wanted to know if he would like to set up a another meeting. He knew this meant preparation for marriage. He told them politely that this would have to wait for his next trip. In later years, Karl thought it was unfortunate that he had "chickened out," and as a result had lost many good opportunities, both on this occasion in Iran, and also later in Sweden, to select a marriage partner. He rationalized that he was waiting for the "right one" among so many fine young women. As a fatalist, he believed it was his destiny to not get married, and in many ways, he was glad he never did. Picturing himself as a husband was a disaster! Later in life, he reflected that a vagabond should remain in his hotel room. His older brother once told him that he thought that mother earth had not yet given birth to a woman who would be worthy of him!

Tristan Und Isolde, 1998

Chapter 18

SEEKING ARCHITECTURAL OPPORTUNITIES

After Karl had established himself as an architect in Stockholm, it occurred to him that he should try to obtain a project in Iran so he could return and work in the country of his birth. While spending three wonderful weeks with his family and friends in Mashhad, he asked his sister's son-in-law, Ghavam Nasiri, the dean of the medical faculty, how to make contacts in his field. After a while, Nasiri suggested that he take a trip to Iran as a guest of Mashhad University to lecture on hospital design.

Consequently, Karl traveled to Mashhad with Ervin Pütsep. On his arrival, he stayed the first two nights at Dr. Mojeeb's home. In 1965 Karl had invited Dr. Mojeeb and Pütsep for dinner when Dr. Mojeeb was visiting Stockholm. They had enjoyed a wonderful evening, and the doctor promised that if Karl was ever in Mashhad, he would be delighted to host him as a guest in his home. Karl stayed at his brother's home, and after two days, Ervin moved to a hotel. The first day they met the Chancellor of the university, and Ervin presented his lecture on general hospital design. They were then invited to visit the hospital and the medical faculty.

THE SHAH REZA HOSPITAL

On the second day of their visit, their hosts took them to look at plans for a new five-hundred-bed hospital. It was still in a preliminary stage, and it did not impress Karl or his boss. The men told the dean of their concern for the poorly designed

CHAPTER 18

facility. In response, the dean offered to go over the plans with them in the near future.

That evening, Ghavam Nasiri told Karl that this project would never be realized. The architect was Mr. Ghiaie, a near relative of the Shah. When the board had approved the project, Sazemane Barnameh of the Ministry for Financing Special Projects decided that they did not have a sufficient budget for this project. When the university wanted to move ahead with building the hospital five years later, Ghiaie was contacted in order to resume the project. At this point, it was ruled that the project was outdated, since medical facilities must be updated every few years, and a new design was called for. Each time there was a revision of the plans, Ghiaie received his fee that was equivalent to half a million dollars, and each time Sazmane Barname rejected the project due to insufficient funds. They were told that they should not put any of their time or money into this project since it would suffer the same fate and be rejected.

Before leaving Iran, Karl and Pütsep met with Asadollah Alam, a member of Parliament, at his mansion residence in Niavaran. They were also invited to meet with Shahpour Ahmad Reza Pahlavi at Saadabad Palace. On their return to Sweden, Karl gave a complete account of their Iranian trip to the Iranian ambassador Akbar Darai. Two weeks later, Darai called Karl and invited him to visit the embassy. Darai told Karl that they wanted to build the first open-heart surgery center in Teheran and that it was going to be financed by the Queen Mother's Foundation. The Foundation would be sending Karl and Pütsep an invitation.

A week later, Karl and Pütsep received an invitation from the Minister Alam and Senator Nafissi, who was the trusted head for the project. Pütsep's firm was selected. Their research had verified that Pütsep's company was one of the leading hospital design companies in the world.

Karl found this set of circumstances almost unbelievable. It was almost like a dream to him, but it was real. Letters from a Minister of Parliament, from a senator, and from a governor. . . . Daily meetings followed with Ambassador Akbar Darai, who was forthcoming, especially with Pütsep, whom he entertained at Operakällaren, the finest restaurant in Sweden. Eventually everything was prepared. Karl and Pütsep had produced an elegant folder of all the hospitals that Pütsep International had built, with copies in English and Farsi. They booked their air tickets and were on their way back to Tehran!

On their arrival in Tehran, they were welcomed by Senator Nafissi's secretary and whisked off to the Tehran Royal Hilton where Pütsep had made reservations. There was an invitation waiting for the men at the hotel from Senator Nafissi to join him at his residence for breakfast. Here they met Shalchian, an engineer who was the Minister of Roads and Communication, and Mr. Irani, the principal architect for the project. After the customary greetings that are usual in Iran—a new experience for Pütsep—it was resolved that Pütsep and Karl would codesign the project with Irani and that they would receive their brief about the details of the project at his office. After breakfast they left for Irani's office that was located on Pahlavi Avenue a short distance from the Hilton hotel.

At the architect's office, a pile of drawings on a table confronted them. After a brief overview, Pütsep asked Karl in Swedish what he thought of the project. Karl told him it would be good for a hotel but that he didn't see a hospital. They asked Irani if all these drawings were for an open-heart surgery center. He responded that these were merely preliminary sketches that they needed to work on. When they asked if he had a schedule of specifications for the project, they were handed a bundle of typed papers ruled with square meters for each room. Karl saw Senator Nafissi flinch with an uneasy expression on his face. Pütsep said to Irani that he did not see a design for a hospital. Could he please explain? He replied, "That is why we need your help."

Senator Nafissi asked Karl in Farsi if he thought anything could be done to alleviate the situation. Karl told him that this design was certainly not meant for a hospital. Then he asked Karl to accompany him to the adjoining room and closed the door. He explained to Karl that five million Toman ($500,000) had already been spent on this project and that it would be desirable if Pütsep International could take over at this point. Karl discussed Nafissi's proposal with Pütsep, but he rejected the idea and said that he could not see anything to work from. After this terse discussion, they agreed to meet again the next day. As they were leaving, Senator Nafissi asked Karl to join him and Mr. Shalchian, the Minister of Roads and Communications, for lunch. Karl took leave of Pütsep to attend the meeting. Five months later, and after two more visits to Tehran, Karl and Pütsep received letters via the Iranian Embassy in Stockholm from Minister Assadollah Alam that they had been awarded the contract for the design of the Queen Mother's Open Heart Surgical Center. Karl was overjoyed!

Chapter 19

A UNIVERSITY IN SAUDI ARABIA

Five months after his adventures with the open-heart surgery center—which caused him to think of how foolish he had been—Karl again received an invitation from Tehran to accompany ten university professors and the vice president of the Pahlavi University in Shiraz on a trip to Riyadh in Saudi Arabia. Ervin Pütsep and Karl had met Prof. Ghawami, the dean of the medical faculty, and Amir Motaghi, the vice president of Pahlavi University, on their previous visit to Tehran. The two men were also invited to the office of Minister Alam at Nivaran Palace. Once there, Mr. Alam explained that the previous year, during his official visit to Iran, King Faisal of Saudi Arabia had invited His Majesty the Shah of Iran to a reciprocal visit to Saudi Arabia. Since Riyadh had no university, the Shah had a plan to present King Faisal, as a gift, a complete project for the construction of the first university to be built in Saudi Arabia. The name would be Pahlavi University. After this short briefing, they were guided to a conference room where they were to meet His Majesty the Shah.

Upon entering the room, the Shah courteously welcomed the party and then proceeded to impress upon the assembled group that this project should be worthy of a king and that he would be presenting the entire project to King Faisal during his official state visit in January 1969. The next day, Karl and Pütsep took off for Shiraz. After two days of visiting the university and meeting with all the heads of the various departments, they were ready to proceed with the design of the new university. It was mid-September before they flew to Riyadh. The airport at Riyadh was not impressive, but they were served a lot of tea. They were ushered into the VIP lounge where the Vice Minister of Education received them with TV cameras rolling. It was the big event of the day. After a ceremonial reception and the presentation of the Iranian and Saudi delegates, along with the two Swedes, they went to their hotel. At that time, Riyadh had few hotels, unlike Tehran that had many fine hotels such as the Hilton, Sheraton, Intercontinental, Hyatt Regency, and Meridian, to name a few. Tehran had been the center of the Middle East—the city that never sleeps. And now, thirty years since the revolution, Tehran still had the above-mentioned hotels that had existed under the Shah. It had a population of four million at the time. It is presently a city of over fifteen million people.

That evening the men attended a dinner reception in honor of the Iranian delegation. The next morning they had a breakfast meeting that continued on at the Ministry of Higher Education. On the afternoon of the third day they were granted an audience with King Faisal at his palace. On the fifth day, they held a morning meeting at which they finalized their decisions and approved the final plans. That afternoon, the dean and faculty of the Pahlavi University left for Mecca on their pilgrimage. Pütsep and Karl remained in Riyadh. In the evening they had a final dinner with the Saudi officials from the Department of Culture and Education.

The next morning, Pütsep left for Sweden, and Karl took a flight to Jeddah. Of all their experiences during their visit to Iran, the men will never forget witnessing the beheading of an unfortunate soul in front of the mosque and the jubilant cheering of the crowd that had gathered to watch the spectacle. On the morrow, after his arrival in Jeddah, Karl underwent the customary ritual preparation and dressing in the sacred garments of a pilgrim. Karl was driven to Mecca by limousine where a guide conducted him to the holy site of the Kabah. After he had paid his respects, he was invited to have lunch with Mecca's cultural director at his residence. His host seated him at a generous table with at least a dozen other guests who sat quietly while Karl and his host ate their lunch. In the afternoon, Karl traveled to Jeddah and then on to Tehran.

A SUMMER VACATION IN RIYADH

In 1968, Riyadh was not the thriving metropolis that it is today. It certainly was not a place where one would choose to spend one's summer. In mid-September, the daytime temperature often exceeded fifty degrees Celsius. It seemed that the only guests in the hotel were members of Karl's party, besides two English gentlemen who took their meals at the same time at an adjoining table. After dinner on the second day, Professor Ghawami, the dean of the medical faculty, got everyone's attention with two strokes of the dinner gong, and then he announced in Farsi, "Gentlemen, we are being watched, and perhaps even spied upon!" Karl translated in Swedish for Pütsep's benefit. He smiled whimsically. He was of the opinion that these middle easterners were too suspicious where the British were concerned. At the last breakfast before they all took off for their various destinations, to their surprise, the two English gentlemen at the neighboring table came over to introduce themselves. One gentleman said that he had enjoyed Dr. Pütsep's recently published book on surgical centers in hospitals. Pütsep was bowled over with astonishment. With a knowing smile, Dr. Ghawami asked what had brought these two gentlemen to Riyadh.

"Vacation!" they exclaimed simultaneously.

Pütsep asked, "How did you come to know about my book?"

"We are working for Wilkins Corporation as specialists in hospital and university building design."

For the next five months, Karl worked hard on the university project. Pütsep's office was a hive of activity as they wrote the program and designed the campus. Karl worked on coordinating the project at his office. He was also responsible for designing perspectives, elevations, and the architect's model. They had to design an entirely new campus from the ground up. During this period, the hospital Professor Ghavami and Saidi from Pahlavi University came to Stockholm to discuss their progress, and they were presented with the first sketches.

In first week of March 1969, Pütsep and Karl flew to Tehran with hundreds of drawings and a large-scale model. The day after their arrival, they accompanied the heads of the various departments of the Pahlavi University to the Niavaran Palace to make a presentation of the project to the Shah. He showed great interest in their work and asked them to explain the details of the project to him. To everybody's astonishment, the Shah was knowledgeable about how a university should be designed. Their meeting lasted over forty minutes, and the Shah was visibly pleased with their presentation. Pütsep went back to Stockholm to make the changes that had been decided upon in Tehran. Karl stayed and worked with Moghtader, their Iranian coarchitect, who had been educated in France. Two days later, the Shah left on an official visit to Kualaluampur Malaysia.

A NOTORIOUS ENGLISH PLOY

While waiting for events to unfold, Karl spent some time discussing the project with Moghtader, their coarchitect. In the evenings, Karl discussed the project over dinner with Amir Motaghi, the head of the university, who had taken up permanent residence at the Hilton Hotel. They became regulars at the Hilton's Shimrann café. After a few days, Karl could see uneasiness in Amir Motaghi. The days went by without any communication from Minster Alams. Eventually, Karl called Minster Alams' office and asked for a meeting. To his surprise, he received a call back minutes later from Miss Oweysi, who had the dubious distinction of being the daughter of General Oweysi, the commander of SWAK, the Iranian secret police. She said that His Excellency would see him at four o'clock that afternoon.

At the appointed time, Karl was guided to the Minister's office. Karl was asked how Professor Ghawam Nassiri was doing, and Karl began to feel uneasy. It was not customary for a Minister of the Royal Court to ask after one's friends. Then he broached the university project with rather a sad expression on his face. At this time he referred to Karl by his father's name, Hadjsadeh, whom he had known personally. Karl's father had helped Alams' father, Shokatolmolk, who had become Prime Minister and Governor during both the reign of Reza Shah and the Ghajar Dynasty. Karl's father had been commissioned to establish a new Persian Sherkate Shargh rug-weaving factory in the city of Birjand. When Karl asked Alam when Pütsep should present the additional drawings for Saudi Arabia, Alam replied, "Arabha dorr afshani kardand." (Translated, this old Persian expression means "Arabs are strewing rubies along the path!")

Bahrain was considered part of Iran, so when King Faisal of Saudi Arabia received the Emir of Bahrain officially as head of state, it caused uproar in Iran. The propaganda war started two days later with newspapers, TV, and radio reports blaming King Faisal for intruding in Iran's domestic affairs. Iran could not tolerate two heads of state and regarded the Emir of Bahrain as simply a governor. Consequently, the Shah's official trip to Saudi Arabia was canceled, and the university project was scuttled. Karl was left in Riyadh with his architectural model and what seemed like kilometers of drawings! When Karl asked Amir Motaghi what he thought their situation was with regard to the project, he replied that it had turned out to be a lost investment and that, unfortunately, Pahlavi University would not be able to recover his expenses. For Pütsep International, this was of no great consequence, but Karl had no contract with Pahlavi University or with Pütsep since Pütsep had refused to sign a partnership agreement with Karl until the project was secured. Karl had to take his leave and suffer the loss of his investment of time and money in the project. He could reclaim none of his losses, and he simply had to walk away from this project empty handed.

A few months later in Stockholm, Prince Akbar Darai, the Iranian ambassador, invited Karl to the embassy. After tea in the ambassador's office, Karl was shown two English newspapers with front-page articles and photographs of King Faisal and Queen Elizabeth II together in the Queen's royal carriage. It was reported that Wilkins Corporation had been awarded the design and building contract for the first university campus in Riyadh! Darai said that this was not the first time that the British had pulled the rug from under their feet.

Chapter 20

A HAUNTING JUDGMENT

In March 1969, Bagher Pirnia, the new governor of Mashhad, who succeeded General Batmanghelich, invited Karl to examine a proposed city plan that was in the final stages of architectural design. By April, Karl and Tanaka, a Japanese architect from Pütsep International, were accommodated at the new Club Complex in Farah Park in Mashhad. This property was owned by the City Water Department and operated under City Hall supervision. At that time, the new Mayor was an engineer by the name of Sharestani. He had replaced General Lieutenant Bani Etemad, the former mayor, who had been very liberal. During Etemad's tenure, there were no restrictions on the serving of alcohol in restaurants and bars and the bazaars that comprised half the city, except around the Holy Shrines. However, Shahrestani was famous for his religiosity. He forbade the serving of all alcoholic beverages and banned liquor stores. Only Armenian liquor stores were allowed to serve alcoholic drinks inside their bars.

The Imam Reza Shrine, one of the holiest shrines for Shiite pilgrims, was situated at the center of the old bazaar that encircled it. Boulevards radiated north to south and from east to west, forming a circle of buildings around the Shrine. These boulevards were each three to four kilometers long and lined with hundred-year-old trees. They had served as the main traffic arteries for the city since the early eighteenth century. This centralized city plan had been the most famous for travelers visiting the Middle East. Even the French Colonel Lebrune mentioned this city and its famous attractions in his travels through Russia and Persia in AD 1723.

After Tanaka and Karl received the drawings and the cost schedules for the undertaking, they started with a systematic review of all aspects of the project. They soon discovered that much of the necessary materials were missing. The project was being built on rough estimates and not on actual cost projections. The design called for two semi-circular buildings that surrounded the Shrine at various heights from six to fourteen stories high. They saw immediately that these buildings were too high and that they would block the view of the shrine and the famous Mosque of Goharshad, dating from AD 1418. Gotharshad was the daughter-in-law of Teimur Lang the Great (1336–1405), better known in the West as Tamerlane, the chief of the Barlas, a Turkish-Mongol tribe.

On the lower level between the two buildings was a circle that would carry all the road traffic in each direction, including all the taxis and pilgrim buses from all parts of Iran. These buses could number several hundred during special religious festivals. Both Karl and Tanaka could immediately see that this would result in unbearable congestion and smog problems since there was no provision for ventilation in the area. The bazaar was moved to a constricted area under one of the buildings with little natural light. They realized that these plans had been put together hastily. Tanaka and Karl spent two days sightseeing in the area in order to assess the traffic volume, the number of people, and the number of shops that would need to be accommodated. Karl already knew the situation quite well, but it was all new to Tanaka.

On the third week, Bourbour the architect arrived from Tehran, and they discussed the project with him in detail. He dismissed their reservations about his plans by saying that these problems would be worked out in the future and that they should see these plans as a preliminary proposal. Two days later it was time to present the findings of their investigation to Governor Pirnia in Bourbour's presence.

The first question put to Bourbour was, "Why did he see it necessary to plan for a city of more than 500,000 people?" He replied that the plans were for a city of two to three million inhabitants. Karl and Tanaka then asked him if he realized that 80 percent of the proposed area would be empty for twenty to thirty years. Governor Pirnia's face changed color as he asked pointedly, "Do you mean we are paying billions to have empty spaces?"

Then Tanaka asked why the budget was so unrealistically low for such a vast undertaking. Pirnia turned to Bourbour with a grim expression on his face. "Tell us!" he demanded. In his defense, Bourbour replied, "All the tenants will be required to supply and install all their own windows and doors after their leases are signed."

Pirnia retorted, "You take everyone for a fool in this city!" and stormed out of the meeting. The entire meeting's conversations had been recorded. Tanaka and Karl spent the next two days putting the finishing touches to their own proposal. Tanaka wrote in English and Karl in Farsi. Karl's

CHAPTER 20

use of English was limited at the time. The next day Tanaka took off for Sweden and Karl flew to Tehran to visit his brother-in-law Mokarram, who was at that time chairman of the city council. Mokarran told Karl over dinner at his hotel that it was unnecessary for Pirnia to be so upset and that they should work it out. He also told Karl that Bourbour's father was an old friend and colleague of his and that they had worked together in Parliament. He then said that Karl and Tanaka were invited to Bourbour's private residence in Darrus in northeast Tehran for tea the following afternoon.

Karl and Tanaka where warmly welcomed by both Bourbour and his son. After the traditional greetings and tea, Mokarram talked about the good old times they both had when they were members of Parliament and things were different. Then they left Karl and Tanaka and went into another room and closed the door. After more than a half hour of scheming, the two old foxes came back and suggested they all go to Bourbour's office just a block away. Bourbour was a wealthy man and enjoyed a large and sumptuously furnished establishment.

His office was elegant and well organized. It was uncluttered, without sketches and drawings on the walls, unlike the architect's offices in Sweden that Karl was accustomed to where each architect had his own cubicle with a personal filing cabinet and a radio on the bookshelf behind him. In Iran, as in the rest of the Middle East, clients and visitors were always impressed by the elegant offices of doctors, engineers, architects, and lawyers. The more costly and ostentatious the office, the more prestige was given to its incumbent. Bourbour's office was no exception to this rule; however, Karl thought, *In Iran, what you see is not necessarily what you get.*

Bourbour again presented the project to the two men and concluded that he was hopeful that as additional partners they would be able to assist him with a new design. He scheduled another meeting with Karl and Tanaka for the next day. Mokarram and Karl left the office. In the car, Mokarram opened the discussion and proposed that Karl should collaborate with Boubour in this project. It would be profitable for Karl and could lead to future projects. At that time, Karl had no idea of what was awaiting him in the coming months. Karl told Mokarram that he was bound to their present arrangement and that Pütsep, his associate in Stockholm, would not like it if he went ahead with this project on his own. That evening Karl called Pütsep and told him of the opportunity that had been presented to him. To Karl's surprise, Pütsep said that they should accept the proposal on his behalf and that Karl should work as his employee and not as an associate on the project. Karl rejected this idea.

The next day, in the presence of Mokarram, Karl called Bourbour and thanked him for the offer but said that it would be difficult for him to join them since he had other projects that he was working on. Later Karl mentioned to Mokarram that he was convinced that this was a poorly conceived project. Consequently, Karl declined the offer, and a few days later, he left Tehran and started work on another project. Karl's judgment of the Mashhad City Center project became a closed episode in his life and was soon forgotten—or so he thought! The year was 1969.

Bostad, 2012

Chapter 21

AT THE SHAH'S RECEPTION FOR PRESIDENT KEKKONEN IN HELSINKI

In September 1969, Iranian Ambassador Akbar Darai invited Karl to lunch at the embassy in Stockholm. During their meeting, the ambassador told Karl that Queen Farah was hoping to invite Alvar Alto, the renowned Finnish architect and designer, to Tehran to discuss the design for a small museum in Tehran. Darai asked if Karl, as a practicing architect, could contact or visit Mr. Alto in order to better explain what the Queen had in mind. When Karl later called Alto, he asked if Karl could come to Helsinki.

The embassy provided Karl with a ticket, and he took off for a meeting with Mr. Alto. At their meeting, Karl presented the embassy's letter inviting him to assist with the design a museum in Tehran. Unfortunately, he did not have any more detailed information to give Alto. Over lunch, Alto told Karl that he could not blindly agree to a project without knowing more about it. Karl suggested that the best solution would be to have the Royal Court of Iran invite him as a royal guest. During their conversation, Karl recounted in detail the bad experience that Pütsep and he had with the Ghasemabad project in Mashhad that had run aground. When Karl returned to Stockholm, he informed Darai that it would be necessary to invite Alto to Tehran.

A month later, Alto called Karl to inform him that he had received his ticket to Tehran but that he had never flown economy class before. Karl immediately called Ambassador Darai to rectify the matter. According to Iraj Diba, a consul at the embassy and a close friend of Karl, confusion reigned at the embassy, and the embassy employees were all blaming each other for this blunder of protocol. Karl knew all along that this was merely a ploy to cover up their predilection for bargain shopping. They sent letters of profuse apology to Alto, and eventually a first class ticket was hand-delivered to him by an embassy employee.

Early in July 1970, Darai again called to ask a favor of Karl. He wanted Karl to accompany Iraj Diba to Helsinki two days before the official visit of the Shah and his Queen to Finland. The Minister of Court, Mr. Alam, had asked if Karl could help with the writing of the guests' seating name cards at the banquet tables for the reception that the Shah would hold in honor of President Kekkonen. Karl politely told Darai that he should find another calligrapher. He'd had enough working his tail off for the futile Ghasemabad project for Mashhad that had been ordered by Governor Pirnia, and he had lost a lot of money as a result of it. Darai told Karl that he would have an invitation to attend the royal reception and that he would receive VIP treatment with all his travel and hotel costs paid for by the embassy.

Karl accepted the offer and traveled with Diba to Helsinki, arriving the day before the Shah's arrival. He spent all day in a room at the Finland Foreign Ministry, writing the names of the guests in Farsi on cards that had already been printed in Latin. The following evening, much to his surprise, and just an hour before the reception was due to commence, Ambassador Darai introduced Karl and Diba to the King and Queen. He mentioned that Karl was their liaison with Alvar Alto and that he had been a great help to them. Karl reflected on the fact that he had only met Alto once and received one phone call from him a month later. Karl supposed that the ambassador had meant well.

That evening there were more than 180 guests at the royal reception. Karl's seat was as far as possible from the dignitaries' table, next to the emergency exit. The lady seated to his side asked him if he could see the King and hear anything of what was being said. Karl told her that he could not, but fortunately he would be able to read all about it in the morning newspaper. He continued that they were not only fortunate in that they were not obligated to wait to shake hands with the King and Queen, but that they were also much safer sitting next to the emergency exit! The next day Ambassador Darai conveyed Mr. Alam's gratitude for Karl's help and said that Alam would like Karl to visit him the next time he was in Tehran since he had something to discuss. After arriving back in Stockholm from Helsinki, Karl visited Darai and asked what Mr. Alam had in mind. He told Karl that Alam regretted the loss that Karl had incurred in the failed Saudi project and that he might be able to suggest a way for him to recoup his losses.

MINISTER ALAM—AN ARISTOCRAT WHO FAVORED OLD FRIENDS

In January 1971, Karl went to Tehran and immediately called Mr. Alam's office. Miss Oweisy, his secretary, told him that he was out of the office until the next Thursday, but that he could visit him at his residence in Niavaran, where he had first visited him with Pütsep in 1963. This mansion was later confiscated after the Islamic revolution and occupied by one of Khomeini's top mullahs. Mr. Alam received Karl in his study, and after thanking him for assisting the embassy in Helsinki, asked if he would be willing to provide architectural help to an architect friend who was in process of designing a hospital project. He emphasized that this time he would be paid up front. Karl expressed his willingness to be of service, and they retired to the veranda where a few more guests were present. After some socializing, Karl left.

Early the next morning, he received a call in his room at the Hilton hotel from someone who presented himself as an architect but would not give his name since he said he preferred to remain anonymous. The man said that he would like to meet Karl for breakfast. Karl told him he was just on his way downstairs to the Shimran coffee shop and that he would be waiting for him. The man arrived fifteen minutes later.

During breakfast, they talked about architecture in general and made polite conversation about the weather. Then the man became more earnest and asked if he could talk with Karl in private. Karl suggested his room and ordered tea to be sent up. Once in the room the man said that a friend had recommended him to Karl and that Karl would be able to help him with his project—a two-hundred-bed hospital. He said that he had never designed a hospital before and that he needed Karl's help with the programming and the scale design, but he didn't want Karl officially as a partner. Karl told him that he would be agreeable to this. Then the visitor told Karl that for the first stage of the project he would be receiving five million toman, equal to three hundred and seventy thousand US dollars, of which seventy thousand was allocated to "unspecified costs." Karl knew that this figure was intended for the inevitable bribe. He indicated that Karl's payment would be two hundred and fifty thousand US dollars, a hundred thousand at once and the rest on delivery.

While the man was explaining his deal, Karl estimated that this was a good offer, and he agreed to the proposal. The man opened his portfolio and handed Karl an envelope containing blank US travelers' checks. They shook hands and Karl returned to Stockholm the next day. Karl started immediately and soon completed the preliminary sketches and final drawings. He received help with the text lettering from his friend and neighbor who worked for Skanska Construction Company and would often help Karl during her free time. After two months, Karl returned to Tehran with all the drawings but void of any company designations, signs, or logos. His anonymous partner had the drawings stamped with his office logo and he paid Karl the rest of the funds. Karl never met him again, but during the course of the next four years, he received similar commissions. They were profitable, and he completed these projects expediently.

Karl continued to work on further projects in the Middle East in which he completed the initial design and then handed his concept drawings over to an architectural office with a large staff to complete the working drawings and building details. He usually received 15 to 20 percent of the architectural fee for developing the aesthetic concept and initial design of these projects. He was not interested in spending endless hours on the technical details of the buildings he designed. The setbacks of his early career were soon overcome, and, in this manner, he could use his free time for his art.

Cosmic Superlative, 2005

Chapter 22

AT THE CROSSROADS OF A NEW CAREER

Karl adopted a private approach to his art and viewed with some disdain the fads and conventions that were so often manifested by the gallery system. He had taken Max Ernst's advice to heart and was committed to working along a wholly independent path. In Iran there had been no art galleries. Piraste was the only artist who had painted portraits and landscapes in his hometown. In Germany, after the war, people did not have much interest or time for art, and they rarely had any art works that could be considered "modern" in their homes. Living rooms and hallways were usually hung with traditional hunting scenes and charming depictions of Bavarian woodcutters in the forests. After the war, all efforts were devoted to restoring the old museums, and plans for more modern facilities were temporarily shelved. There was little talk about "modern art."

As a student at the Art Academy in Stuttgart, Karl had been exposed to and become part of the modern art movement. He was fully aware of what had been taking place in Paris and was familiar with the work of Yves Klein, and even with Jean Tingley's work in Switzerland. He had met Leonor Fini during his surrealist period and dedicated a painting to her. After Karl had settled in Stockholm, one of his friends invited him to visit some of the galleries in the old city of Gamla Stan. Although hesitant at first, Karl was soon thrilled by the expansive range of contemporary art that was represented in the colorful galleries in this quaint environment. His architect friends were fully committed to the more contemporary works that were sold through these galleries, decorating their own homes with abstract, Expressionistic, and Constructivist paintings in profusion. Soon Karl was visiting galleries on a regular basis. Every Saturday and Sunday he would stroll through the galleries. He still had a strong interest in the transcendental qualities of surrealism but was not able to get fully engaged in painting due to the continuing demands of his architectural work.

By 1965, Karl had become well acquainted with the modern art in all of Stockholm's galleries. He had studied original paintings and prints by Picasso, Miro, Dali, and the pop artists. He found his gallery visits stimulating and inspiring. At the opening of an exhibition of Luigi Fontana's works in Stockholm, he bought three of his characteristically sliced white canvases, with a bank loan that he had obtained with the help of his boss Ervin Pütsep, who cosigned the loan agreement. A few years later, Karl sold these works for three times what he had paid for them. He bought other works, among them another large Fontana with three cuts, which he resold at a handsome profit for $8,000. Years later he was shocked to hear that the same work by Fontana had changed hands at Christie's in London for over a million dollars. In 1967 he visited exhibitions by Jean Fourtier and Antonio Tápies, from whom he also bought a painting. He became enthusiastic about his art dealing and about the profits he was making as a side interest.

By now, Karl's professional career as an architect had been established, and a whole new life opened up to him. He took business trips to France, Austria, Switzerland, Italy, and Spain on architectural assignments. He noticed that Swedish homes generally had more original art works than the reproductions he often encountered on his travels in other countries. *Scandinavians generally tend to have better taste in these matters*, he thought. He attended public lectures by Carlo Derkert, one of the curators working under Pontus Hultén, the director of Stockholm's Moderna Museet. During these years, Hultén was innovative and progressive, turning the Moderne Museet into a trend-setting institution. He introduced pop art to Europe in a notable exhibition in 1962 and a short while thereafter mounted controversial exhibitions by René Magritte and Jean Tinguely. By the time he showed Niki de Saint Phalle's huge reclining woman in 1966, he had developed the *Moderna Museet* into an authoritative museum of modern art. Karl respected Hultén, because he had the courage to put on provocative exhibitions.

Karl's circle of architect friends would often invite Carlo Derkert to speak to them at arranged gatherings where they discussed recent developments in contemporary art. Karl and his colleagues felt that they had a responsibility to furnish the hospitals that they designed with good art works; therefore, they needed to be fully informed on modern movements in the visual arts to do a good job. As architects they were responsible for implementing the "one-percent for art" legislation that allowed for one percent of the total construction cost of

CHAPTER 22

each public building to be spent on artistic and decorative adornment. Consequently, they tried to keep in touch with the latest developments in contemporary art and particularly with the new generation of artists whose works could be purchased for this purpose.

Karl's architectural assignments took him to different parts of Europe, and he would always visit the museums in the cities he stayed in. Germany was undergoing serious reconstruction, and new galleries were coming to the fore. Within a few short years, Germany rose from the ruins of war to become an exemplary modern state. Then, in 1965, Karl decided to give up his job with Ervin Pütsep. He reasoned that if he was self-employed, he would be free to travel and work on his own art. He was hoping to get a significant commission in Sweden, but the project did not materialize. An opportunity presented itself in Iran, and he traveled back to the land of his birth with Pütsep. They met with the Shah's Minister of Culture and were granted a large hospital project. However, Pütsep took the entire project for himself since Karl had neglected to draw up a written contract confirming what he had thought was a partnership arrangement. He had always believed that a handshake was good enough to seal any contract. This would not be the first time that Karl's trusting nature would jeopardize his ambitions. However, he saw this as a temporary setback and was not daunted in his desire to be self-employed.

Karl rented an office in Stockholm and worked on freelance work. During this time, he continued to assist his old firm from his new office. His office soon expanded to become a retail showroom. As a result of his special knowledge of Persian rugs and artifacts, he opened a boutique in the front of the office, displaying expensive art works and exclusive artifacts. He even mounted several Persian folk art exhibitions that he traveled to different parts of Sweden. One of his exhibitions was hosted by the Swedish Iranian ambassador in the northern city of Sundsvall and opened by Lands Hövdingen, the governor of Sundsvall. This show was successful and included Persian miniatures, silver crafts, and Persian rugs. Karl used the profits from this show to enter some architectural competitions. Then, in January 1969, he received his first commission to build a small hospital. Immediately after this project, he received several large commissions to build hospitals in the Middle East and in North Africa. During this period, he accumulated considerable amounts of money.

During July and August 1976, Karl had started to produce lithographs, working with Leif Nielsen, a talented lithographer who had come to Sweden from Denmark. Karl had found that lithography was not bound by the limitations and boundaries set by architectural hospital design. Nielsen was the founder of Gallery Prisma, an experimental studio during the 1950s and 60s. He exhibited the finest avant-garde work and was an important figure in presenting the latest trends to the public. His gallery attracted many significant artists of the day. It was while Karl was working on a lithograph at Nielsen's studio that he was introduced to many significant artists and critics, including Stig Johansson, the art critic for *Svenska Dagbladet,* the Swedish morning newspaper. Johansson was a good friend of Leif Nielsen.

The long-standing relationship between Karl and Stig Johansson began when Nielsen introduced the two men over lunch at Den Gyldene Freden. The Michelin Culinary Guide noted this establishment as one of Stockholm's oldest and finest restaurants situated in Gamla Stan, the eleventh-century town renowned for its historical preservation. The restaurant was owned by a Mr. Wedholm at the time and was frequented by artists, singers, songwriters, and important cultural personalities. Nielsen presented Karl as an architect who had been printing lithographs at his studio. He mentioned that Karl had studied at the Stuttgart Kuntz Academy as a guest student and that he had worked with Max Ernst for a short time. He also said that Karl was an opera and theater "nut" and was printing his first lithograph of four interpreting Richard Wagner's *Die Ring des Nibelungen.* (Karl would again express this theme in his oil paintings for his Homage to Shakespeare and Wagner suite that he completed in the 1980s.)

After their first meeting, Johansson viewed Karl's lithographs and was impressed. The men spent the entire afternoon discussing art, architecture, and the cultural life of the city. Later meetings followed at local bars or coffee shops. When Karl was in the city, he often joined Johansson's art walks to local galleries and museums as he prepared his weekly Saturday art reviews for the *Svenska Dagbladet* morning newspaper. Karl enjoyed these walks and particularly the discussions that often followed in local bars with other artists who were in the company. Karl reciprocated by inviting Johansson to the concerts that he often attended in the city and for which he held annual subscriptions. This routine was interrupted four years later by Johansson's heart surgery. However, the men continued to communicate by telephone. Karl called Johansson the last time from his Palm Beach home in 2013 to wish him a merry Christmas. In January 2013, Stig Johansson passed away shortly after his ninetieth birthday.

In 1977, Karl completed his final architectural project in the Middle East. He decided to take a few months off to contemplate his future, while leaving in abeyance a small project that was under consideration in North Africa. He calculated that he had earned enough money to live off the investment returns of his funds. He was forty-three years old, and the constant traveling between the Persian Gulf states, Sweden, and the United States had become too much for him. He felt an unresolved inner conflict. His architectural career, although lucrative, did not give him the satisfaction of his artistic talent. More than 80 percent of hospital design was comprised of functional details, and even the building itself could rarely be seen as an artistic creation. He finally decided to subcontract the North Africa project to a German company. He was liberated!

Karl bought a powerboat and resolved to go boating and to travel. He would see the most important art exhibitions in Europe and the United States. His first trip was by car, which he took with Stig Johansson to visit art exhibitions and museums in Copenhagen, Hamburg, and West Berlin. Johansson had never visited these cities and had not even visited his summer home in more than thirty years. He had to convince his wife that he indeed wanted to go on this trip with Karl.

The Kunsthalle Museum in Hamburg was hosting the first large retrospective exhibition of German art. Among the artists represented were the founders of the Bauhaus, including Karl's favorite, Oskar Schlemmer. Karl had seen a retrospective of Schlemmer's work in Stuttgart Art Academy, and he remembered that it was on that occasion that he had been introduced to Max Ernst by Professor Pfenninger.

Karl and his companion Stig Johansson set off for West Berlin in July 1977 in Karl's new Volvo. Stig could not speak a word of German or English and had never set foot outside Scandinavia. It had been a year since the two men met. As they drove, they conversed about Schlemmer's work. He had been one of the most important members of the Bauhaus. He had worked with architects and had done groundbreaking work with set design for the theater. In his paintings he used figurative elements as design and compositional elements. He would also create total artistic environments that included sound. His work epitomized the spirit of Gesamtkunstwerk—a perfect synthesis of all the arts. His ideas still pervade the work of modern theater and opera designers.

As they drove along, they soon got stuck in a long line of cars, mostly Trabants, on a narrow highway leading to East Germany. The Trabant was East Germany's prestige car, but it was slow and unreliable. After about twenty miles of crawling along the narrow road, sandwiched between what looked like an endless queue of Trabant motor cars, they were pulled over by traffic police. After checking their passports and driver's licenses, Karl was informed that they had exceeded the twenty miles per hour speed limit by seventy miles per hour. The penalty was two hundred West German marks in cash. Karl protested. "How could I be speeding when I was stuck in a line of over twenty slow-moving vehicles?" The traffic officer's response was curt: "You did! Either you pay or follow us to the police station!"

Karl new the reputation of the Stasi and the East German police, so he paid the penalty and the two men continued on their journey to West Berlin. It was during this trip that Stig tried to convince Karl that he should work more as an artist and prepare for an exhibition of his work. They finally reached Berlin, and after crossing the boundary at Checkpoint Charlie, it was as if they had entered a totally different world. They checked in at the impressive Hotel Kempinsky. Karl was still on the payroll of hospital design, so he thought he would treat his friend and enjoy the luxury. It turned out that Karl could not have found a better traveling companion than an art writer and critic for visiting the fifteen art museums on their itinerary. Stig's father was the legendary architect and art critic Gotthard Johansson, who came to prominence in Sweden during the first half of the twentieth century. He was a renowned authority on modern architecture and one of the few supporters of Kaminski. Johansson's cousin Hubert Johansson was the sole printer of all the museum catalogs published in Sweden, many of which are collector's items today. His last commission was to print Karl's *MOMEN* catalog for his exhibition at the Haus auf Lutzöwplatz Cultural Center in Berlin. He was close to Gotthard, and he also printed all the books that Gotthard published on modern architecture and art.

Karl and Stig spent a week in Berlin and attended the most important art exhibition in Europe at the time: the Tendenzen der Zwanziger Jahre, Fifteenth European Art Exhibition, under the auspices of the Council of Europe and the Akademie der Künste at the Grosse Orangerie at the Schloss Charlottenburg in Berlin (August 14, 1977–October 16, 1977). The two men were duly impressed with the new National Gallery, built by Mies van der Rohe, the legendary architect, the largest modern museum in the country. The museum had a glass façade and synthesized the architectural styles of Le Corbusier, Marcel Breuer, Bruno Taut, and Oskar Schlemmer. They also attended the famous Pergamon Museum that held the largest collection of art works from the antique world of Babylon, Egypt, Persia, Greece, and Italy. They of course also visited the Bauhaus and Gropius's home. They took a special interest in the art of the Cubist Period, the Russian avant-garde, and Dadaism. They viewed works by the Expressionists Max Bachman, Otto Dix, and Otto Gross. After each day's long walks through the galleries Stig and Karl would find a bar restaurant on Kurfurstendam and enjoy a Berliner Weise beer. This beer had a mixture of sweet and sour flavors and soon became Stig's favorite. In the evenings, they attended performances of the Berlin Philharmonic and the German Opera, which performed Fidelio during their visit. This remarkable performance had one of the most unforgettable stage settings that Karl had ever seen. It was as if a brick wall surrounded the entire stage and the soldiers were all dressed in 1920's revolutionary guard uniforms. The governor of the jail was costumed like Mao or Stalin, and the décor bristled with metallic gray tones. Sitting in this performance, surrounded by the Ulbricht Wall, was so surreal and haunting that Karl had difficulty sleeping that night.

During their days in Berlin, Karl ran across numerous friends from the art world in Stockholm and Stuttgart. They also bumped into some of Stig's friends. They all seemed to have congregated in Berlin for the special occasion of the Retrospective at the National Gallery—the largest of its kind that Germany had ever hosted. Even Karl's former boss Ervin Pütsep was here. Karl recalls that Pütsep was one of the most intellectually gifted people he had ever known. He was an incredibly fast reader. During their trips to the Middle East for projects in Iran and Saudi Arabia during the 60s, Karl saw him read five or six newspapers in three or four languages on one flight. On one trip in 1963, Karl saw him read *The Godfather* in no more than two hours. Karl could not read English at the time, so when he asked Pütsep if the book was available in German, he responded by buying him a German copy when they landed in Zurich. It took Karl almost a week to read it. Pütsep had published three books on the subject of surgical center design. One of these became the best reference book for hospital design architects. Karl's old office colleagues would call him "Mr. Know-All." Every morning at the office, he would relate the latest developments from all over the world, from news about new concerts and theater performances to American football scores. That evening Pütsep hosted Karl and Stig at dinner. After some spirited discussion and several glasses of good wine, Pütsep saw occasion to take issue with Stig's latest art review in the *Svenska Dagbladet.* During these days, Karl found that he too disagreed from time-to-time with Stig's assessment of a particular show or exhibition. However, the two men always showed respect for each other's points of view and agreed to disagree on some subjects. Over the last while, Karl had become even more convinced that he enjoyed art more than architecture, especially his specialization of hospital design that involved even less architectural work. He also became convinced that the time had come to say goodbye to his architectural incomes.

After returning from their visit to Berlin, Karl spent an entire month boating in the Stockholm archipelago with his friends. During this time, he also managed to subcontract a new commission for a small doctor's daycare center. By the end of September 1976, Karl was exhibiting the lithographs he had printed at Leif Nielsen's printmaking studio. This exhibition was held at Gallery Nielsen, owned and operated by Nielsen and his wife in Gamla Stan. It was also the first time he had shown a print that contained his iconic image of a stylized tree. This image had already appeared in his major paintings from 1974 after being developed in his perspectival drawings of his architectural period.

Karl continued to participate in Stig Johansson's gallery walks, and as he visited new exhibitions, he established new friendships with gallery owners and their staff. He began to enjoy his new artistic life, free from the demands of a busy travel schedule and the stress of his former profession as an architect. Leif Nielsen recommended that Karl book an exhibition at the Mälargalleriet for January 1978. This was a large and spacious gallery that would accommodate most of his large seven- and eight-foot paintings, such as *The Detonation* and *Structural Change*. The show had a successful opening with a generous buffet of snacks and drinks. Most of the attendees were Karl's former architectural colleagues, friends, and neighbors. The Iranian ambassador to Sweden, Issa Malek, also attended. At the time, the Shah was still in power, and there was no sign of the forthcoming Khomeini revolution. The ambassador bought two paintings for the embassy that are still seen from time-to-time on the walls of the reception rooms of the embassy in Stockholm. The show received good reviews in several newspapers, including *Svenska Dagbladet*, and notes in the Dagens Nyheter Northeast section. Although this show produced good returns for Karl, the first two years of his career as a full-time artist were financially negative. However, his monetary returns were not as important to him as the direction of his new artistic path. After a highly successful architectural career of twenty years, he was not concerned about his financial situation going forward into the future.

Dream Island Suite, 2008

The Lonely Road, 1967

The Last Church, 1968

Chapter 23

AN ARTIST AT LAST

It was against the rich background of modernism that Karl began to paint in a serious and committed manner. He moved into a double-storied villa in Stockholm with a small studio on the upper level. Because he was independent of the gallery system, he could afford to go his own way with his paintings. He would often destroy work he did not like. His work was personal and even idiosyncratic. One of the earliest works from this period is *The Lonely Road* (1967), depicting a road disappearing over the horizon, a subject prompted perhaps by his personal feelings of loneliness and of his heightened awareness of himself standing at the threshold of his new career as an independent artist. The road is walled on both sides, indicating that there is no escape to left or right as the viewer's eye is moved toward an unknown future in the distance.

The following year he painted *The Last Church* (1968). Karl was an avowed agnostic at the time and often took issue with the hypocrisies of institutionalized religion. This work was painted at the height of the Cold War between Russia and the United States. It was also the era of the Vietnam War and of growing tensions between Arabs and Israelis. In this painting of a deserted chapel with a dilapidated poster depicting an apple on the wall, the apple is the only emblem of veneration. It symbolizes the Earth that has become the subject of materialistic control and acquisition. It has also become the prize over which competing political and religious interests wage war. Ironically, the earth is despoiled in the process, hence the neglected appearance of the apple in the poster. Karl had a keen sense of social justice and of environmental issues. His paintings often became a vehicle for his response to environmental issues of universal concern.

Karl's artistic sensibilities were profoundly influenced by his early exposure to the artists of the Russian avant-garde, some of whom were later associated with the Bauhaus. The cityscape represented an inexorable and unresolved tension. Its powerful forms and severe geometry at first fascinated Karl. This was at a time when new technology and scientific developments were celebrated as evidence of the new age of steel and speed. *The Lifting Crane* and *The Chimneys,* both painted in 1969, celebrate this new technology and the dynamism of the city in the manner of the Italian futurists.

In his work of this period, there is a clear and carefully stated concern with the impact that the materialistic world has on all things organic, including the human spirit. His awareness of this conflict is clearly seen in his *Dawn at the Center of the City,* painted in 1973. This painting depicts a severe cityscape that acts as a foil for the four independent and unrelated individuals depicted in the painting. A prostitute stands propped against a wall. A man in a suit is seen sitting alone in a second-story hotel room, silently gazing into the distance. A vagabond lurks at the end of the city street, and a uniformed policeman stands motionless in the foreground with his back to the viewer. None of these individuals appear to be aware of each other. Each is motionless as if immobilized by unseen forces hidden within their environment. The relationship between the figures and their passionless architectural setting is awkward and strained. They are isolated and estranged from each other, as lone individuals unable to act or move. Moreover, these figures are representative of clearly defined and stratified social classes. Not surprisingly, this painting caused quite a stir when it was first exhibited in Berlin at the Haus am Lútzowplatz Gallery in Stockholm in 1979.

Karl's work drew the attention of Adereas Kap, the art critic of *Der Tagesspiegel.* Kap accused him of being critical of the ideals of the Swedish social democratic system. Karl had exposed some of the inherent shortcomings of an order that relied heavily on social engineering to achieve its egalitarian goals. He had confronted the viewer with a scene

The Crane, 1969

The Chimneys, 1969

Dawn at the Center of the City, 1973

poised on the brink of social pathology in which individuals are subordinated to a dispassionate city environment with its debilitating and inhumane checks and controls.

He had become aware of the inherent conflict between harmonious organic systems in a benign and ordered universe on the one hand, and the contrived world of man-made technology that confines the human spirit on the other hand. This conflict between man and machine, or between nature and technology, was highlighted during the 1960s and 70s by a generation of young people who espoused anti-establishment views. This movement was violently opposed to the rapid proliferation of dangerous technologies that had the potential of destroying the world and enslaving the human spirit. Karl felt these issues deeply.

In 1962, geometric forms resembling stylized trees first made their appearance in his architectural drawings while he was working at Pütsep's office. As a practicing architect at the time, he had been designing the institute of pathology for the Karolinska Institute in Sweden. Architects often make use of abstracted impressions of shrubs and trees as landscape elements in their renderings of proposed buildings. Karl had developed a stylized interpretation of a tree that used a trunk supporting spheres of differing sizes. These spheres often gently impinged on each other like under-inflated beach balls that flatten at their points of contact. This particular abstraction recurred in his architectural renderings of trees that he produced at his office in Sweden during the 1960s.

In *Structural Change* (1973), the stylized tree becomes symbolic of universal organic growth in the face of destructive man-made technological and dehumanizing institutional forces. The tree stands on a flat plane and is threatened by the symbolic explosion that occurs on the horizon, represented by a large sphere breaking through layers of containment. This is Karl's allusion to the awesome power of the atomic bomb and the threat it poses to all living things, including the earth itself. The forms are harmonized and interrelated by their uniformly crisp shapes and are presented in close proximity to each other. This stylized form of a tree would become fully realized as the subject of his largest and most controversial sculpture *The Tree of Utah,* constructed thirteen years later in the Great Western Desert in North America.

The awful threat of imminent nuclear destruction during the height of the Cold War also became the subject of his painting *Detonation.* This work was also completed in 1973 and is significant, because it contains the first inclusion of a treelike form with simplified and abstracted trunk, branches, and sphere-like protuberances that would often recur in Karl's work.

Karl's inquiry into the dichotomy between technology and the elements of an organic world was evident in *Detonation.*

Structural Change, 1973

Detonation, 1973

This painting was exhibited at various international galleries, including the Haus Am Lützhow Platz (the Berlin Culture Center) in Berlin in 1982, and then again at the Striped House Museum in Tokyo in 1985. It made its debut at the Salt Lake Art Center the same year in Utah. Again we see the symbol of organic unity represented by the stylized form of a tree on the left of the composition. However, instead of an atomic explosion on the horizon, we see the man-made structure of a city with its familiar rectilinear forms. The architecture of the city is severe and abstracted, presenting an austere and even hostile environment for human habitation.

The subtle influence of surrealism was still present in these early works, prompting Karl's mentor, Max Ernst, to remark, "Dali is still alive in the work of Momen." In his painting *Shangri-La,* also painted in 1974, Karl expressed his Utopian dream—the ideal cityscape. *Shangri-La* has remarkable similarities to the Frank Gehry-designed Guggenheim Museum in Balbao, Spain. Both structures are constructed with interconnected curvilinear forms contained by highly articulated yet harmonizing sheer planes. Although designed as buildings for human habitation, both structures are consciously sculptural when seen as constructions in space. Although Gehry's museum was designed twenty-three years after the *Shangri-La* painting, both structures employ multi-planar geometry, with remarkably similar intersecting curvilinear forms, making Gehry's design curiously coincidental.

Working with the conflict between man-made and organic orders, Karl completed *Intrusion* in 1975. This work also caused a stir among the art critics of the day, including Stig Johansson, the respected Swedish art critic who was positively impressed with the poignant symbolism. The dingy brown architectonic form represents the evolution of humankind's technology reaching blindly and menacingly toward the tree. The tree is stunted and has truncated limbs, indicating the deleterious effects of technological and institutional confinement. This represents the tension between organic creation and contrived technological progress.

Karl befriended Leif Nielsen, a local gallery owner, who introduced Karl to other galleries and was able to give him good advice about getting established as an independent artist. The two men remained friends throughout Karl's career. Nielsen introduced Karl's work to the influential Málargallery and Galeri Bleue. Later Nielsen was instrumental in introducing Karl to Julle Hammer, the director of Haus Am Lützhow Platz, which resulted in three successful exhibitions at this important venue.

In 1977, Karl completed *Distance,* a much larger work that was to become the capstone of this early career. Again the theme is derived from the unresolved

Shangri-La, 1974

Intrusion, 1974

relationship between the organic nature of humankind and the alienating forces of technocracy. This work indicates Karl's affinity with the forms and constructs of his early hero, Oskar Schlemmer.

All these early works were painted in Karl's tiny studio at the top of his villa in Stockholm. They were all assembled for his first major exhibition at the Millir Gallery in Stockholm in January 1978. The exhibition was well received and gained much positive critical review in the local press. Karl recognized the auspicious nature of the moment and decided to make the final break to become a full-time artist. He was invited to show the collection at the Haus Am Lützplatz in West Berlin the following year. He went to work with newfound passion. He felt that he had made his breakthrough and nothing could hold him back from pursuing his dream. Max Ernst's admonition came ringing back to him:

"Do your own work. Only that should be good enough for you!"

Distance, 1977

Chapter 24

COMING TO AMERICA

In 1978, Karl delivered his last architectural project. After succeeding as a successful German-trained architect after World War II, he soon decided that he would move to the United States and work the rest of his life as a full-time artist. It was inevitable that this avowed bachelor and adventurous traveler would voyage to the New World where he would become enraptured by the contrast of vibrant cities and the wide-open expanses of Utah's Great Western Desert. America would become his artistic home, and it would be here that he would execute his most notable sculptural piece, the eighty-seven-foot-high *Tree of Utah*. The odyssey of his travels had exposed him to the entangled complexities of nations and the human condition, across time, place, and cultures, inciting a lifelong humanist impulse that would infuse his modernist oeuvre.

In the United States, unfettered by the constraints of his former profession, he discovered freedom and inspiration for his art, diving headlong into the affair of his life's work. The great masters of modernism had educated and influenced him, but he never relinquished the seminal influences of his youth in Mashhad, Iran, where he grew up surrounded by complex rug designs and the hues of colorful dyes in his father's Persian rug workshop. It was also here that he was exposed to the world of Russian avant-garde art. He had drunk deeply from this fountain of inspiration.

Karl was both adventurous and impulsive. He had been traveling to the United States as an architect, doing consulting work since the beginning of the 1970s, mostly in the San Francisco Bay Area, but this was his first trip as an artist. Now he could settle down and devote the rest of his life to his art. In San Francisco, he quickly reestablished an old friendship with Erland and Christine Jannesson. Erland was a civil engineer he had known since he first started working in Stockholm where the men had offices in the same building. The Jannessons had immigrated to the US in the mid 1960s, and Karl had stayed with them at their home in the Bay Area a few times. He had taken a liking to Sausalito on a previous visit. On this occasion, the Jannessons introduced him to a realtor, who showed him various townhouses in the area. He quickly settled on one in particular. It was well situated on a hill, overlooking the bay on Harbor Drive. The two-thousand-square-foot townhouse had two bedrooms on the top floor, a living room and kitchen on the ground floor, and a large balcony with a spectacular view. Within a few days, a contract was signed. He purchased furnishings from a Scandinavian design store in San Raphael and moved into his new residence.

He was quick to purchase artist's materials, set up his new studio, and start to paint. He also contacted some of his family and friends from Iran who now lived in the States to say that he had relocated. He enjoyed the association of his relatives and renewing old friendships. He contacted Ghasem Hadjtarkhani, a dear friend he had last seen in 1967 when Ghasem was a student in London. He now operated a successful rug business in Maryland.

A cousin, Akbar Farivari, was an air force colonel and a military attaché to the Iranian Embassy in Washington, D.C. Akbar and his family had moved to the United States after the Islamic revolution in 1979. Farivari's children and grandchildren had all become highly qualified professionals working in Maryland. In order to be close to his family, Karl decided to purchase a small, one-bedroom apartment in Washington, D.C., on New Hampshire Avenue near DuPont Circle. Here he could reconnect with his large extended family, including dozens of second cousins who lived and worked in the area. On his visits to DC, he would often accompany his relatives to parties and receptions at the Iranian Embassy. Karl kept up this DC apartment until October 1985, when he was forced to sell in order to raise funds to complete the building of the *Tree of Utah,* his most significant sculptural achievement.

Ghasem Hadjtarkhani also operated his rug business in the San Francisco area, and on a visit to Karl's studio, he mentioned that he knew William and Mary Geguiboare, the owners of Cobra Gallery in Napa Valley. He arranged a meeting for Karl. The Geguiboares were impressed with Karl's work. They soon arranged a large exhibition of his work at their gallery. The exhibition was well received, with good reviews in the local press. The Gegiboares went on to sell over eighty of Karl's paintings and sculptures to collectors and corporate buyers in the Bay Area. William and Mary later divorced, and William moved to the Eastern United States.

Karl traveled between Stockholm and his properties in the United States on a seasonal basis. After his first exhibition at Gallery Málaren in Stockholm and a favorable reception by the media, he decided to seek out opportunities for exhibitions that were further afield in the United States. He had established a base for himself on both the east and west coasts, and this would be a good time to explore modern art museums and art centers in the New World. In Stockholm, Karl had lunch with Leif Niellsen, Stig Johansson, and Bengt Törnebom, the owner of Gallery Prisma. He mentioned that he was thinking of traveling to the United States in June or July of that year to view museums and to make contacts for possible shows in the future. On hearing this, Stig embarked on a long preamble extolling the virtues and personal benefits he received from his trip to Germany with Karl and how this had totally changed and enriched his perspective of art internationally.

Stig asked Karl if he could join him on this trip since he would love to go on his own but the English language barrier prohibited him from doing so. Karl approved of his proposal. They could use Karl's townhouse in Sausalito and his two-bedroom condo in Washington, D.C., on their travels. A week after Karl arrived in Washington, Stig called Karl to say that he was going to purchase an airline ticket from Stockholm to New York. They agreed to meet in New York City. Stig asked Karl to book an economical hotel room for him. Karl responded by inviting Stig to stay in New York as his guest. He booked two rooms at the Waldorf Astoria, a hotel he was intimately familiar with having stayed there on numerous occasions when he was working as an architect. He was often in the company of engineers and other professionals in those days, and they would often have their meetings at the Waldorf. Consequently, he was able to book two adjoining smaller rooms with a shared shower at a special rate.

Karl arrived at the hotel a day before Stig's departure from Stockholm, and he arranged to meet Stig on his arrival in the lobby. On Stig's arrival, Karl helped him register at the front desk and asked that Stig's room be charged to his own account. After checking in, the two men enjoyed a drink at the bar and then went for a walk in the city. They walked to Park Avenue and then to Fifth Avenue. The sights of the city overwhelmed Stig. He loved the atmosphere and the hustle and bustle of the crowds. After dinner, they decided on their schedule of visits to art museums and places of interest.

On their first day, they went directly to the Museum of Modern Art (MOMA)—a visit that lasted most of the day. To Karl's surprise, Stig had already made an appointment for 10:00 a.m. that morning with one of the museum curators through the *Svenska Dagbladet* newspaper in Stockholm. They were received by one of the curators at the reception desk of the museum at the appointed time.

CHAPTER 24

When Karl mentioned to her that Stig could only speak Swedish and French, she proceeded in French and guided the men to her office. Here she presented Stig with a museum catalog and gave both men a pass for a week's free attendance to the museum. She also invited them to a special reception for museum patrons the following evening. However, the men had to excuse themselves since they had planned to attend a performance by the New York Philharmonic Orchestra that evening. After their meeting with the curator, the men proceeded to the main exhibition hall on the first floor where they were confronted by Picasso's *Guernica* that was on show at the museum until 1981. Stig was dumbfounded as he sat on a bench in front of the painting and could not move for at least five minutes. He appeared to be paralyzed. Eventually Karl asked if they should move on, "Please go and have some coffee. I am not finished," Stig replied.

After half an hour, Stig had finished contemplating the Picasso, and they were able to continue viewing other galleries. They had lunch at the museum and then decided to continue on to the Guggenheim Museum where they stayed until closing. They returned to the hotel that evening to freshen up and have dinner. Then it was time to go strolling on Broadway. They dropped in at the Sheraton for a drink and then continued on to see Marc Chagall's painting *The Magic Flute* in the foyer of the Metropolitan Opera.

The week in New York was soon over after multiple museum, gallery, and concert visits. The two men then boarded an Amtrak train for Chicago. They enjoyed the unique luxury of a sleeping compartment, a reading lounge, and the famous bar and restaurant. These amenities created a nostalgic moment for the two middle-aged men, with recollections of similar settings in movies such as North by Northwest and several Alfred Hitchcock movies. Forty years later, Stig still reflected on being served fancy cocktails in this fine restaurant on wheels. Karl wondered if today's young people ever have time for nostalgia. He reflected that things change so rapidly nowadays that there doesn't seem to be enough time to file things in one's memory.

Upon their arrival in Chicago, their first stop was to view Picasso's "head" sculpture that stands fifty feet high in Daley Plaza in the Chicago Loop. It was the first such major public artwork in Downtown Chicago and had become a well-known landmark at the time of their visit. After this stunning experience, they were off to the Art Institute of Chicago, where the men were equally enthralled by Rodin's sculptures. Karl came to regard the United States as his artistic home. He thought this to be the most egalitarian country in the world and became an American citizen in 2003.

Chapter 25

DEVELOPING A PERSONAL ICONOGRAPHY

Working as an artist in Sweden, Karl had shown his work in several cities and received consistently good reviews. However, in the beginning, his exhibitions did not produce many sales, mainly because he did not want to part with his paintings. He was financially independent and did not need an income from his painting. Consequently, his prices were high. He was more interested in experimenting with his work and did not want to sell everything he produced. He had never been one to affiliate with art groups. His strong sense of individuality and his desire to be his own man made him fiercely independent, not wishing to work collaboratively with other artists.

The Swedish art world was replete with exclusive communities of artists, each grouped around a leader who represented that particular group's ideas. Groups would exhibit together and not take kindly to interlopers. Consequently, as an outsider who did not seek affiliation, Karl was soon branded a loner by the prevailing art establishment. Nevertheless, he had no shortage of galleries who wanted to show his work. In Stockholm, Galleri Nielsen, Mälargallcriet, Galleri Bleue, and Boibrino all mounted exhibitions of his paintings. In 1985, he ventured to the new world of the United States and held exhibitions at the Metropolitan Museum and Art Center in Miami, the Old Town Gallery in Park City, the Salt Lake Art Center, and the Springville Museum of Art in Utah. He also went east and showed work at the Striped House Museum in Tokyo.

His work became more abstract, thereby losing figural references altogether.

CHAPTER 25

In 1989, he held a retrospective exhibition of all the paintings he had completed during the previous decade. All surrealistic references had disappeared. Instead, Geometric Abstraction had opened the door to symbolism and strong figure-ground relationships. Even his palette reflected this change. Karl's colors became purer and bolder and his compositions simpler. *The Loosening Cage,* painted in 1986, represents a conscious attempt to destabilize the conventional order of his earlier compositions. Billowing clouds are introduced as a counterpoise to the strong architectonic forms that rise up in his compositions. Solid masses dissolve into two-dimensional shapes and begin to float, accentuating the sense of airiness in the composition. The tone of this work is also a great deal lighter than his earlier surrealistic paintings. The decorative qualities of some works and their primary colors echo the work of the pop artists.

Shangri-La 2000, painted in 1980, indicates how far he had progressed since his earlier work completed in 1974. The composition has opened up, and all the elements float against a deep, blue sky. Architectural elements are captured in a state of dynamic flux as they whirl around a central blacktopped pylon with no reference to a horizontal axis. Kandinsky's *Small Worlds* IV (1922) and *In Blue* (1925) make use of similar compositional devices in depicting dynamic abstract elements cast against a flat background. The concept of the ideal city existing on the horizon has been subsumed within a metaphysical depiction of symbolic elements encircling a central vortex.

This painting also introduces an important technical innovation in Karl's painting technique. For the first time, the plane surfaces are textured with an evenly applied gestural mark similar to the abstract texture arrived at by using a small scraper on freshly stuccoed plaster. This treatment gives the forms corporeal weight against their fast-receding blue background. *Shangri-La 2000* signaled an important shift in Karl's work. Rather than depict surrealistic scenarios reminiscent of Oskar Schlemmer's stage settings, he now chose a vocabulary of geometric forms that are ordered in highly evocative abstract compositions. These paintings are iconic in their uncompromising frontality, but they also become mandala-like in their powerfully suggestive symbolism. They reverberate with the Bauhaus masters' preoccupation with significant form.

El (Eleazar) Lissitzky (1890–1956) had become an exemplar for Karl. It was from El Lissitzky that he learned to manipulate geometric abstraction within the confines of perspectival illusion. Lissitzky began his career by studying engineering in Germany and later significantly influenced the integration of the non-objectivism of Russian Suprematism, Constructivism, and De Stijl in the work of the German Bauhaus. In *Captive Giant,* completed in 1986, a red sphere is partially encased in an encircling

The Loosening Cage, 1986

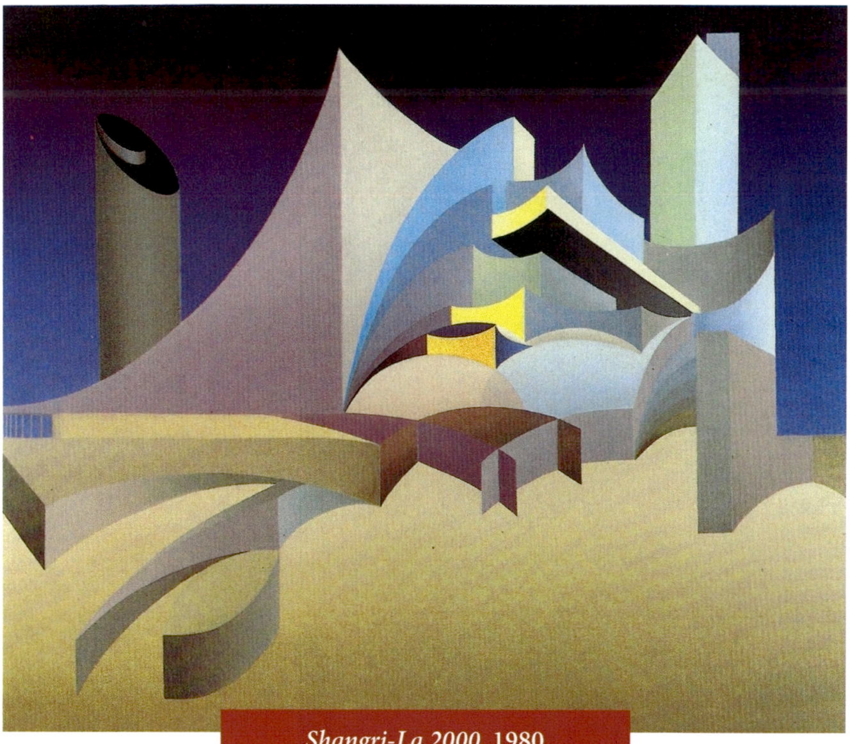

Shangri-La 2000, 1980

Captive Giant, 1986

form to the right in the composition. The title *Captive Giant* speaks of the fact that the forces of organic creation are held captive by the architectonic world of technology. Hovering over the scene is a crosshatched grouping of linear elements that appear to mediate between the sphere and pylons. This painting also represents Karl's first use of metallic luster in his oil paints. The metallic luster gives each individual brushstroke a sheen that changes with the spectator's viewing angle, creating a dynamic play of light and texture.

Also completed in 1986 was *Voyager*. This composition is directly related to Karl's most important sculptural work, *The Tree of Utah*, completed in the same year. After the successful completion of this sculpture in Utah's Great Western Desert, Karl withdrew to his Sausalito studio and painted almost ceaselessly. By the end of 1987, he had completed a number of significant works, including *The Hammer*, *The Red Angle*, *Prism Pyramid*, *Clock Tower*, *Evening Prayer*, and *Cage*. *Evening Prayer* and *Clock Tower* are both inspired by religious considerations.

Clock Tower, 1987

Prism Pyramid, 1987

Voyager, 1986

The Red Angle, 1987

The Hammer, 1987

City in the Far, 1986

Blue Tower, 1986

Demolition, 1986

Urban Night, 1986

Evening Prayer was shown in an ecumenical exhibition because of its recognizable religious connotations conveyed by its simple centralized composition and reverential tone. Although not an adherent of any religious philosophy or creed, Karl thought if he ever wanted to choose a religion, he would choose Christianity because of the edifying art and musical compositions that have been inspired by this faith over the centuries.

The painting *Cage* was also completed in 1987. The symbolism of the cage, represented in this work by the forceful descent of dark blue bars impinging upon a square base, is to remind the viewer that we are all confined and hedged about by modernism—the twentieth century's most pervasive and most influential art movement. Modernism has dramatically affected the way we see the world about us and has changed how we think about and create art. All of Karl's works completed during this highly productive year were included in a successful exhibition held at the Haus Am Lützowplatz in West Berlin in 1989.

Karl's work had progressed away from three-dimensional rendering toward a clearer and more assured use of two-dimensional elements in his paintings. His highly abstracted geometric images became a combination of Persian and Western perspectives. His vocabulary of circles, hemispheres, straight lines, and rectangles echoed his early vocation as an architect, practicing in Sweden, a country known for the purity of its design. The largest of these works, the *Tree of Utah,* was to become a permanent feature of Utah's desert landscape.

Evening Prayer, 1987

Cage, 1987

Chapter 26

A BILLIONAIRE AS PARTNER

Karl inherited the best and the worst of his father's character traits—his artistic talent, and his impulsive decision-making that often had economic repercussions with catastrophic results. He was born when his father was eighty years old, so most of his catastrophic business decisions were made before Karl was born. Karl's oldest brother told him of one such event that was occasioned by his father's gross miss-calculation. He had been trying to reduce the operating costs of his Mashhad rug factory, which was the largest in Mashhad at the turn of twentieth century. The production of this factory included a small percentage of silk rugs. He had to buy raw silk to produce these rugs, and he blamed himself for having to pay such high prices for the silk. It occurred to him that he should produce his own silk.

He purchased a forty-acre mulberry orchard, planted additional trees, and after three years, introduced silk worms with all the hazards and shortcomings of a novice. He eventually succeeded in producing sufficient quantities of silk for his silk rugs. However, after calculating the costs of producing his own silk, he found that it was now costing him three times the price for the silk that he had paid previously!

There were other examples as well. Once he grew two five-hundred-pound watermelons in his orchard to send to the governor and to Mashhad's Member of Parliament as gifts, at enormous expense. The locals were still talking about this episode years later.

Karl met Stig Johansson, the time-honored art critic of the Swedish newspaper *Svenska Dagbladet,* for the first time at Leif Nielsen's printmaking studio in 1975. Johansson's wife was also a journalist at the same newspaper. Their friendship grew, and they soon became

CHAPTER 26

lunch companions, a liaison that continued for many years. They traveled together to Denmark and Germany, and Stig visited Karl at his homes in Washington, D.C., and Sausalito. Together they traveled to various art museums in the US to see important exhibitions. In the fall of 1978, Stig asked Karl if he would be interested in seeing the collection of one of the best art collectors in the world. Karl agreed, and the two men set off by road to the city of Sandvik, the headquarters of the multinational Sandvik Steel Company, about two hundred kilometers north of Stockholm. Here they would meet Carl Eric Bjőrkegren, the vice president and financial director of the company.

They set out at 10:00 a.m., with Karl behind the wheel since Stig had no driver's license. Karl thought Stig was an ideal passenger. Like all others who don't have driver's licenses, Stig was calm while enjoying the passing scenery and didn't continually try to give Karl instructions. They arrived and parked in front of the impressive red brick building that was the head office of the Sandvik Company, one of the finest steel producers in the world. They were ushered into Bjőrkegren's office, and the secretary announced their arrival to Carl Eric Bjőrkegren. He was a presidential-looking gentleman and, after giving Stig a long handshake and inquiring after his general well being, he turned to Karl and gave him a warm welcome. He said that he already knew much about Karl thanks to Stig. He invited the two into his office, where he immediately presented Karl with an ornate penknife that was etched with Vikings symbols and Sandvik's name and logo.

He had a painting by an avant-garde painter of the 1920's prominently displayed on the wall of his office. After coffee, they departed together for the short drive to his mansion. Here Bjőrkegren's elegant wife, Ala-Britt, welcomed them, and after a glass of sherry, they enjoyed a delicious lunch prepared by the Bjőrkegren's chef. After lunch, Bjőrkegren showed Karl his collection. Stig was already familiar with these works. His collection was impressive, with works by the most significant Swedish artists from the twenties and thirties. They were of good quality, and Karl could see that Bjőrkegren preferred paintings with bright colors. Among the Swedish artists, he had several works by Matthias Grünewald. Then he showed Karl some of his own paintings. They were good for an amateur, but Karl could see they were not all painted by the same hand.

Bjőrkegren said he knew that Karl collected Persian rugs and asked if he had any high-quality ones that he didn't have space for that he could buy. Karl said that he had two rugs: one that was a three- by six-meter semi-antique Tehran rug that would be perfect for his dining room. Bjőrkegren said that he would be in Stockholm the next week and would stop by to see Karl. When he turned up at Karl's house the following week, he brought with him a man by the name of Gőran Utterstrőm, who introduced himself as Bjőrkegren's butler. When Karl showed the rug to Bjőrkegren, he liked it immediately and asked his driver to put it in the trunk of his limousine. He said that he needed one more for his living room and invited Karl to have dinner with himself and Gőran the following week when he would also settle the purchase of the rug.

The next week, Karl picked up Uttersrőm and drove to Sandviken. They had a pleasant dinner, and Ala-Britt Bjőrkegren was happy with the rugs. She told Karl that he must be a magician to show her husband an item that he was satisfied with. Many dealers had been out to their home but without success in selling any of their wares. After an excellent dinner, the party retired to the library to discuss the payment for the rug. After a little arm-twisting, he gave Karl a check. When they rejoined the others, Utterstőm said to Bjőrkegren that Karl had been caught out by a professional since anyone who could do business with an Arab could get the better of anyone!

That night before Karl left, Bjőrkegren asked him to let him know if he ever came across a rug that would suit his living room. Karl told him that he was leaving for London in a few weeks for a meeting with a representative from the Middle East to go over the final stages of an architectural project in the Persian Gulf. He would visit a few top dealers on High Street Kensington since they usually carried top-quality rugs. He also knew one of the biggest wholesale dealers in London. He mentioned that he could look out for a rug that would match their interior décor now that he was familiar with their home. Bjőrkegren turned to his wife and asked if she would like to accompany Karl and himself on a trip to London. She responded, "Why not!"

In London, after checking in at the London Hilton, the party agreed to meet again in the lobby in fifteen minutes. Ala-Britt announced her destination as, "Harrods, where else?"

Laughing, Bjőrkegren turned to Karl and said that this was why she married him. Her quick response was, "Why else?" Again they laughed, and then Ala Britt said, with a broad smile across her beautiful face, "That is why he is still in the stream and ready to be caught!"

The concierge hailed a taxi for them, and Karl gave their destination as the Klaty Oriental Rug Company at London's customs and excise depot. The building was four stories high, and the four-thousand-square-meter facility was filled with rugs. The owner was originally from northeastern Iran. He was a tall, well-dressed, middle aged man with a large black chapeau hat that he never took off. He welcomed the three, and after the customary tea, which in this case was served by a young man, he and Karl exchanged some pleasantries in Farsi. Karl expressed a hope that Bjőrkegren

A PARTNER

would find what he was looking for, and then Bjőrkegren introduced the party to two of his assistants before excusing himself to attend to other waiting clients.

CHAPTER 26

Bjőrkegren did not find a suitable rug for his living room, but he was interested in a silk Mashhad rug he saw. The three-by four-meter rug was smaller than he needed, but its shimmering red colored got his attention. When he asked Karl what he thought of it, Karl told him that he had seen a similar rug just a year ago in New York. "It was offered to me but the price was far over my budget," Karl said.

Bjőrkegren asked, "How much was it?"

Karl replied, "The dealer in New York wanted four hundred thousand dollars." Bjőrkegren looked at Karl in disbelief, "Is that possible?"

Karl replied, "Yes, and here you must pay much more, because that was the wholesale price!"

The owner returned to join the party and confirmed that some of Karl's father's work would be even more expensive. Bjőrkegren looked stunned and said to Karl in Swedish, "I am finding it difficult to decide on a purchase when there are so many rugs to choose from, and since the rugs are all folded, I cannot see an entire rug to make a decision."

Karl told him that rug dealers do not need to see the whole rug to make a decision. Then he said he should wait until he could find him the right one.

The party returned to the hotel, and while waiting at the bar for Ala-Britt, Bjőrkegren told Karl that he was going to retire in a year's time and move to Stockholm. He was already heavily invested in three hotels in Stockholm. He had acquired a reputation for buying up small industrial companies and then stripping them of their assets for a quick profit.

Ala-Brit eventually returned from her shopping spree later that afternoon. She was laden with so many boxes and shopping bags that the bellman had to help her carry her load. She turned to her husband with a self-satisfied smile and simply said, "Expensive!"

Bjőrkegren returned a knowing smile and nodded his head. Ala-Britt added, "I will need at least an hour to dress myself to accompany you two snobs to the restaurant for dinner!" She kissed her husband and moved toward the elevator with her cache of boxes and bags and with the bellman in tow.

Bjőrkegren ordered another whiskey, and Karl phoned an art agent he knew in London to ask him if he still had Marc Chagall's *Harlequin* that Stig Johansson had told him about. He replied in the affirmative, and Karl made arrangements to view the famous painting with Bjőrkegren.

Bjőrkegren knew that Karl was going to visit New York in a week's time and asked him to let him know if he should come across a top quality rug there, because he trusted Karl's judgment.

The following afternoon, after viewing the Chagall painting, the Bjőrkegrens went back to Sweden, and Karl had his meeting with the structural engineer who was consulting on his hospital project.

In November 1979, when Karl was in New York, he visited Fayaz, a wholesale rug dealer, to ask if he knew of anyone who might have a top-quality rug for sale. Fayaz later called Karl to tell him that he knew a person on Fifth Avenue who had a large collection of extraordinary top quality rugs. The following day, Fayaz accompanied Karl to the dealer's office. Rad was a tall, elegant, middle-aged gentleman. He didn't look like the average rug dealer to Karl. The men were welcomed and offered the customary tea. Rad's daughter was also elegant and served as his secretary. She knew about Karl's architectural projects in the Middle East. Both father and daughter behaved in a relaxed manner and were not pushy or overbearing as many rug salesmen tend to be.

Then Rad escorted Karl and Fayaz from his office to the adjoining store. There they saw piles of exquisite rugs—not of the kind one would find at a dealer. Karl had never seen anything like this before. He picked out two rugs that would suit the Bjőrkegrens' needs perfectly. One was a rare Tabriz that was antique peach in color and six by four meters in size. It was perfect for his home and his taste. Karl called Bjőrkegren and described the rug to him over the phone. When Bjőrkegren asked the price and Karl told him it was expensive, "About six figures," Bjőrkegren asked Karl if he could bring it to show him in Stockholm. Karl told him that he would have to buy it before it could leave the US. He said that if Bjőrkegren did not like it, he would buy it from him and keep it for himself. Bjőrkegren wired the funds, and Fayaz took the rug to Stockholm. He liked it. When Karl returned to Sweden, Bjőrkegren invited him and Stig Johansson to dinner. He proudly showed off Chagall's *Harlequin*, and the rug looked wonderful in his living room. This time Ala-Britt appeared even more excited about the rug than her husband.

Karl continued traveling back and forth between Stockholm and Sausalito in the US. On one of these trips, he found Bjőrkegren another top-quality Tabriz rug.

In the spring of 1980, Bjőrkegren purchased a four-hundred-square-meter mansion in Strandvagen, the most fashionable district of Stockholm, opposite the American Embassy. Before they moved from Sandviken, he had the house extended by two hundred square meters to accommodate a library and a gallery for his art collection.

CHAPTER 26

ONE MUST CHOOSE ONE'S PARENTS WISELY

Bjőrkegren was an elegant man who wore tailored suits in the manner that conservative Swedes liked to dress, much like their English counterparts. He typified the stingy unemployed billionaire. He offered his guests mineral water in Sherry glasses. However, he was pleasant and good-humored, always ready with a witty comment that often bordered on sarcasm, but he was never offensive. His demeanor made him a popular guest at all of Stockholm's high society parties. He thoroughly enjoyed advising people to choose their parents wisely, as he had—his parents were billionaires! He asked Karl on many occasions to buy him fine rugs. On one such occasion, both Bjőrkegren and Uttersrtrom asked Karl if he could find them some additional fine rugs and that they would be happy to purchase them from Karl. Karl accepted their offer, and on his next trip to Rad in New York, he was able to find and purchase a top-quality, twenty- by fifteen-foot Tabriz rug for Bjőrkegren.

Karl asked Rad if he had some high-quality Mashhad rugs. He was a little reserved at first, but then he asked Karl to accompany him to another heavily guarded storage facility. There he showed Karl two Muod rugs from Sherkate Shargh Brigand, a rug factory that had been established by Karl's father in the early 1900s. He then showed Karl a hundred-year-old Mashhad rug that was one of finest ever produced. It had originally been crafted for Sigari, the most highly ranked businessman in northern Iran at the time. Rad also showed Karl a fine Esfahan rug. They both measured ten by fifteen feet.

Karl called Utterstrőm and described the rugs to him. He asked Karl to purchase them. Again, Bjőrkegren wired Karl the money, and the deal was closed. Mr. Fayaz took the rugs to Stockholm. They never asked Karl how much he paid for the rugs, and Karl never disclosed their price. They were overjoyed with the purchase; however, Utterstrőm wanted to test Karl's estimation of the rugs and invited Jack Francis, the internationally famous expert on rugs, who was also Sotheby's representative in Stockholm, to inspect the rugs. Francis was thrilled to see them and suggested they should be placed on auction in Dubai. A special catalog was printed for the four rugs, and the selling price of each was estimated at 250 thousand dollars. They were not sold at auction, because Utterstrőm had placed a high reserve price on each of them. Karl knew all the while that he was just trying to confirm that Karl's recommendations were correct.

Chapter 27

JUMPING WITHOUT A PARACHUTE

In the summer of 1989, Bjőrkegren invited Karl to lunch at the Vedholm Restaurant and mentioned in his telephone call that he had a splendid idea he wanted to discus with him. They met at 1:30 p.m. and found that the restaurant was not crowded. After ordering lunch and a glass of wine, Bjőrkegren explained that since he was now retired, he had more time on his hands. He wanted to start something new, like an art gallery, an interior design studio, or even a high-end furniture store. As an architect, Karl's preference for him was to start with an exclusive furnishing and interior designing company; however, Karl told him that it would be difficult to find one. Bjőrkegren replied that he had been to Harald Westerberg, the famous and top-ranked furnishing store, where he had ordered some furniture for his new Stockholm home. Hans Westerberg, the owner, had complained that he was getting old and going to retire soon. He said that he was thinking of perhaps selling the company.

Harald Westerberg was established at the turn of the twentieth century as the most exclusive furnishing company in Sweden, with high-quality Scandinavian, English, and Italian furniture.

Karl said that he was not prepared to run a shop. Bjőrkegren responded that neither of them would be required to run it. They would only need to put in the capital. Karl was not convinced that this was a good idea. After coffee, Bjőrkegren suggested that they walk to the store, which was located nearby at Kungsgatan, one of Stockholm's major business streets. The store was large and elegant, with tastefully arranged furnishings of high quality. The owner, Hans Westerberg, greeted the men,

CHAPTER 27

and Bjőrkegren gave him a wish list of furnishings for their new home that his wife had prepared.

Bjőrkegren did not waste time. As a leading industrialist, he did not need to soft-start his purchase proposal. He told Westerberg that he and Karl wished to buy his company. Westerberg was surprised and asked how Bjőrkegren knew that he wanted to sell. Bjőrkegren replied that Westerberg had mentioned two weeks previously that it was his desire to sell the company and retire. Bjőrkegren told Westerberg that he would not find two more qualified buyers. At that moment, Karl thought to himself that this was obviously a tactic that the "big guys" used. After not more than two hours, the purchase contract was signed for a price equal to four hundred thousand US dollars for the company name, the store with all existing pieces of furniture in the showroom, and all stored goods. Also included was the provision that Hans, his brother Christer, and two other employees would keep their jobs with present salaries and benefits for twelve months.

Before signing the sales contract and before any decision was made, Karl said that he wished to talk with Bjőrkegren in private, and they walked over to the Hotel Anglais bar just two hundred yards from Westerberg's showroom. There Karl asked Bjőrkegren how he could be so sure that he would be a partner in this deal. In response, Bjőrkegren told Karl that he had already calculated that the existing investment in merchandise would be more than 80 percent of their purchase price, and if they were to rent the showroom, it would cost more than one hundred fifty thousand US dollars per year. Karl asked him how he knew all this in just two hours. Bjőrkegren's reply was accompanied with a loud laugh. "I had a financial expert evaluate the company two weeks ago. You didn't think I would jump without a parachute, did you?"

As he spoke, Karl did a mental calculation for himself. It was not a bad business, and besides, he had the funds in his bank account. The two men returned to Hans and signed the deal. Bjőrkegren's lawyer suggested that they register a company with fifty-fifty stock holding and a starting capital of nine million Swedish crowns, about 1.5 million US dollars. They decided to finalize the name of the company within one week and that Harald Westerberg AB would be an important part of the name. In the end, the company was named "Birco."

Chapter 28

ADDING CHINESE RUGS TO THE INVENTORY

Bjőrkegren suggested that Karl should go to China, do some research, and buy some Chinese rugs directly from the factory to supplement the inventory of their store. It was mid-March, and if Karl were to travel to China, it would have to be before the Persian New Year on March 21. Karl went to the Chinese Embassy's commerce division and explained to them that their company wanted to buy rugs directly from China. The clerk told him that he could get a visa only when he could present a letter of credit. Karl mentioned that he could easily arrange that. He also mentioned that he was a director of Birco and that he intended to spend two hundred thousand dollars in Beijing. In those days, that was a significant amount of money. The clerk became exited and asked Karl to wait. He returned twenty minutes later with a man who looked like a high-ranking official. The man ushered Karl into a large meeting room and offered him tea.

Karl provided information about Birco and himself and mentioned Bjőrkegren's name. They seemed to know who he was, which came as no surprise to Karl since Bjőrkegren was the most well-known industrialist in Sweden. The official then told Karl rather earnestly, "It normally takes a week to have a visa issued, but because we know Mr. Bjőrkegren, your visa will be ready tomorrow."

The next afternoon, Karl received a call from the Chinese trade council to inform him that his visa was ready and that he should bring his letter of credit with him. To his surprise, they had made special arrangement for him to be picked up at the airport in Beijing. When he told Bjőrkegren of these developments, he said that they should not waste any time. However, Karl was not sure if it was wise to act so hastily. He explained to Bjőrkegren that he thought the local Chinese were hoping for a kickback from a cousin in China for any business they transacted under their auspices. It would be better if he went to look for an agent himself. He would go from city to city, since he understood that the provinces were independent from the central government and in competition with each other. Bjőrkegren agreed but thought this process might take too long and they might end up without any Chinese rugs at all.

They agreed that Karl should go to China. The visa was in order, and Karl took an SAS flight to Hong Kong. From there he left on a China Airlines flight to Beijing. When he disembarked at the airport, he was immediately met by a gentleman, Mr. Tzu Wong, and a companion Karl referred to as "Madame X." They met Karl at the arrival gate. Both were fluent in English, and after welcoming him to Beijing, they ushered him into a black limousine. It was night, and they drove down quite a dark road toward the city. As they reached Tiananmen Square, the entire road before them was illuminated as if by the midday sun. They drove to Hotel Beijing, the only big hotel in Beijing. The hotel reminded Karl of Stalin's Soviet style architecture with its massiveness exuding overbearing power.

Mr. Wong and his companion helped Karl check in and were back again at half past eight the following morning to take him to the warehouse. He was shown many rugs until he came across a pile of rugs that he thought had the best designs for Swedish tastes. When he wanted to select some of these rugs, he was told that they had already been sold to a Mr. Barghi, a Swedish rug dealer. Karl said he preferred the style of these rugs to the more flowery designs in the warehouse. Mr. Wong's response was negative. Karl then said that he would like to go back to his hotel. He thought if they could not provide him with quality rugs of his choice, he would return to Sweden.

Barghi was an established rug dealer in Stockholm. His Chinese rugs were specially designed for Swedish tastes, with geometric abstract patterns and neutral colors. Karl guessed that Barghi had already warned Mr. Wong of potential future competition.

Karl went back to the hotel and talked with Carol, his Chinese friend in Washington. He asked her about her cousin, and she said that her cousin would meet him at the hotel at about 2:00 p.m. He waited in the lobby until 4:00 p.m. but nobody showed up. He should have known from the outset that with all the controls in China, one couldn't have even a simple conversation from this hotel without the authorities knowing about it.

Later, Mr. Wong arrived at the hotel and informed Karl that they had found some rugs that would suit his taste. He seemed nervous as he spoke to Karl. He said that Karl could see the rugs the following morning and that the vice chairman of the company had invited him to dinner the following evening. The next morning after breakfast, Karl was conducted to another warehouse ten kilometers from the city that looked like a weaver's workshop.

The rugs they showed Karl were of higher quality and similar to the rugs that had been set aside for the Barghi Co. Karl selected a few, but he was still not satisfied with this option. After an hour of looking, he told his hosts that he would like to have a meeting with the director of this workshop. That afternoon they took Karl to the Ming Mausoleum, which was impressive. The approach to the tomb is lined with hundreds of horses, camels, and elephants, all carved in sandstone and marble, twice their normal scale. Karl's companion and tour guide was the Chinese woman "Madame X." She also accompanied Karl to the Forbidden City, the Summer Palace, and a Ming temple. She never offered an opinion about the rugs, but when the driver was not present, she asked Karl many questions about the political system in Sweden. Did Sweden have a cooperative system and how did socialism work in Sweden?

The next day was April 3, and in the afternoon, Karl saw on TV that the British Navy had sunk an Argentinean battleship in the Falklands War. That evening at 7:00 p.m., Mr. Wong and Madame X picked up Karl. After driving down some narrow streets, they eventually entered a crowded teahouse. The smoke-filled establishment was relatively dark, but it seemed fashionable judging by the clientele. They pushed past some tables and came to a small room with a narrow spiral staircase that led to an upper floor. The narrow staircase emerged into a large upper room with a huge circular table in the center. Heavy traditional chairs that were ornately carved surrounded the table. Also in the room was a large and imposing portrait of Chairman Mao. Mr. Wong offered Karl a chair, and a waiter served them tea. After a wait of about ten minutes, a middle-aged man entered the room in the company of another official who remained silent throughout the dinner. Both were wearing the obligatory Mao caps and battleship gray Mao tunics. Mr. Wong presented Karl to the director and his companion. Karl failed to remember his name for longer than two minutes. The man talked aloud in Chinese for at least eight to ten minutes without interruption, all the while pointing at Karl. All the others in his party looked on silently. After the director finished his monologue, Mr. Wong translated what the director had said. "The director welcomes you and hopes that you buy a large quantity of rugs from his cooperation." The other three applauded loudly, and Karl joined in.

After the director's speech, five or six servers rushed into the room. They looked like an invasion of Chinese warriors, each carrying the spoils of war. They brought in numerous dishes of fish, duck, pork, chicken, soups, and various vegetables. It was enough for a large party of forty to fifty persons. The director poured two successive cups of shark fin soup for Karl and then proceeded to serve him with his own chopsticks from the spread of dishes. Karl remembered that Tanaka, his friend and colleague, had once told him that when a host offers you food with his own chopsticks, he uses the opposite ends from the ends that he eats with. Karl enjoyed the meal immensely. Unfortunately, he could not taste all the dishes and missed the American tradition of carrying leftover food out of the restaurant in a doggy bag. Finally, after a week of negotiating, Karl was able to purchase enough high-quality rugs that would make a fine addition to his company's inventory back in Sweden.

THE *TREE OF UTAH* UNDER CONSTRUCTION

Chapter 29

THE *TREE OF UTAH*

Karl Momen's most ambitious sculptural work was not created in Sweden or anywhere else in Europe or the Middle East. In the summer of 1981, Karl embarked on an adventurous road trip that would take him across the North American continent from east to west. The American ethos of freedom and democracy appealed to his deeply rooted sense of individualism. He had become disillusioned with the unsuccessful development of the socialist idyll in Europe. It was in the United States that he would conceptualize and construct the most challenging but most significant product of his oeuvre—the *Tree of Utah* (1986). This monumental work would not only pay homage to the unique landscape of the Great Western Desert, but it would also typify his architectonic style. This sculpture was to become the consummate statement of his Constructivist vision.

After his arrival in the United States, Karl decided to travel by car across the breadth of the continent, from Washington, D.C., to California, so that he could become better acquainted with the topography of the vast American landscape. He arrived in Salt Lake City after a week of cross-country driving in the sweltering heat of late summer. After a night's rest and an early morning breakfast at a local hotel, he was faced with two choices about which route he should take for the remainder of his journey to the pacific coast. He could travel south on Interstate 15 to Los Angeles via Las Vegas, or he could travel west on Interstate 80 via Reno and Lake Tahoe to San Francisco. Although he entertained a passing interest in seeing the sights of Las Vegas, he eventually decided to proceed on to San Francisco, across the Bonneville Salt Flats.

This part of the world has had an interesting geological history that sets it apart from most other geographical areas on the planet. In prehistoric time, this region, known as the Great Basin, was covered by a vast expanse of water of approximately twenty thousand square miles in area. Geologists know this vast inland ocean as Lake Bonneville. As precipitation decreased over eons of time, the lake gradually grew smaller, leaving only a small remnant of this vast body of water. This remnant is known today as the Great Salt Lake, which has become one of the saltiest bodies of water in the world and the largest inland salt-water lake in the Western Hemisphere. The shoreline of the prehistoric Lake Bonneville can still be traced high up on the mountainsides that now border the dry valley that was once the lake bed. The receding waters left behind a vast plane of saline deposit known as the Bonneville Salt Flats, site of the fastest and most popular automotive speedway in the world. It was here that Gary Gabelich drove his rocket-powered car, *Blue Flame,* to a world speed record of 620 miles per hour in 1970.

Standing on the Flats, one can see the curvature of the earth. It has been said that the Great Western Desert is a place of extreme speed, heat, cold, and boredom! Interstate 80 stretches west for one hundred twenty miles from Salt Lake City to the Nevada border. The last fifty-mile segment of this highway is arrow-straight and relentlessly monotonous to motorists. It was in this region that Nancy Holt (1938–2014) worked from 1973 to 1976 on a forty-acre parcel of desert, framing the Great Basin landscape with the large concrete circles of her *Sun Tunnels* (1976). Her husband, the late Robert Smithson (1938–1973) created the now-famous *Spiral Jetty* (1970) near Promontory Point in the Great Salt Lake. There is a timelessness about this region where the elements are manifest in silent and motionless testimony of the greater universe. Here a few visionary men and women have found the impetus and the space to give expression to their most cherished dreams and aspirations. It was into this epic and severe environment that Karl Momen introduced his bold and optimistic work that is steeped in a heritage of geometric abstraction and rooted in a distant world of Russian Constructivism.

After an overnight stop at a local hotel in Salt Lake City, Momen was on the road again. It was nine o'clock on the morning of August 20, 1981, and it was already hot. He stopped briefly as he was leaving the outskirts of the city to buy some tomatoes, lettuce, and a bag of ice as light refreshment for the long car journey to the California border. Momen soon left the city far behind, and after a few hours of uninterrupted travel, he found himself traveling along the dead straight I-80 highway to his first rest stop at the border town of Wendover. The car glided along almost silently, and for a while, he lost all sense of motion. He became aware of the surreal desert landscape that floated around him. The desert heat and blazing sun would have been unbearable but for the air-conditioning in the car. Forcing his faculties to focus on his surroundings, it appeared to him as though he was driving over a gigantic, flat, sun-blanched canvas. The dead straight disappeared toward the horizon, but the heat eddies in the air obliterated the distant mountains. He was driving through vast, limitless, white space, almost as if he had left the planet.

After a while, Karl reached for the tomatoes and the lettuce he had brought with him. Then he realized that he did not have salt for the tomato. The thought crossed his mind that he could wait until he reached Wendover where he would be able to buy some salt. Then it dawned on him that he was traversing the largest dried salt lake in the world, which appeared to be an endless expanse of the white substance in every direction.

Karl pulled over and stopped the car on the shoulder of the road. He got out of the vehicle and was instantaneously blasted by the searing hot air. It was as if he had opened the door of a furnace. His shoes crunched over the white surface. The thought came to him that it was not unlike snow but for the 120-degree temperature difference! He stooped down, took a pinch of the white crystalline powder, and sprinkled it over his tomato. He ate in haste, fearing that the tomato might get scorched in the inferno of hot air and the reflected heat rising from his white surroundings. After taking in the alien panorama for a few moments, he returned to the welcome air-conditioned comfort of his vehicle and resumed his journey.

As Karl drove, he watched tiny, shimmering, black dots in the distance grow into large vehicles and then disappear as they sped past him on the eastbound lane of the highway. Then it occurred to him that the monotony of this seemingly endless journey could be relieved by focusing his attention on the desert—something that would arrest the eye against

KARL MOMEN ON THE SALT FLATS

CHAPTER 29

the featureless foil of the desert and provide a point of reference for it and perhaps the entire soul. It would have to be some kind of psychological injunction to act as a counterpoise—the ultimate figure/ground relationship. And who better to come up with such a grandiose stratagem than he, the artist!

Thoughts and images flashed through his mind as he slowly grasped the implications of his musings. He felt as if he was on the verge of a unique and powerful new discovery. Something had to be done, but what? All of sudden, it seemed, he found himself entering the outskirts of a town. He had arrived in Reno and pulled into a local hotel.

That night as he lay in his hotel room, images of that morning's poignant experience kept flashing through his mind. The next morning after a troubled night's sleep, he continued his journey, but awhile before he reached San Francisco, he stopped the car on the side of the road. He found a pencil and a scrap of paper in the car and made a rough sketch of what would become the *Tree of Utah.*

Karl had envisioned a large structure in the form of the stylized tree that had so often appeared as a symbolic element in his paintings. It would rise up from the flat desert terrain and be visible for miles around. The concept of the *Tree* was now fully realized. The perpendicular trunk would hold spheres high above the flat plane of the desert. He recollected that the stylized image of such a tree had appeared in his architectural drawings in the early 1960s and later in the early 1970s in some of his major paintings. This iconic symbol had emerged from his subconscious as if it had been planted there from time immemorial.

To Karl, the tree was a symbol that represented the natural order of all living things—an order that was under assault by the effects of rampant industrialization and urbanization. Although the tension between the organic world of nature and man-made technocracy had consistently been the subject of his painting, he had never conceived of a sculpture along these lines, least of all one of such enormous dimensions. Momen became increasingly excited about the concept but had no idea of how he should proceed. This was an ambitious project that would require support beyond his resources.

After some inquiries, he was referred to the Utah Arts Council. He telephoned the Council in early September 1981 from San Francisco and spoke in turn with Ruth Draper and Arley Curtz, the director and assistant director respectively at the time. They asked Karl to mail in a written proposal for consideration by the Council. He immediately went to work and produced a series of drawings as well as a small maquette of the *Tree* as he had envisioned it adjacent to the highway near Wendover. He packed his travel bag and, with the model under his arm, boarded the first flight to Salt Lake City.

Within hours he was speaking face-to-face with members of the Arts Council—only two days after his initial telephone contact. At this meeting members of the Arts Council could hardly believe that this stranger, with whom they had only spoken briefly on the telephone, was seriously committed to such a unique and unexpected undertaking in an inhospitable environment so far from his home country. Karl, however, was determined.

The members of the Arts Council were initially excited about the project, and Arley Curtz sent Karl an encouraging letter offering Karl all the assistance that the Council could muster. After this meeting, Karl returned to Stockholm to consult with engineering colleagues in order to refine the design and work on the final dimensions of the structure. In the initial design, he had envisioned a structure between seventy-five and eighty-five feet in height. The news media wasted no time in publicizing Momen's proposal for a large sculptural project in the Great Western Desert. Karl's plans received immediate coverage on Swedish television news broadcasts. Photographs of Karl's model were publicized far and wide. That April 1982, a public announcement about the launch of the project was made at the Haus am Lutzowplatz Cultural Center in Berlin. The director of the Center organized a special reception in Karl's honor and presented him with a ten-foot-high cake shaped in the form of the *Tree*. There could be no going back for Karl at this point.

Not long after this enthusiastic reception in Europe, Karl received a chilling letter from the Utah Arts Council informing him that the Council was distancing itself from his project and, although council members would not stand in his way, they would not be able to give him any direct assistance. Upon receiving this disconcerting news, Karl immediately returned to Salt Lake City to discuss the matter with the Council. Dennis Smith, the chairman of the Council's visual arts committee at the time, said that the Council was dedicated to the assistance of Utah artists only and would not be able to assist materially or work with a foreign artist in this project. They would, however, act in a consultative capacity, offering advice and general guidance as the project developed. Karl was obviously being treated as an interloper by conservative Council members who did not want to be implicated in a venture beyond the limited scope of their financial and creative capacity, notwithstanding the fact that Karl had assured the Council that he would fund the project entirely from his own substantial personal financial resources at the time. Nevertheless, Karl and Dennis Smith became good friends and met often during this period.

Karl thought he should not be discouraged about the Council's rebuff. In his experience, boards often rejected ideas at first, only to reverse their decisions later. He thought he should probably plan on being at the next meeting in the spring of 1984.

After receiving the Council's letter, he called Dennis Smith from Stockholm and asked him why the Arts Council had changed their decision. Smith told him that he and Abravanel, the chief conductor of the Utah symphony, who was also on the board, had voted in favor of the project, but the other members thought that the project might pose a financial burden on the Council. The chairman of the board had the final say and had voted against the project. Then Smith asked Karl if he knew the chairman of the board. Karl replied that he did not. He explained that he felt inspired to complete the project. He saw the vast barren landscape as a large canvas upon which he could create a sculpture as a metaphor for life and growth in stark contrast and as a counterpoise to this otherwise inhospitable environment. It would provide a focus of color and relieve the monotony of sixty miles of uninterrupted flat terrain. It would also provide an intriguing artwork for travelers to enjoy and contemplate in their journey across this barren expanse of desert.

Karl explained to Dennis that he did not agree with the notion that land art should be inaccessible to average people, deriding the notion that such works should "only be accessible to art lovers with flush wallets, rented SUVs, and guides with GPS compasses."[3] He thought that for thousands of years art had served a public purpose. The Greeks, the Romans, and even during the Renaissance, all forms of art had been created with public access in mind. He did not agree with the views of some "phosphorescent, self-illuminating art gurus who manipulate the minds of the gullible with money and false rhetoric and hold that land art should be so inaccessibly hidden that one has to be a jackrabbit to experience it."[4]

When the time came for the next Arts Council Board meeting in the spring of 1984, Karl was invited to attend. Upon entering the boardroom, Karl was greeted by Ray Kingston, the chairman of the Council. To Karl's great surprise, Kingston spoke to him in Farsi and asked Karl when he was last in Iran! Karl told him it was about eight years ago. Then he gave Karl the floor to explain his justification for the artwork and to report on how far he had proceeded with the project. Karl provided the information and again asked for the Arts Council's endorsement. In response, Kingston said that the Arts Council had no budget to assist artists with their private projects. Karl replied that he was not there to ask for money and was willing to make a contractual agreement that the Arts Council would not be imposed upon financially. He would take sole responsibility for all financial obligations. All he wanted was their endorsement of the project as a new public sculptural venture being constructed in the interests of the community and the state. Kingston told Karl that the Arts Council could not provide such an endorsement. At this point, Abravanel challenged the chairman and asked why the Council could not provide its blessing. Kingston responded

KARL WITH THE *TREE OF UTAH* PROTOTYPE

that the Council could not shoulder such a responsibility, whereupon Karl asked him to elaborate on what kind of responsibility he was anticipating. Kingston replied that he wanted to protect the Council from media gossip. Karl thought that Kingston's tone was somewhat sarcastic and unbecoming his office as chairman of the Board. Karl pressed him for a more definitive reason for his rejection. He retorted that the decision had already been made. They had communicated that decision to Karl by letter and nothing would change their ruling. Karl was surprised by Kingston's heavy-handed and negative response and the apparent stranglehold he exercised over the other board members. Karl had attended many board meetings for multi-million dollar projects before CEO's of multinational corporations and heads of state, but he reflected afterward that he had never experienced such an overbearing chairman; however, this episode did not change Karl's determination to complete the project.

Undaunted by his lukewarm response from the Arts Council, Karl turned his attention to securing a site for the sculpture in the desert along the I-80 freeway. Dennis Smith accompanied Karl to a meeting with representatives of the Utah Land Board. At this meeting, Karl learned that since he was not a US citizen, he would not be allowed to own land in what was considered a "strategic area" due to its proximity to two US Air Force bases. The specious nature of this argument was brought into sharp focus by Karl's observation that he had recently purchased a condominium in Washington, D.C., a few miles from the White House!

CHAPTER 29

The Land Board representatives referred Momen to Kosrow Semnani, a local entrepreneur in Salt Lake City, who owned large tracts of land in this arid region. Semnani was intrigued by the idea of the sculpture and generously offered to sponsor the project by donating the land upon which the *Tree* would be constructed. Semnani, who happened to be an expatriate Iranian, would ultimately become the project's chief benefactor. He assisted Karl in preparing the numerous applications and submissions to the various local authorities to obtain the necessary permits for the structure. The Federal Aviation Administration's approval also had to be obtained because of the height of the *Tree*.

By October 1983, Karl had called for tenders for the construction of the sculpture. He received several estimates ranging from $300,000 to $500,000. However, he was not able to get a firm estimate because the condition of the subsoil at the site was not known at the time. In working with various local authorities, Karl soon discovered that people had mixed feelings toward the project. Some people were excited and helpful, while others were negative and resentful about his plans. In October 1983, Momen received a construction proposal from Don Reimann, a Salt Lake contractor who had the reputation of being the finest concrete caster in the state of Utah. The Reimann family had been in the stone-casting business from the days the first pioneers entered the Salt Lake Valley, and had worked on a variety of imposing structures throughout the region, including the Provo Temple of The Church of Jesus Christ of Latter-day Saints. Moreover, Reimann was one of the few concrete casters in the industry who was willing to attempt the daunting task of casting concrete spheres over thirteen feet in diameter.

A building permit for the *Tree* was granted at the end of January 1984, and Karl took a permanent suite at the Hilton Hotel in Salt Lake City. He also hired Frank Harris, a cameraman from California to document the entire construction process.

One of the most important considerations Karl had to resolve at the outset of the project was the choice of finish that would be used on the surface of the large concrete spheres. Initially, Karl and Reimann had contemplated using some form of ceramic tile. Tiles were not a satisfactory solution since tiles would crack and break over time. In March 1984, after lengthy discussions and numerous inquiries about various materials, Karl and Reimann discovered that anhydrous copper silicate, known more commonly as chrysacolla, was ideal for their purpose. Moreover, this unique material was indigenous to Utah. The blue and green rocks were quarried in southern Utah about three hundred miles south of Salt Lake City. Don Reimann contacted the owners of the quarry, who agreed to donate one hundred tons of the stone to the project. However, Reimann's team would have to collect the materials themselves. Later that month, Reimann

CHRYSACOLLA

and his eight sons spent three days hauling the stone from southern Utah using two large trucks. A stonecutter was contracted to cut the stone pieces to size with the aid of a diamond saw, and soon thereafter, the Reimann family set to work with the casting of the enormous concrete spheres.

Each sphere would require a purpose-made mold. In order to make the molds, wooden jigs were constructed over which plaster of paris was carefully applied, using hemispherical screeds that pivoted at the north and south axes of each convex former. Once the plaster had set hard, the surfaces were treated with a special release agent to prevent the concrete from sticking to the plaster, and then concrete was cast over the convex forms. The inside of the concrete forms would serve as concave molds for the finished spheres. The molds were produced in quarter segments, allowing four successive castings to be welded and bolted together to make a complete sphere. Each of the six spheres was constructed in this way.

WOODEN JIG FOR SPHERICAL MOLD

WOODEN JIG FOR TUBULAR TRUNK MOLD

The trunk of the tree was cast in like fashion. A tubular form was used to make a mold that would cast three longitudinal sections. The sections would be welded and bolted together on site in the desert in order to create the central trunk of the *Tree*.

Good fortune and propitious circumstances were soon to be overshadowed by some of the most daunting challenges that Karl had ever encountered in his career. A few months into the project, it was discovered that the amount of steel reinforcing bar required by the structure had been underestimated. New calculations by Devon Stone, the structural engineer hired by Karl, now indicated that the final weight of the piece would far exceed the one hundred tons originally estimated. It was also at this critical moment that the media became interested in the project again. Local TV stations sent crews out to interview Karl and to obtain footage of the construction site near Wendover. A flood of articles and television reports heightened public interest. The publicity brought with it controversy and debate about the artistic merits and appropriateness of the sculpture as a public structure. Due to the technical difficulties with the steel reinforcement of the sculpture, Karl moved the completion date of the *Tree* from June to October 1984. He had already sent invitations to numerous civic and national dignitaries, including President Reagan, who graciously declined the invitation but nevertheless sent a personal message wishing Karl great success with his project.

At the height of this intense media attention, Karl received news that would cause his blood to run cold. Devon Stone, the structural engineer, reported that the soil tests indicated that the selected site was wholly unsuited to supporting the finished weight of the structure. Although original plans had indicated a modest concrete platform at the base of the structure, new calculations called for a ninety-foot-deep foundation comprised of twenty reinforced concrete piles with a diameter of twenty inches each. The piles would in turn support an eight-foot-thick reinforced concrete slab. This was an unexpected setback and a totally new ball game for Karl who, at this time, thought he had the end of the project in sight. This new revelation would result in a delay of at least six months, at more than double the cost of the project. Karl weighed the options before him. He could possibly redesign the *Tree*, scaling down the size and mass of its main trunk, its branches, and the spheres. Thoughts of canceling the project crossed his mind. If he did cancel the project, this action would give the lie to all his detractors and to the increasingly vociferous opponents of the project. If he pressed on, how would he be able to afford the escalating costs? After this fateful turn of events, journalists Elaine Jarvik and Jim Wolf reported extensively in the local press on this major setback to the project.

Karl took a few days off to ponder his predicament and finally decided that there was no going back or opting out of the project. He and his associates had committed themselves to completing the sculpture. The work would go on, and the *Tree* would be completed as planned. He decided to sell the condominiums he had recently purchased in Washington, D.C. He also sold his cabin in northern Sweden and some prized pieces of his personal art collection. With the funds raised by liquidating these assets, Karl was able to instruct the construction team to make the necessary changes to the original design and to proceed with the construction as planned.

Word about Karl's unexpected obstacles and shortfalls soon got out. Suddenly suppliers refused to deliver materials. Some suppliers demanded prepayment before considering an order for the project. However, Karl's additional funds became available, and he set about ordering the twenty-inch steel pipe for the piles. The pipe was supplied in thirty-foot lengths, and three sections had to be welded together to make up the full length of each pile. Because of the excessive length of the piles, there were not many companies who were equipped to drive these long pipes into the ground. A large crane was brought in from out of state. Because of the unknown conditions of the subterranean soil at these depths, Karl could not get a fixed estimate for the pile driving, and he proceeded on blind faith. It turned out that the piles sank easily and quickly through the soft residue of the prehistoric lakebed. Reinforcing steel was placed inside each pipe, and they were filled with concrete. This operation occupied Don Reimann and his sons for three continuous weeks. By the end of fall, they had thankfully also poured the enormous foundation base. With the onset of winter, the crew withdrew to Reimann's Salt Lake factory to work on the large concrete spheres.

The next important decision was to determine how the colored striations on the large spheres were to be made. There were no natural materials available locally that matched the colors that were specified in Karl's design. After considerable deliberation, he decided to import the finest quality ceramic tiles from Italy, again at great personal expense. Because of the scarcity of the high-quality tile, the order had to be prepaid before it was shipped. The best means to attach the tiles to the concrete spheres also had to be determined. Reimann identified a special brand of epoxy as the most suitable adhesive. It turned out to be the most expensive product of its kind. For the first three months of 1985, Don Reimann and his workers occupied themselves with first gluing the ceramic material and then gluing the blue and green chrysacolla, piece by piece, to each concrete sphere.

As soon as the spheres were completed, work commenced on the trunk and supporting limbs of the *Tree*. However, Karl's cash reserves had run dangerously low by this time, and he was compelled to seek various loans to complete the project. A loan raised in Sweden was not enough, and he turned to his local artist friends Dennis Smith and Gary Smith. They agreed to cosign a $30,000 loan from Copper State Saving and Loan Company to aid Karl.

The project lurched precariously forward, but Karl was soon forced to again turn to his good friend Kosrow Semnani for yet another loan of $150,000. The end was not yet in sight, and by early September 1985, Karl had exhausted these funds as well. At this late stage in the project, he was compelled to call a halt to the operation, and Don Reimann and his team were called off the job. Work came to a stop, and Reimann moved on to other projects. Eventually Karl

GLUING CHRYSACOLLA PIECE BY PIECE

was successful in raising another $30,000 in Sweden, and work on the *Tree* was resumed. The project was now nearly completed, and plans were being made to erect the structure on its base. However, just before this final operation, Reimann discovered that the *Tree* would need cathodic protection to prevent the steel reinforcing materials from being corroded by the salt environment. Momen was barely able to find the money for this unexpected expense. Then, in what seemed like a cruel twist of fate, just when Momen and his team thought that they had accounted for every outstanding contingency, it was discovered that the structure would also have to be equipped with lightning protection. Miraculously, Karl was able to come up with sufficient funds to pay for this as well.

The physical dimensions and mode of construction of the *Tree* are impressive. As a manifestation of engineering virtuosity, the *Tree* stands as a significant example of the finest practices in steel frame and precast concrete construction. The *Tree* consists of a central steel-reinforced concrete trunk supporting six large precast concrete spheres, the largest of which measures thirteen feet, six inches in diameter and weighs sixty tons. Thick-walled diagonal steel pipes, or limbs, penetrate the spheres and continue through their hollow cores to the opposite surfaces. These steel limbs are secured to the vertical surface of the trunk by the dual means of bolting and welding to steel plates on the trunk's surface. The steel plates are secured by horizontal reinforcing bars embedded within the concrete trunk. Each weld was heat-treated several times to relieve stresses in the metal, otherwise the joints would eventually fail. Allowance was also made for the expansion and contraction of the materials as a result of the wide range of temperature variations in the desert. The combined weight of the spheres, the limbs, and the main trunk came to 875 tons, all supported by an eight-foot-thick concrete foundation. The foundation is supported in turn by twenty-five steel-encased concrete piles that were driven ninety feet into the loosely compacted desert clay to ensure permanent stability of the structure.

20 CONCRETE PILES WERE SUNK 90 FEET TO REACH THE BEDROCK BENEATH THE SALT FLATS

The *Tree* is located adjacent to the westbound lane of Interstate 80 as this highway cuts across the desert approximately twenty-six miles east of Wendover and seventy-five miles west of Salt Lake City. By the time the project was completed, the structure had consumed 100 tons of chrysacolla rock, 4 tons of epoxy, 160 tons of steel, 15 tons of colored cement, 18,000 imported ceramic tiles, 5 tons of welding rods, 7 tons of timber for mold formers, and 20 tons of plaster of paris. The structure cost 21,000 man-made hours of labor. The project had also cost Karl over one million dollars ($2,250,000 in today's currency), which was more than twice the amount he had budgeted for. The entire amount was eventually paid for from his personal funds.

The sculpture was finished in September 1985—just seventeen months after the commencement of construction. Karl immediately set about organizing a dedication ceremony, and on a wintry January morning, Saturday 18, 1986, Utah became the beneficiary of this unlikely public sculpture. Over a thousand people gathered to hear outgoing Utah Governor, Norman Bangerter, accept the *Tree* from its maker on behalf of the people of Utah. The dedication was a celebratory event. Also in attendance was Anna Greta Leijon, the then Swedish Minister of Labor.

Notwithstanding the cultural conservatism of the state and the reticence of local arts agencies to acknowledge this extraordinary manifestation of one man's

UTAH GOVERNOR, NORMAN BANGERTER WITH KARL MOMEN

artistic vision and resourcefulness, the *Tree* soon became a permanent feature of the barren desert landscape and was acknowledged by the arts establishments in Europe and the Far East.

Rising 87 feet above the Salt Flats, the structure was built to withstand desert winds gusting over 130 miles per hour and earthquakes in the order of 7.5 on the Richter scale. In 2002, the local Highway Patrol estimated that two million cars traveled past the *Tree* annually, and every hour, five to seven cars stopped so that their occupants could study the *Tree*. On a clear day, the *Tree* is visible to travelers on the highway at a distance of about 12 miles. Motorists first see the multicolored spheres as though they are suspended by seemingly invisible means above the desert. In warm weather, the trunk is lost in the convection currents of hot air rising from the blanched desert floor. Only the spheres shimmer mysteriously and silently in the arid air. On nearing the *Tree*, the trunk becomes visible and the balls are elevated high above the surface, changing hue with the prevailing conditions of light and weather. Some critics referred to the *Tree* as one of the boldest pieces of visual art to be conceived in this western state. It certainly joined Robert Smithson's *Spiral Jetty* as its most significant.

TREE OF UTAH
DEDICATION (1986)

Chapter 30

CONTRARY VOICES AND PRAISE SINGERS

Even before ground had been broken for the foundation of the *Tree*, media interest had descended on the project, straining to identify any aspect that could lead to something sensational in the local press. Newspaper headlines such as "*Tree* artist wants to put more flavor in the 'salt'" and "Utah Mulls over Karl Momen's Monumental Meatballs" proliferated. Not to be outdone, the *Wall Street Journal* carried a headline that read, "Sure, the Redwoods Grow Taller, But They Don't Have Coconuts." Other writers referred to the *Tree* as "a coagulated mushroom cloud" or as "giant scoops of ice-cream."

These statements by the media were indicative of the derisive attitude adopted by many critics as they applied their own sensibilities to interpreting the *Tree* to their largely uninformed readership. Similes of "meatballs," "ice-cream scoops," and "coconuts" drawn from pantry vocabulary were typical of the level of discourse in these publications. Many of these self-appointed critics took it upon themselves to voice their condemnation of the *Tree* simply because it was something new that they did not understand and that had suddenly sprung up in their midst. It was contrary to anything they had experienced. These critics often lacked the conceptual apparatus to adequately contextualize the sculpture or to apply appropriate constructs to its interpretation. It is also a fact that there had been no "buy-in" by the public.

The public had never been consulted or invited to contribute to the realization of Momen's artistic vision. Derision is often the response of those who feel left out or disadvantaged by their own ignorance. The state's art and museums apparatus remained mute and distanced themselves from any engagement or meaningful interpretation of the *Tree*.

Unfortunately, the American public education system leaves the populace largely uninformed about matters art historical. A utilitarian general education curriculum and the lack of appropriate educational standards have left this country at a distinct disadvantage in comparison to other developed countries. Depreciated standards have done little to provide the average citizen of even a rudimentary understanding of the defining characteristics and origins of their own built environment. It is also true that it does not require any significant measure of talent, aptitude, or education to find fault or to criticize another's endeavors. This is particularly true in a conservative ethnocentric community. Significantly, several well-known and respected local artists, namely Frank Riggs, Gary Smith, Dennis Smith, and Neil Hadlock—all gave their support throughout the project. Unfortunately, Karl was seen as an interloper by the state's arts agencies.

Although the *Tree* stood in a swirl of uninformed local controversy that was often derisive, worldwide interest was also aroused, and within a year, more than six hundred individual publications would eventually carry news of a much more positive nature. The Swedish press gave the *Tree* intense media coverage, largely because of Momen's Swedish citizenship. The Japanese media also showed surprising interest. Numerous positive articles appeared in international art and architecture magazines. Significantly, overseas interest was more informed than local reports. The local media sought to sensationalize their reporting of the *Tree*, often presenting the *Tree* as a bizarre phenomenon. Ironically, the *Tree* may have attracted more critical awareness overseas than in Utah itself. It was perhaps for this reason that Elaine Jarvik, a local critic, noted that the *Tree of Utah* was arguably Utah's most visible and internationally well-known piece of art. The growing awareness of the *Tree* by the public media prompted some advertisers to think of the *Tree* as a ready-made advertising opportunity. It could qualify as one of the world's most striking billboard locations. Momen received proposals from some Nevada casinos to hang signs from the boughs of the *Tree*. He also received offers from film companies to film commercials at the site and to build a snack bar at its base. Momen dismissed these proposals as crass commercialism.

Opinions about the work varied, from critics who saw the *Tree* as an unfortunate intrusion upon the serenity of the desert, to others who heralded the work as a sophisticated piece of environmental art. Some cynical reports questioned Momen's generosity in embarking on such a costly endeavor and then magnanimously donating it to the people of Utah. Proposals to construct a pullout for motorists at the site were condemned by some for encroaching on Utah's skimpy road finances at the time. However, many applauded Momen for his innovation, his generous spirit, and his artistic genius. Katherine Metcalf, a local art critic, proclaimed the work to be the product of a sterile Bauhaus aesthetic reflecting a "pre-ecological, monument-making consciousness that is far from the 'site-determined' works that are created in the western desert by younger artists such as Nancy Holt, James Turrell, and the late Robert Smithson." However, others saw an opposite point of view. Namely, that the *Tree* was in fact site-determined, that it was the product of a particular reading of the stark landscape, and that it engaged the landscape in a unique and elemental phenomenological discourse. It could be said that the *Tree* was in fact prompted by its maker's particular experience of this unique and specific environment. There is no doubt that Momen was a product of the abstract Constructivist movement as expressed through the work of Russian artists such as Naum Gabo, Anton Pevsner, and Kashmir Malevich. The aesthetic of pure form that characterizes Momen's work is not an anachronism as much as it bears witness to the profundity of significant form and the tenacity with which this aesthetic prevails. The fact that the *Tree* did not please everyone does not detract from its function as a significant public sculpture, as Carol Nixon noted: "The artist's job is not to create something that will satisfy everyone. It's to 'create dialogue' and present new ways of viewing the world."

Utah environmentalists did not seem particularly concerned about the *Tree*. Utah Wilderness Association coordinator Dick Carter proclaimed, "With all the important environmental issues facing the state, I'm stunned that anyone is making a fuss about it." Environmental activist Alex Kelner commented somewhat sarcastically that he was "not offended" by the sculpture. "I'm much more offended by high rises in the canyons—they're much more permanent!" Kelner expected vandals to deface the sculpture and thought it was just a matter of time before the marshy environment eventually claimed the *Tree*. Momen was unmoved by his environmental critics. "What about Mount Rushmore?" he countered at the time.

An avid supporter of the project, Scott L. Beesley wrote to the editor of the *Deseret News* that he thought that Momen should be made "an honorary prophet of his adopted state of Utah." Springville Museum Director Vern Swanson appreciated Momen's work as "architectonic" and thought that it was Momen's intention to "enlarge the dot on the Utah map of art history that Smithson had created." Other more utilitarian views were expressed by those who saw no value in the expenditure of money on anything that did not result in materialistic advantage to the poor and needy.

Olle Granath, director of the Royal Academy of Art in Stockholm, stated, "There is a kind of poetic craziness in the project which ought to get encouragement." As far as he knew, there was no Swedish artist who had made such a large international creation. Stig Johansson, a prominent Swedish art critic and writer, saw the *Tree* as "a sparkling mosaic giving life to something generally the most sterile that exists." On the other hand, Janet Koplos, writing in the *Asahi Evening News* condemned the *Tree* as something "drained of life." She saw it as something "petrified," consisting of "spheres attached to a column without the least intimation of growth, movement, or even grace." Significantly, Koplos had never seen the *Tree* in the desert, and her response was based upon a photograph of an early painting that Momen had executed in 1974.

Momen always reserved judgment on his creation, allowing people to form their own opinions. He knew that people would have their own interpretations, and it was for this reason that he had, at an early stage, contemplated naming the piece "Metaphor." He proclaimed that the tree was the most elemental symbol of life and that in this work he brought together the disparate elements of space, nature, myth, and technology. He acknowledged that we live in a world in which technology had taken the helm, and the *Tree* represents the tension that exists between the natural world and the world of technology. On another level, the *Tree* also represents the elemental confrontation between life and death, hope and despair. Momen did not want to load his icon with too much literal meaning. In the end he proclaimed, "I don't want to be a messenger. I'm just an artist."

Cyber Superlative, 1994

CHAPTER 31

Chapter 31

A GHOST FROM THE PAST

Almost fifteen years after the fiasco of the Masshad City Center project, and fifteen thousand kilometers away on the other side of the globe, the ghost of revenge lurked in a new and unexpected guise. Those affected by the loss of the Masshad City Center project would seek to exact vengeance with a slick ploy that was often the nature of vendettas in the architectural profession. The unfortunate troublemaker would become the victim of a carefully contrived stratagem. He would be singled out and punished in the most unexpected and unlikely manner—as if strangled with an invisible silk stocking! Karl would have to pay a price for destroying an opponent's pet project!

In mid-August 1984, Karl received a call from Katherine Nelson, an art writer for *Utah Holiday* magazine. She wanted to interview him for an article on the *Tree of Utah*. They met several times, and she wrote a complimentary article that was published in the September issue of the magazine. Some weeks later, she called Karl to invite him to a party that her Iranian friends were organizing. Karl arrived in the company of Katherine Nelson and her husband. The hostess was an elegant Iranian woman who welcomed the Nelsons in French and Karl in Farsi. The welcome was repeated by their host, Mr. Khazeni, who also spoke to the Nelsons in English and to Karl in Farsi. The name Khazeni did not ring a bell at first with Karl. He learned that the man was an architect and educated in Salt Lake City. Then he recognized Ray Kingston, the chairman of the board of the Utah Arts Council, who was also in attendance. Kingston greeted Karl in Farsi in a surprisingly friendly manner.

During the presentation of the guests by Mrs. Khazeni, one Iranian gentleman who turned out to be a structural engineer came across to Karl and started a conversation about Masshad. He asked Karl if he knew architect Kahzeni. Karl could not recollect the name. The engineer replied, "That's funny! You should know that name!"

Then the man told Karl that Mr. Khazeni was a partner of Boubour, the architect in Masshad, and that Tanaka and Karl had scuttled the plans for their new city plan, deeming it unrealistic and overpriced at the time. The engineer told Karl that he had a tape recording of that fateful meeting. He said that Karl's negative review had been a blow to a large and profitable project. Then he mentioned that Ray Kingston had been an associate architect in the project and stood to make a lot of money from it. As Karl heard this new information, his blood ran cold—and his thoughts turned to Goethe and Faust!

At that moment, Karl did not know what to believe. The next day he called Dennis Smith and asked him if he knew why Ray Kingston had so adamantly dismissed his request for acknowledgment of his project by the Arts Council. Smith replied, "Perhaps Ray Kingston doesn't like Middle Eastern people!"

At the time, Karl did not want to blame anybody or anything with regard to his rejection by the Arts Council. Ray Kingston was a successful architect and a highly respected official in the state of Utah, and he did not want to cast any aspersions in his direction. A few months after the party, he met Katherine Nelson for a cup of coffee at the Roasting Company in Salt Lake City. He detected an air of uneasiness in her attitude toward the *Tree*, which was new to him. Katherine Nelson had been educated in France, and she knew Mrs. Khazeni. By that time, she most likely knew that Karl had been instrumental in putting an end to Kingston's lucrative architectural project in Masshad.

With Norman Bangerter replacing Scott Matheson as governor of the state, and Ray Kingston leaving his position at the Arts Council, the situation was moderately improved. Carol Nixon, the incoming director of the Arts Council, had enormous enthusiasm for Karl's project. Although Karl did not receive any financial aid or grants toward his enormous personal expense, she did assist with recommendations for dealing with various state departments and provided constant encouragement. She assisted with the organization of the dedication of the *Tree*. Governor Bangerter had likewise given his support.

However, Ray Kingston's out-of-hand dismissal of Karl at the time had cast a lasting shadow over his project and soured his reception by the state arts organizations. Nevertheless, Governor Bangerter officially accepted the *Tree* on behalf of the state of Utah at the dedication ceremony after Karl donated the *Tree* to the state. The state art departments tasked with the custodianship of the state's public art collection turned a blind eye to its curatorial responsibility for this internationally lauded public sculpture. It was left to Utah's Department of Facilities and Construction Management, which had oversight for the construction and maintenance of state buildings, to assume the responsibility for the *Tree of Utah*'s curatorship and interpretation—a task for which this department was patently unqualified.

Chapter 32

A FATEFUL SECOND TRIP TO CHINA

At the time Karl was dealing with the Utah Arts Council in Salt Lake City, he also undertook a second trip to China to purchase a collection of Chinese rugs for a big sale at Kosmos Rugs, a retail store in Stockholm with which Karl had become affiliated. He was trying desperately to find a means to raise funds to supplement his savings in order to pay for additional expenses incurred by the *Tree*'s construction. He was investigating the possibility of getting a sponsor to build the *Tree*, the largest sculptural work he had ever attempted. He also needed to obtain a building permit.

During the flight from Stockholm to Salt Lake City, Karl evaluated his entire involvement with the new partnership he had established with Bjőrkegren, a Swedish entrepreneur, in the rug business. Karl asked himself how much time he should spend with Birco, the new company they had established. Then, as if from nowhere, he got an idea. Why not carpet large hotels in the United States with Chinese handwoven rugs? Before the plane landed in San Francisco, he had worked out how to produce handwoven rugs that could be custom-made for individual rooms and banquet halls in a hotel.

The day after his arrival in Salt Lake City, he called Bjőrkegren to explain his idea to him. Bjőrkegren quickly saw the potential and excitedly agreed to Karl's proposal. Karl called Mr. Wong, his contact in China, and explained the idea to him. Two days later, Wong called Karl to tell him that the Chinese Minister of Trade and Exports was excited about his idea and asked that Karl send him detailed plans. Karl thanked him and set about writing all the technical details for a prototype of his production process.

In between dealing with the Utah Arts Council, he contacted the corporate head office of Marriott Hotels with his idea for carpeting their hotels with custom-made Chinese rugs. He was directed to a gentleman responsible for the interior flooring department and eventually spent an entire afternoon presenting his plan to representatives of the company. The hotel people liked the idea, especially the fact that they could have the Marriott logo woven into the rugs as needed. They agreed that Karl would get more details about prices and terms of delivery, and then they would have another meeting. Before Karl left their corporate offices, the hotel executives told him that they would only deal with Swedish Birco and not with any Chinese suppliers or intermediaries.

Karl returned to Sweden and had a late lunch with his partner Bjőrkegren. Karl explained his design to Bjőrkegren in detail and filled him in on his discussions with Marriott and the Chinese. The two men agreed to have a meeting with Eric Willers, the Birco lawyer. Willers liked the idea but suggested that the best arrangement would be for Birco to open an office in New York. Consequently, they decided to register a company in the United States. However, they would need someone who was both knowledgeable about the rug business and familiar with the American market. Karl knew a young Iranian man who was educated at George Washington University in business administration. His name was Jamshid, and just a month earlier, he had told Karl that he was hoping to start an export/import business. He would be excellent at managing their office, and Karl had implicit trust in him. Jamshid also spoke with a fine Bostonian accent. Karl called him and explained their plan. He was interested and wanted to know more.

A few days after Karl's telephone conversation with Jamshid, he traveled to Washington, D.C., and invited Jamshid to meet him at his condominium on New Hampshire Avenue, close to DuPont Circle. Karl told him about the organization of Birco and presented him with a ten-page written draft of their plan.

After they had dinner, he called Bjőrkegren and told him that they should all have a meeting in New York. Three days later, he checked in at the Plaza Hotel and Bjőrkegren arrived in the afternoon. They had a light dinner at the Oak Bar and went over the agenda for the next day's meeting. Jamshid arrived at ten o'clock the following morning. It took only a few minutes for Karl to see that Bjőrkegren approved of his choice of Jamshid as manager of their New York operation.

During the first hour of their meeting, Jamshid presented a financial plan that seemed elaborate, but it impressed Bjőrkegren. (Karl thought it too advanced for an architect such as himself.) The meeting continued for another four hours after lunch, and they decided that Karl should go to China again and strike a deal with the rug merchants. The following day, Karl had a telephone conversation with the same representative of Marriott Hotels that he had met with previously at their corporate offices. The hotel executive confirmed that they were definitely interested, and if everything went well, they would introduce the new carpets into one of their big hotels in the Midwest. They calculated that it would be an order worth six to eight million US dollars.

At the end of June 1982, Karl went back to Beijing to try to work out an agreement with the Chinese for manufacturing approximately two million square meters of carpeting for a twenty-four-floor hotel. He arrived the day before the World Soccer final and received a royal reception at the Beijing airport by Mr. Wong and a mysterious woman that Karl referred to as "Madame X." Mr. Wong was forthcoming and pleasant, but he seemed rather nervous. The next morning, he and Madame X joined Karl for breakfast at 8:00 a.m., after which they traveled to the Ministry of Trade and Export.

At the meeting, Karl was greeted by the director, who had hosted him so generously on his previous visit, and three high-ranking officials. Karl presented their plans for the project in English, but for some reason, he had forgotten to bring the detailed technical designs of how the hand-knotted rugs of different shapes and sizes could be produced by a simple and effective method. Their initial questions focused on how this was possible, and they wanted him to make a drawing and explain his method. They also insisted on knowing the name of the company that he wanted to make the rugs for. After two hours, they could not agree on an agenda, and Karl postponed the meeting until the next day. He told them that he needed to discuss the matter with his partner. Karl was uneasy about how the negotiations were going. The Chinese were aggressive this time around and appeared to be in a hurry to co-opt this multi-million dollar project. The atmosphere was laced with post-cultural revolution hostility.

Karl called Bjőrkegren and explained to him how things were going. Karl said that the Chinese were aggressive and were pressing him for his exact method of production, the name of the company the carpets were intended for, and the name of a contact person at that company. The men agreed that if the Chinese didn't want to deal on their terms, Karl would return to Stockholm. Karl endured two more grueling days of meetings with the Chinese, during which they persistently tried to get the name of his client out of him. Finally, Karl explained that his partner had invited them all to come to Stockholm where they could show them the design and draw up an agreement. Consequently, Karl returned to Sweden. Bjőrkegren was not pleased that Karl was not able to get the Chinese to sign an agreement. Karl explained that it was not his doing and that they had refused to sign. Karl challenged him to do better himself, and if he thought he could, then Karl would be willing to accompany him on a trip back to Beijing. With this unfortunate turn of events, the multimillion-dollar project slipped out of Karl's grasp.

Cosmic Universe, 2004

Chapter 33

FORTUNE-TELLING IN TOKYO

While the construction of the *Tree of Utah* was going ahead, Karl was also planning two exhibitions of his artworks, one at the Salt Lake Art Center (SLAC) in Utah, and the other in Tokyo. He was fortunate that the SLAC was able to accommodate his exhibition in April 1984. Karl got the idea that he should also do an exhibition in Tokyo since it would not cost much more to include Tokyo in the shipping itinerary for his works traveling from Stockholm to Salt Lake City. He called Sigrid Falkman, the cultural attaché at the Swedish Embassy in Tokyo, and introduced himself. She already knew about the *Tree of Utah*. Karl explained that he would like to do an exhibition in Tokyo and asked if she could give him some advice. She explained that it was difficult for the embassy to arrange an exhibition. It would have to be organized by the Arts Council in Sweden. She said that the only way she could help Karl was to give him a list of museums that he could contact directly.

It was April 5, and Karl had the Utah winter behind him. It was also just two days after his birthday. He never celebrated his birthday, and on many occasions, it had passed quietly and unceremoniously. Birthdays were not a tradition in Iran when Karl was young. Most people didn't even remember what day they were born. It was during the 1960s, when many European- and American-educated Iranians came back to Iran, that they brought this western tradition back with them. It spread like wildfire among middle and upper class families. Birthday gifts soon set records, and a million-dollar gift was not unheard of among the wealthy.

Karl decided to take off for Tokyo, and the next afternoon he was on a United Airlines flight with a stopover in Seattle.

From Seattle he called Mrs. Falkman. He mentioned that he was going to be in Tokyo the next day and that he would like to meet her. After a long silence, she agreed. Karl imagined her pointing to her head and telling her colleagues that the same nut who had asked her for the names of art museums the previous day was now on a plane from Salt Lake City to meet her. When he asked her if she could recommend a hotel, she mentioned Hotel Ocura. Karl asked the clerk at the United Airlines service desk at the Seattle Airport if they could make a reservation for him. They did! Years later he silently reflected on the fact that if a passenger made the same request today, they would call airport security!

The next day, Karl arrived at Narita Airport in Tokyo at 4:00 p.m., and after an uneventful taxi ride, he checked in at the Ocura hotel. He had a quick shower and proceeded to the bar for a drink and a salad before retiring for the night. However, Karl soon discovered that the world is sometimes not as big as it seems. Hotel Acura's lobby was rectangular, with the front desk facing the main entrance. To the left of the entrance were the elevators, and to the right was the bar and coffee shops. Karl had exited the elevator and was walking briskly toward the bar when he almost collided with a gentleman in the middle of the lobby. They looked at each other in disbelief and froze momentarily as they realized they knew each other. Karl had literally bumped into his dear friend and former colleague Hisashi Tanaka from Stockholm.

Tanaka went by the nickname "Q." It must have been more than three years since they last met. Simultaneously they asked each other what had brought them to Tokyo, and then they both laughed. Tokyo was Q's birthplace, and he returned there every year. They agreed to meet in the bar in fifteen minutes. Q returned in the company of another Swedish gentleman. After they introduced themselves, it turned out that Q and his business companion had arrived the previous week to find a partner for a business enterprise exporting Swedish prefabricated wooden houses to Japan. Karl mentioned his dealings with Sigrid Falkman of the Swedish Embassy and that he was due to see her in the morning, whereupon Q said he knew Sigrid and that they could go together since he was free that morning.

The next day the two men met Sigrid Falkman—a charming and enthusiastic woman who appeared to be happy to see them. Karl thought her change of attitude was occasioned by the fact that Q had taken the time to inform her about him. At their meeting, she called the directors of two museums and set up meetings for Karl. The next morning, Karl met with Mr. Kanasawa, the managing director of the Hara Museum of Contemporary Art, and in the afternoon, he visited Mr. Sukuhara, the director of the Striped House Museum. Both museums were in Ropongy, the most fashionable district of Tokyo. This was also near to where the Hotel Acura and the Swedish and American Embassies were located.

The Hara Museum was the most important contemporary art museum in Tokyo and was privately owned by a real estate tycoon. The Striped House Museum was operated by a private foundation. Mr. Kanasawa of the Hara Museum first said that his exhibition schedule was fully booked until 1987. Karl could get a provisional booking for 1989 or 1990. Mr. Sukuhara was a famous photographer and a professor at Tokyo University. He liked Karl's work, and they eventually decided on a show in April 1985.

Q had also arranged meetings for Karl that Friday with Dr. Miki Tamon, deputy minister for the Department of Arts and Culture, and Toke Aiba, the director for culture at NHK, Japan's major TV station. Karl became a dear friend of Toke Aiba, an intellectual icon in Japan and the author of two books on Ingmar Bergman. He was a thorough gentleman and a textbook example of Japanese decorum. In 2002, Karl received a New Year's card from him; however, Karl's last letter in 2003 remained unanswered.

A SHINTO TEMPLE FORTUNE IS REALIZED EXACTLY ONE YEAR LATER

That Thursday, Karl and Q spent the entire day sightseeing. First on Karl's wish list was the most important Shinto Temple in Tokyo; it had a breathtaking view. The serene atmosphere of this sacred edifice made a deep and lasting impression on Karl. Q provided a complete history of the temple, explaining a little of the Shinto philosophy as they went along. Then he told Karl to take a fortune slip. In accordance with Shinto tradition, Karl knocked three times, took a thin bamboo shoot with a number on it, and exchanged it for a rice paper fortune with the corresponding number from the special table piled high with hundreds of such papers. Karl gave the paper to Q without reading it. Q looked at it and almost shouted out loud in disbelief. Karl said that he hoped that it had not foretold the last day of his life. Q said that it was unbelievable and proceeded to translate the slip of rice paper for Karl. The fortune was titled "The Most Lucky One" and stated that Karl was on his way to "create something on a high plateau that the world would take note of and be amazed by"!

That afternoon, they visited a cemetery that was filled with people on blankets under the fully blossomed cherry trees. People were eating, drinking sake, and dancing to music to celebrate the arrival of spring and pay homage to their deceased family ancestors. It was the most beautiful tradition honoring the dead that Karl had ever encountered. He thought this was also the most dignified way to remember their deceased family and friends. Close to the cemetery was another thousand-year-old Shinto Temple. As they walked across the manicured grounds toward the temple, Karl jokingly asked, "How about one more fortune?"

When they entered the temple, Karl put some coins in a bronze urn and took a bamboo shoot in the same manner as he had done previously. He took the slip of rice paper and gave it directly to Q, again without reading it. Q glanced at the paper and almost immediately started jumping up and down. He called to Karl to hold up the fortune paper he had received at the first temple, and then he showed both papers to the growing crowd of bemused visitors who had gathered to see what all the excitement was about. Both papers bore the same message! The chances of such an occurrence were almost zero.

As Q turned so that all could see the papers in his hands, he beamed at the crowd of over a hundred onlookers with his inscrutable Japanese smile. After working many years in the same office with Q, Karl had grown accustomed to his incomprehensible smile. Now almost fifty years later, he still could not tell whether he was serious or just teasing. Q immediately called his wife in Sweden and Mr. Sukuhara to tell them of Karl's unbelievably good fortune. For a moment Karl had become an instant Japanese celebrity. His destiny had been pronounced as if by the finest soothsayer or oracle in the country. *As it has been written, so may it be*, he thought. As for the exhibition—two months before the opening, Mr. Sukuhara called Karl to tell him that he had obtained the Swedish Embassy's patronage for the show. Both Karl and Q were grateful for the embassy's support.

One year later in May 1985, Karl traveled from Salt Lake City to Tokyo to attend the opening of the exhibition. Q arrived from Stockholm. He had invited Miki Tamon, who was at that time director of the Osaka Contemporary Art Museum. Karl was gladdened to see Mr. Aiba, the president of NHK among the guests. The show was well received and drew positive articles, reviews, and TV news reports. Karl felt deeply indebted to the Shinto Temple's prognostications!

While traveling to Tokyo in 1985, Karl found himself booked on a United Airlines flight in business class, seated in the upper level of a Boeing 747. To his side was a Japanese gentleman with whom he had struck up a light conversation over dinner. Afterward, when the cabin services were over, the passengers settled down for the overnight flight. Karl could not sleep, so he took his A4 drawing pad from his portfolio and started making some abstract sketches in different colors with his Uniball pen. He completed half a dozen sketches and then slept for a few hours.

The passengers were awakened for breakfast about two hours from Tokyo. Karl's neighbor and fellow passenger noticed the sketches he had made during the night and asked Karl about them. He told the man that he had an exhibition at the Striped House Museum and that these sketches would be on sale at the museum bookshop. The Japanese gentleman became excited and said that he had seen the advertisement for Karl's show and had read an article about the *Tree of Utah*. He asked Karl how much the sketches would sell for, and Karl replied that they would sell in the store for between seven hundred and one thousand US dollars, but that he would only get 60 percent of their selling price. The man then offered to buy all six sketches for a total of $2,500. Karl accepted his offer. They shook hands, and the man handed over twenty-five one-hundred-dollar travelers' checks. Karl read this as a confirmation of his good fortune. It was also the first time he had earned his airfare while traveling on board a plane.

Composition II, 2004

Chapter 34

A MISSED OPPORTUNITY

Karl had misjudged situations and lost opportunities many times in his life. The one such event that he would never forget occurred a few months after starting construction of the *Tree of Utah* in July 1984. Karl was living at the Salt Lake Hilton when he received a phone call early in the morning from the secretary of a gentleman by the name of Wendell Ashton. She said that Mr. Ashton would be pleased if he would join him for breakfast at the Alta Club the following morning at 7:30 a.m. Karl thanked the lady on the phone, and a few hours later, he asked Don Reimann, the head of the construction company commissioned with building the *Tree of Utah* if he knew a gentleman named Wendell Ashton who had invited him for breakfast at the Alta Club. Karl knew neither Wendell Ashton nor the Alta Club.

When Karl mentioned Ashton's name and the Alta Club, Don and his sons gathered round him with expressions that were a mixture of respect and dumbfounded disbelief that he had never encountered before. They told Karl that Mr. Ashton was the CEO of the *Deseret News,* one of the largest newspapers in Utah, and one of the most influential people in Utah. Later, when Karl mentioned this meeting to Semnani and Dennis Smith, they too were astonished.

The next morning Karl arrived at the Alta Club at 7:15 a.m. The club was situated in an impressive building in downtown Salt Lake City, not far from historic Hotel Utah. Karl waited at the receptionist's desk, and at exactly 7:30 a.m., Aston arrived. He was a distinguished-looking gentleman, about sixty years of age. He welcomed Karl, and they were ushered by the director of the club into the dining room. During the breakfast, Ashton asked Karl about his education, his occupation, and the reason for his decision to build the *Tree of Utah*.

Karl give him a short resume of his educational history and what he had been working on but stopped short of providing the reason for his interest in building the *Tree*. At that time, he had no clearly reasoned response to this question. Karl could not explain what his goal was in constructing the *Tree* other than admitting to the fact that it was his destiny to build it. He told Ashton that after arriving in Salt Lake City on his trans-American road trip, he had arbitrarily decided to cross the desert toward San Francisco on Interstate 80 rather than to proceed south on Interstate 15 to Las Vegas and then on to Los Angeles. Ashton looked at Karl with disbelief and astonishment. "Was that the only reason?"

"No, not exactly," he replied, and Ashton laughed loudly. Karl told him that to that day he had not been able to determine the reason for his decision. He mused that perhaps he would find out one day.

Ashton probed further, "You must be a brave and courageous man to put all your time and money into this project."

Karl responded, "It came as an instantaneous vision that struck my mind when I walked on the Salt Flats for the first time."

"What name will you choose for this work?" asked Ashton. Karl told him that his first choice was "Tree of Life" as a tribute to life in the barrenness of the desert. However, the media publicity that later erupted around the *Tree* resulted in it finally becoming known as the *Tree of Utah*.

Ashton said that he liked the idea of putting some color in the desert. He asked Karl if he had seen the inside of the LDS Salt Lake Temple. Karl responded that he had not. Ashton told Karl that he would organize a time the next week to take him to the temple and maybe get an audience with Spencer W. Kimball, the President of The Church of Jesus Christ of Latter-day Saints at the time. Karl thanked him and told him it would be a great honor to get the prophet's blessing on his project.

A week later, Karl went to the *Deseret News* building, and Ashton accompanied him to the Church offices. Ashton told Karl that President Kimball was ill but would see him briefly. Karl thought it a special honor to be introduced to President Kimball and to shake his hand. Kimball appeared to be interested in Karl and gave him his blessing. He was then introduced to Gordon B. Hinckley, and Karl gave him a short description of the *Tree*. Hinckley commented that the *Tree* would be a good thing for the young people and wished Karl success with his project. After they left the Church office building, Karl took leave of Wendell Ashton and a Church official conducted Karl on a brief visit to the Salt

Lake Temple. They entered a side door and Karl was ushered to a room on the first floor of the building. At the time he thought this was a great privilege—one that he would always remember.

Two days later, he again met Wendell Ashton at Salt Lake's Abravanel Hall, where Karl was presented to Josef Silverstein, the new chief conductor of the Utah Symphony Orchestra. Karl later became good friends with Silverstein through their mutual Salt Lake City friends, Daniel Mattis and his wife, Naomi. Until 2005, they often had dinner together at a Chinese restaurant owned by a Greek engineer in Bountiful.

The following day Karl received a call from Elaine Jarvik, the staff writer at the *Deseret News*. She wanted to interview him. They met at a coffee shop opposite the newspaper's office. Karl was impressed by Elaine Jarvik's youthful and energetic appearance. She was always highly animated with a ready smile that encompassed her entire demeanor. She was casually but elegantly dressed. She was incurably curious and seemed to be searching for answers to everything Karl said. In later years, Karl would observe that her joyful demeanor never changed. Karl got the impression that she was constantly analyzing and judging him. She would listen intently to everything Karl had to say, and when he responded to one of her questions, she would say "Really!" as much to acknowledge that she understood what he had said as to egg him on to reveal more. He often wondered what she really thought of him and his project. She was a good listener and a good storyteller in her articles. However, when he read her articles he could never determine what her point of view was. He thought that she possessed the most beautiful, happy, poker face that he had ever encountered. She never committed her own feelings about the *Tree* in what she wrote. Karl found it interesting to find out that she was married to the inventor of the Jarvik artificial heart. Their first meeting resulted in a positive and intriguing full-page article about the *Tree*, depicting Karl as a man who reveled in great personal challenges.

Karl was again invited to have lunch with Wendell Ashton two days after Elaine Jarvik's full-page article was published in the *Deseret News*. Ashton met Karl at Lamb's restaurant at exactly noon, and they were shown to their table. This restaurant would become a favorite of Karl's. He often had lunch there with various friends and associates, including Kosrow Semnani and various journalists, and Jim Wolff from the *Tribune* newspaper. Wolff covered the *Tree*'s progress with all its technical and financial challenges.

Ashton and Karl ordered lamb chops, the restaurant's specialty. Karl thanked Ashton for presenting him to the Church leaders and for the privilege of seeing the temple on Temple Square. Ashton resumed his questioning of Karl.

"Was your decision to build the *Tree* entirely the result of your arbitrary choice of which freeway to take to California?"

Karl repeated his earlier statement. "Yes, it was. And then I was so overwhelmed with the serenity of the desert, and somehow I had a mental vision and felt a powerful impulse to realize the inspiration I had received."

Ashton responded pointedly and deliberately, "You should read the Book of Mormon. Perhaps you will find the answer to your vision!" He then gave Karl a copy of the Book of Mormon with marked pages.

He asked Karl what date he had set for the dedication, and Karl said that it would probably be toward the end of September. Then he told Karl that the Utah Symphony Orchestra was his pet project and suggested that Karl become a patron. He suggested that if Karl gave a donation then the symphony orchestra could give a special concert on the evening before the dedication at which they could play Beethoven's Ode to Joy. The two men agreed to another meeting before the dedication. Karl had planned on making a donation of twenty-five-thousand US dollars to the choir.

Karl would always regret that he did not immediately read the pages in the Book of Mormon that Ashton had marked for him. At the time his mind was preoccupied with issues relating to the construction of the *Tree*. It was only after the *Tree* was completed that he eventually read the appointed pages to find a complementary and literal account of the "Tree of Life." If he had known of these things at the time that he had his desert epiphany, he would not have even considered the involvement of the Utah Arts Council. He would have approached the Church directly, without hesitation, to inform them of his plans. That a total stranger not at all familiar with The Church of Jesus Christ of Latter-day Saints, its religion, and the Book of Mormon should be influenced in the way that he had been to construct such a powerful symbol of the Church's faith was truly remarkable. Ashton had said that he should read the book as soon as he had the time. Karl later reflected that he had not been sensitive enough to receive the prompting that Ashton had given him. Consequently, he had forfeited the help and recognition that the Church could have given his project.

Karl met Wendall Ashton again just before Ashton left the *Deseret News*. Karl expressed his concern about the technical and financial problems he had been having. Then Ashton asked again, "Have you read the book?"

Karl replied that he had started. Ashton smiled and said, "One of those pages was marked for you!"

Unfortunately, Karl had left the book at the Hilton Hotel when he moved across to the Orleans Inn Apartment Hotel that spring.

CHAPTER 34

On January 24, 1985, Karl's exhibition opened at the Springville Museum of Art in Utah. It was the same exhibition that he had shown at the Salt Lake Art Center. On the afternoon of Saturday, January 26, Wendell Ashton came to the museum to congratulate him and the museum director, Vern Swanson, on the wonderful show and mentioned that he thought more people should see it. The following Monday, Richard Christenson, the art critic of the *Deseret News* called Karl to make an appointment to interview him at the museum. Three days later, a full-page article with color pictures appeared in the newspaper.

Karl had sometimes been too slow to grasp an opportunity when it presented itself. He was in Stockholm for a few weeks in April 1984 before taking off for Salt Lake City where the *Tree of Utah* was under construction. His apartment was at Östermalsgatan, close to Humlegården behind the Park Hotel. One evening Karl's neighbor Dr. Winblad, also on the first floor of the building, called him to invite him to have breakfast with her since she wanted to introduce him to a Mrs. Osher, who lived on the other side of the street, and who, like Karl, also had a home in Marin County, California. Upon entering the home, Dr. Winblad introduced Karl to Barbro Osher. She had shoulder-length blond hair, was good looking, and was elegantly dressed with an obvious fashion sense.

They enjoyed a pleasant breakfast and were joined by Dr. Winblad's college-aged daughter. They chatted about what it was like living in San Francisco's Marin County. Karl took Barbro Osher's address and phone number and promised to call her when he was in the States again. The next month, Karl called her from Salt Lake City, but her secretary told him she was in southern California and would be back in two weeks' time. She asked if Mrs. Osher could call him back on her return. Karl said that he had no phone number that she could reach him at—cell phones were few and far between in those days. Karl was wrestling with technical problems with the construction of the *Tree* on a daily basis and time went by. When he returned to the Bay Area a few months later, he had unfortunately lost Barbro Osher's contact information.

Some years later, in the summer of 1998 Karl visited Olle Granath, the director of the Moderna Museet in Stockholm. They decided to have lunch, and as they walked toward the restaurant, they both noticed Barbro Osher leaving the restaurant. Olle Granath greeted her and was about to introduce Karl to her. He asked, "Do you know Karl Momen?"

She laughed. "Oh yes, but he doesn't dare to call me as he promised some years ago!" Karl was frozen in embarrassment and was at a loss for words to find an appropriate excuse. By now he had come to know a lot about Barbro Osher—that she was the president of the Barbro Osher Foundation in San Francisco, the largest sponsor of the San Francisco Opera and the San Francisco Modern Art Museum (SFMOMA). She was also one of the founders of SVEA, the Swedish National Women's Association, and publisher of *Vestkusten*, the weekly newspaper.

A few days later, Ambassador Ingrid Iremark called Karl to tell him that SVEA had their annual conference in Stockholm's Skansen Conference Center, with more than a thousand members in attendance. Claus Oldenburg had been invited as guest of honor. But more important for him, Anna Greta Leijon, a former Labor and Justice Minister, who was at that time the director of Skansen and chairperson of the Board of *Moderna Museet*, had given the keynote address. She had spoken enthusiastically about taking part in the dedication of the *Tree of Utah* with Governor Norman Bangerter on January 18, 1986, at the Great Salt Lake in Utah. She also said that this singular event would occupy two pages in her autobiography titled *Alla rosor ska inte tuktas* ("All roses need not suffer opposition").

A month after meeting Barbro Osher, Karl received a call in Sausalito from Bridget Brink, a staff writer for *Vestkusten*, the bilingual Swedish newspaper in California. She interviewed him in his studio, and a week later, a half-page article on his art appeared in the newspaper. Karl sent Barbro some of his catalogs and thanked her for arranging the interview. After that, Karl met Barbro a few times for lunch, and one day she visited him in his studio in Sausalito. Karl asked if her Pro Sevecia Foundation could jointly sponsor his new book *Homage to Shakespeare and Wagner.* She responded that, unfortunately, since the book was a private publication, the foundation would not be able to sponsor it.

However, when *Arts & Artists,* the curatorial company based in Washington, D.C., arranged a traveling show of Karl's artworks to four museums in the United States, the Barbro Osher Pro Suecia Foundation sponsored these exhibitions. Other sponsors included the Illinois Arts Council, Chicago City, and the National Endowment for the Arts. Osher also sponsored his exhibitions at the Krasel Arts Center in Michigan and at the Tech Museum of Innovation in San Jose, California. She was gracious in also sponsoring the catalog for his retrospective exhibition at the Royal Academy of Fine Arts in Stockholm in 2009. Karl would always be grateful for Barbro Osher's generous contributions to his exhibitions.

Chapter 35

WORKING AS AN ARTIST IN THE UNITED STATES

After successfully completing the *Tree of Utah*, Karl returned to his Sausalito studio in San Francisco to work on a new series of paintings and sculptures. Neil Hadlock introduced Karl to the director of the Salt Lake Art Center while he was building the *Tree of Utah*, and this meeting resulted in his first museum exhibition in the United States. Karl had recently been interviewed by KUTV, and the director of SLAC was impressed with an exhibition that Karl had at the Striped House Gallery in Tokyo and with his 1982 exhibition in Berlin at the Lützow Cultural Center. He asked if Karl could bring the exhibition to his museum. Karl complied, and the exhibition opened in July 1985. The exhibition received positive local TV coverage by TV journalist Chris Vanocker.

After the opening of his exhibition, Karl met Vern Swanson, director of the Springville Museum of Fine Art. He too asked Karl if he could show the exhibition at his museum. The exhibition opened in Springville, Utah, in September 1985.

In January 1991, after five years of intensive studio work, he received an invitation to exhibit at the Marisa del Re Gallery, an upscale venue on 57th Street in New York City. Marisa del Re had a reputation for showcasing significant contemporary artist's work. Karl exhibited nine large paintings and four bronze sculptures. The sculptures were cast by Neil Hadlock, an accomplished sculptor and foundryman who Karl had discovered while working on the *Tree of Utah.* Karl was of the opinion that the quality of Hadlock's casting was equal to the best he could find in Europe.

By this time, Karl's paintings had become forcefully abstract. All references to a horizon line had been abandoned. Simple geometric forms float in a compressed pictorial space as if seen through a telescope against a dark impenetrable sky. Modeling was kept to a minimum, allowing the viewer just enough visual information to read the forms as corporeal objects. These paintings have a brooding intensity that underlies the simplicity and elegance of their compositions. The sphere became a recurring visual icon in his works during these years.

In his painting *Separation in Red,* completed in 1990, Karl depicted the two halves of a bisected sphere in a nearly symmetrical composition. A rectangular bar rendered in rich gold separates the two red hemispheres. Seen against the velvety texture of the deep blue background, these red and gold elements glow with emotive intensity. The schism created by the bisection of the sphere carries with it connotations of disunity that is designed to contradict the essential nature of the sphere as a symbol of completeness and wholeness. This unsettling aspect is succinctly captured within the visual harmony of the composition. It could be said that we gain a more complete comprehension of the wholeness of the sphere as a result of its fracture. We also come to a fuller understanding of the tension that exists between the two halves of the sphere and the intrusion of the bisecting bar, like opposing magnets held in balance. The effect is heightened by the isolation of the simple geometric forms against the dark background. The sphere has come to represent the organic world of spontaneous creation—the primordial human condition. The fact that the sphere is fractured indicates the dislocation that has resulted from the intrusion of the gold bar. The bar represents the world of dehumanizing technocracy. Karl's concern with the tension between human actions pitted against the unfeeling world of institutionalized ideology continues in these later works.

Karl found a ready analogy for the collision between conflicting ideologies in the account of Galileo Galilei's (1564–1642) unsuccessful challenge to the authority of the Catholic Church. Galileo, the Italian astronomer, physicist, and philosopher, had defended Copernicus's theory that the Earth revolved around the Sun—and not the other way around, much to the chagrin of the prevailing prelates of the Holy Roman Church. A year after the publication of his *Dialogue on the Great World Systems* (1632), Galileo was brought before the Inquisition on charges of proclaiming and defending the Copernican system, which had been denounced as heretical. Unwilling to sacrifice his remaining years and his work to a fruitless heroism, he recanted his views. Legend has it that as he did so, he muttered "Eppur si muove!" (And yet it moves!)—referring to the Earth's motion around the Sun.

Karl saw in Galileo's story the essential features of his central thesis, namely the conflict between the freedom of individual creativity and institutional hegemony. In the series *Galileo's Discovery, Galileo's Window,* and *Galileo's Verdict,* all painted in 1990, a red sphere symbolizes the integrity of Galileo and his theory. In *Galileo's Discovery,* the sphere is still intact and coexists with the cross symbolizing the might of the Church. However, in the second work, *Galileo's Window,* the symbol of the cross appears ominously at Galileo's window, and the sphere is dislocated, as a portent of Galileo's ultimate demise.

In the final painting in this series, *Galileo's Verdict,* we see a large cross hovering threateningly over a bisected square representing the effect of the Church's final verdict on Galileo. Stig Johansson, the Swedish art critic, commented on this series in an essay he wrote for the exhibition catalog:

Galileo's Discovery, 1990

Galileo's Window, 1990

Galileo's Verdict, 1990

"There in the sacred gold color of the icon, the cross appears again and again, frequently in dramatic conflict with the sphere, which transforms the picture into a single dynamic field of forces where conflicting will, beliefs, and knowledge struggle. This all symbolizes the continual crisis, both spiritual and temporal, of the ideologies. Although the artist can hardly solve that nexus of problems, he can make art out of it. This is precisely what Karl has succeeded in doing!"[5]

Karl also showed four bronze sculptures at the Marisa del Re Exhibition. He maintained an uncanny ability to remain entirely steadfast in the underlying conceptualizations that energized his work. This consistency is evident in the bronze sculptures *Hagen's Cliff* and *Fafner's Pass*, executed in 1989 and 1990 respectively. Both pieces are strong formal statements. Each demonstrates Karl's two conflicting paradigms pitted against each other. In each case, this is achieved through formal means. In both pieces the organic form is compromised by straightforward bisection.

Fafner's Pass, 1990

Hagen's Cliff, 1989

In *Fafner's Pass,* the interaction between organic and technological forms is subtle, relying on a wavy profile in the bisection to contrast with the rough surface of the cube-like form. Both pieces make use of organic texture, juxtaposed with machine polished surfaces, to further amplify the tension between the two opposing worlds of organic creation and machine-driven technology.

Significantly, it was in these two pieces that Karl first began his investigation of subject matter drawn from the world of the opera. *Hagen's Cliff* refers to the cliff where Hagen is reputed to have murdered Siegfried his half brother in Wagner's four-part opera *Der Ring des Nibelungen.* In the opera, he changes himself into a fire-breathing dragon to guard over his ill-gotten gold booty. The erosion of the bronze form is reminiscent of the destructive effect of the dragon's breath on the metal. Again we see organic forces engaging the man-made cubic construction of the form in this work.

Karl also exhibited a maquette of his large bronze sculpture *Metropolis* that had been exhibited in the 1991 Venice Biennale. This piece echoes the dynamics of conflicting and opposing forces, represented by two hemispheres separated and by a smaller sphere placed between them. A bronze band encircles the unstable configuration and serves to contain the composition. This work reminds us of the physics of the atomic bomb that is designed to release unimaginable energy from components that are similarly configured. The work conjures up the dynamics of

Metropolis, 1990

elemental forces captured at their moment of crisis or release.

In 1995, Karl was invited to exhibit paintings and sculptures at the new Museum of Art at Brigham Young University in Provo, Utah, that had recently opened. His exhibition included the Nibelungenlied sculptures, as well as some significant new paintings that marked the beginning of his exploration of the world of theater. This group, represented by *Andre Chenier* and *Flame from the East,* was completed in 1994. Each of the works in this group employed simple yet highly charged symbolism to convey their elemental messages. Karl's dramatic color palette and textured brushstrokes had reached a state of refinement that combined with the lyricism of his subject matter to create graphic psychological injunctions.

While exhibiting at Brigham Young University Museum of Art in 1995, he was commissioned to produce a sculpture for the museum's sculpture garden. He obliged

Temple of Mercury, 1995

with *Temple of Mercury,* a large bronze piece that would occupy a prime site against the striking façade of the building. Again we see the consistency of Karl's conceptual approach. Two long angular forms with organically textured patina point skyward while cradling a brilliantly polished stainless steel sphere in the triangular space between them. The angular forms become the resting place, or temple, for Mercury, the messenger of the gods. A fleeting and transitory moment captures these great mythological forces in the silent immobility of cast bronze and stainless steel.

Karl also exhibited several paintings for the first time that alluded to planets and other stellar forms in a cosmic environment. Significantly these works produced from 1993 to 1995 relate powerfully to the early works of both El Lissitzky and Kandinsky, referred to earlier in this text. *Cosmic Superlative III* and *Centaurs Behind the Curtain* are examples from this period. Both works were completed in 1994 and are fine examples of geometric abstraction using brilliant color and pure form that evoke the essence of Suprematism. The sphere predominates in these works and becomes agitated, or acted upon, by

Cosmic Superlative III, 2000

Cosmic Superlative, 2001

Centarus Behind the Curtain, 1995

cataclysmic forces that are contained in an elemental universe in dynamic motion.

At this high point in his career, Momen had progressed away from three-dimensional rendering toward a clearer and more assured use of two-dimensional elements. The pictorial space in his paintings flattened out and the areas between his "objects" became increasingly charged with psychological tension. His highly abstracted geometric images reflect a unique combination of Persian and Western sensibilities—the quest for spiritual transcendence through the contemplation of ideal form, grafted with the modernist concern with formal elements and the expressive intent of the artist.

This confluence of disparate worldviews imbued Momen's geometric abstractions with a reverential and iconic character that is further enhanced by their uncompromising frontality and by the metallic luster of carefully patterned brushstrokes on their gleaming surfaces. His compositions are rooted in the visual language of formalism, the aesthetic movement that dominated modernist thinking after World War II. Clive Bell, the English aesthetician, is credited with coining the notion of "significant form"—a concept that found new meaning in Karl's sparse but scrupulously conceived compositions that balance simple geometric shapes within elegantly crafted figure-ground relationships.

***Dream Island Suite: Summer,* 2008**

Chapter 36

RETURN TO THE CLASSICS

In typical epicurean fashion, Karl was a lover of good food, classical music, the opera, and the theater. During the 1960s and 70s, he had traveled widely in Europe and the United States. He would attend theater or opera performances wherever he went. He acquired a keen sense of the subtle nuances of expression that characterized familiar pieces as they were performed in different languages at various locations. He had acquired a rich heritage of folklore from his father's mix of ancient Russian and Persian cultures. As a child he had spent many hours listening to the aged patriarch recite Persian poetry from pre-Islamic mythology—tales that were filled with heroes, kings, and demons. These accounts were often infused with ancient Russian folklore.

In later years, Karl was surprised to learn how similar ancient Persian mythology was to Norse mythology. He also learned that although it appeared as if they had been shaped from the same material, they were different. In the Nordic tales, the gods were the central focus, whereas in the Persian tales, the kings held center stage. This fundamental difference is evident in Wagner's most extensive work *Der Ring des Nibelungen,* which is based on Norse mythology and which became one of Karl's favorites. Although he had read hundreds of novels by French, Russian, German, English, and American writers during his adolescent years, Karl had never made a serious study of the theater or the opera. This changed when he moved to Germany to undertake his art and architecture studies. In Stuttgart he become absorbed by the theater world.

"It was as if I was being sucked into a black hole with a gravitational pull from which it was impossible to escape. It was a case of paradise with Dante's Inferno in each corner!"[6]

While visiting London in 1964 he discovered a small recording company that had been recording the best Broadway and West End plays for the previous decade. Karl snapped up over 150 recordings ranging from Euripides' *Media* and Sartre's *No Exit,* to Becket's *Waiting for Godot.* Karl thrilled to the prospect of being totally immersed in the world of the theater. Reflecting on his fortunate circumstances at the time, he declared,

"Sometimes I sensed how privileged I was. What joy to be able to listen to these kings, angels, devils, oppressors, victims—the good, the bad, the comical, and the tragic. I could feel them near me. When I heard them, it was as if they were right in front of me. They were at my disposal and shared with me their wisdom of a thousand years—sane as well as insane thoughts—laughter, tears, hope, and despair. And I would not let them down. I cannot say that I understood all that they uttered. Often the content was complicated, and these ancient thoughts may have better suited a god or a philosopher—things that I am not. But I refused to give in, and I followed as best I could. I was already inside the door, and no one could throw me out!"[7]

It was inevitable that Karl would eventually turn to the drama of the theater and the opera for inspiration in his art. Not surprisingly, he chose Shakespeare's tragedies because of the breadth of human experience embraced by these timeless plays. Wagner's operas were also an obvious choice because of Wagner's fascination with the mythology of fairy tales and with the richness of his compositions. In these operas, Momen found a complete statement of "Gesamte Kunswerk"—the full integration of art forms.

In Shakespeare, Karl found all the facets of the human condition, with rapid transitions from the tragic to the comical. Karl admitted to his own inadequacy in his use of the English language but recognized Shakespeare's genius.

"I have read and listened to Shakespeare performed in the German, Swedish, and English languages hundreds of times. To comprehend philosophy, the knife-sharp and precise German language best serves one. But the majesty and grandeur of the English language, with its richness of expression, renders Shakespeare's genius more versatile, and his plays become prismatic. Each time one experiences a performance, it is perceived through a different color of the multifaceted prism. The English language is my fourth language, and with this handicap, I cannot expect to get even a bronze medal!"[8]

Karl completed his suite of eighteen paintings coincident with the Wagnerian festival of 1998 in San Francisco. The complete suite was first exhibited in the San Francisco Opera House, comprising eight works inspired by the Shakespearian tragedies, and ten works devoted to the Wagnerian operas. The exhibition coincided with the release of Karl's illustrated text *Homage to William Shakespeare and Richard Wagner.*[9] Karl's love for drama and his vivid imagination allowed him ample opportunity to identify with his protagonists and to enter into their world of intense psychological engagement. Writing about his inspiration for his painting *Hamlet* he said,

"It was in 1969 that I first visualized the entire play. All day long I walked about Kronborg Castle in Helsingor. I saw the traveling theater company performing in the reception hall of the castle. I visualized the King and Queen in their confusion and embarrassment at seeing the reenactment of their own dark tragic deed, with Hamlet observing them all the while as he planned his revenge. I saw the stabbed body of Ophelia's father behind the curtain in the Queen's chamber. Outside the castle I imagined Ophelia's empty grave with the bishop refusing to grant her a Christian burial because she died no longer a virgin. In the final act I saw the large hall—the dying Hamlet throwing the poisoned sword through the air. I saw it piercing the king's back. Then I awoke from my reverie with the heady taste of ambition, adultery, thievery, revenge, and murder still in my mouth."[10]

In 1997, Karl completed *Hamlet* in deep muted tones that contrast with the livid scarlet of Hamlet's sword hanging center stage in the sparse composition. Karl is a master of restraint as he presents the emblems of the drama in a stark but perfectly ordered composition. The crown, high up on the left of the painting, represents a monarchy that has been compromised by the scandalous events that have transpired. The scarlet-bladed sword is poised at the center of the composition and contrasts dramatically with the muted tones of the background. Behind the gilt handle of the sword, we see the shadowy silhouette of the head and shoulders of Hamlet rendered in the vertical bars of a cage or prison cell.

The simple motif of the vertical bars is echoed by the two broad bands on the surface of the canvas that serve to further subject the figure to the sword and also gives the viewer the feeling of looking through bars at the subject within. At the lower left is a shadowy depiction of the bottle of poison that became the instrument of so much grief. It is not accidental that the placement of the bottle in the composition serves to counterbalance the crown in this carefully considered composition. The bottle is dissected and dislocated, a familiar device that Momen had used in earlier works to represent fractured emotions and powerful feelings of disunity or alienation. The other paintings in this series are just as emblematic.

Erland Josephson, a noted Swedish actor and head of Stockholm's Royal Dramatic Theater for many years, also commented on Karl's uncanny ability to capture the essence of the drama that is played out before him.

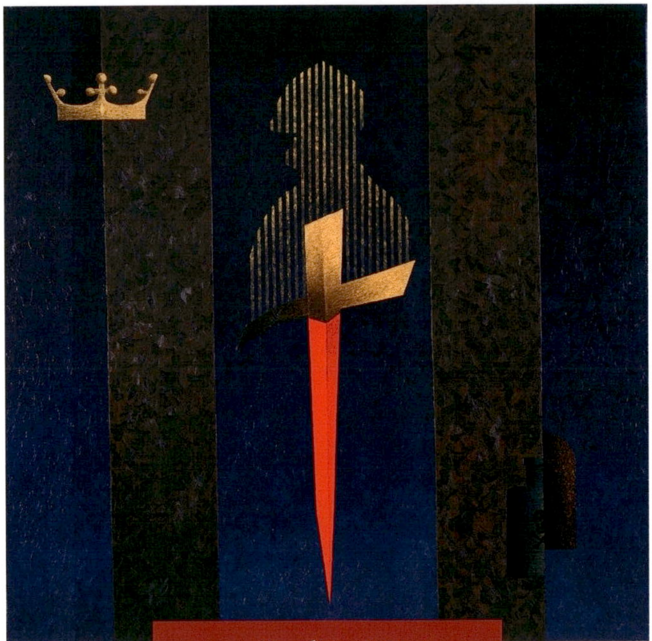

Hamlet, 1997

"Momen is the artist painter as actor. Within the self-imposed rigor and internal order of his indefatigable style, there is an inherent and pervasive intonation that rises first to gesture then becomes at once interpretation and confession. The dynamic compositional elements of his paintings ebb and flow as their changing relationships reflect the timeless flux and transformative power of Shakespeare's masterful characterization of the human condition."[11]

James Mason, a respected musicologist and founding director of the Brigham Young University Museum of Art, commented on Karl's use of symbols and the manner in which his color values aligned not only with the themes of the dramas, but also with the tonal scale of Wagner's musical masterpieces.

"Wagner held his works together with recurring concise themes or 'leitmotifs' that were varied and developed throughout his music. Momen uses geometric elements such as spheres, cubes, and cones in a similar way for their symbolic and unifying value . . . Where Wagner was a master of orchestral color with few equals, the same claim can be made about Karl's use of enlivened subtle graduations of color, vibrant hues, and textures."[12]

In *Parsifal*, painted in 1998, we see Karl's elegant depiction of the Holy Grail, symbolizing the ascendance of spiritual values over worldly ambitions. In this simple iconic composition, we sense the metaphysical connection between the vessel and all that is holy. The Christian cross, placed obliquely to the side, is emblematic of the Grail's sacred contents—

Parsifal, 1999

both the wine of the Holy Sacrament and the redeeming blood of Christ, captured from the wound inflicted in His side at the time of His crucifixion. In March 2006, the Nordic Heritage Museum in Seattle purchased Karl's entire Wagner suite for the museum's permanent collection after hosting Karl's touring exhibition *Nexus*.

Karl's art is made all the more tantalizing by the drama and mystery that plays out in his compositions. His bold use of color speaks of vivid childhood memories of the dyes in his father's Persian rug factory. The simple iconic forms and textures are a reminder of the Russian icons with which he was so familiar. Together these influences imbue his compositions with gravitas and a particular kind of soulfulness that communicates spiritually rather than intellectually. These elements also all work together in his paintings to evoke the brooding dynamism of cataclysmic forces held in abeyance. He is the master of the understated tension between coexisting opposites. His work exposes the nemesis that lurks within us all but to which we never admit. The protracted path of his journey toward his artistic goals pays tribute to the truism that there needs be opposition in all things.

The narrative of Karl's artistic development became an odyssey that would carry him over many cultural boundaries. In Karl's work we see the unity of the ancient Persian folklore of his youth, with the expressions of a finely tuned sensibility tutored in the complexities of a post modern world that is caught up in a collision between technocracy and the human spirit.

Chapter 37

AN AUSPICIOUS MEETING

Erland Josephson was an actor, author, and director of the Royal Drama and Theater Company in Stockholm for many years. Karl had seen his performances on stage, in Ingar Bergman's films, and in scenes with various actors including Liv Ullman. Karl had often bumped into him at a local antique dealer since both men were interested in Russian icons. On these occasions, they often chatted about the icons and the Persian rugs on display. Orima, the antique dealer, was Iranian and knew both men. Josephson soon got to know Karl as an avid collector, theatergoer, and artist.

Karl finished his Homage to Shakespeare and Wagner Suite in 1989 and was compiling the catalog for these paintings. He already had a commitment from James Mason, director of the new Brigham Young University Museum of Art, to write an introduction for the Wagner paintings, but he still needed a similar catalog entry for his Shakespeare works. It occurred to Karl that he should ask Erland Josephson. So one afternoon, he called the Royal Dramatic Theater and asked to speak to Josephson. When Josephson answered, Karl introduced himself, whereupon Josephson immediately asked if Karl had purchased the large *God's Mother* icon by Dimitri from Orima the antique dealer.

Karl responded, "No, but I would like to ask you a favor."

"Do you want to become an actor also? Meet me tomorrow on the fourth floor of the theater at four o'clock."

The following day, Karl was directed to Josephson's office, and the two men exchanged pleasantries about the icons they were both interested in. Then

Josephson asked, "What can I do for you?" Karl responded by opening the portfolio he had brought with him and took out eight large photographs of his Shakespeare suite.

"Is this a gift for me?" asked Josephson.

"No," Karl replied. "I would like you to write the introduction for a book about this suite of paintings."

"But I am not an art critic," replied Josephson.

"And that is exactly why I am asking you! I want you to write what you see in these paintings!" came Karl's immediate response.

Josephson looked at Karl in surprise. "How did you become interested in Shakespeare?"

Karl then told Josephson of the history of his exposure to the literary classics from a young age, starting with *Oliver Twist*, *The Three Musketeers*, and then on to Zola, Tolstoy, and Shakespeare. He told Josephson of how he had read *Romeo and Juliet* in Farsi as a youth but had never fully understood the passion in this tragedy until he read the play again later in English when he was forty years old. Josephson was amazed at Karl's perceptiveness and exclaimed,

"Why did we not think of this difference in the reception of our performances for the young and the old before?"

He asked if Josephson could contemplate the photographs for a few days and then write a few lines expressing his feelings about the plays the paintings referred to. Josephson mentioned that he was not an art critic. Karl said that he was aware of that but he was not asking for an aesthetic critique but rather how well the paintings exemplified elements of the dramas they referred to.

Josephson then asked, "How is it that you became so interested in the theater? I have often seen you at concerts and operas. I have not seen many Iranians at these performances." Then he mentioned with a smile "But I forget that you are an architect—the highest art!"

Karl told him that his father was a Persian rug designer and producer. He went on to recount how as a child he spent time with the Russians when Iran was occupied during WW II. He told him of attending music and theater productions at the Russian Vox Cultural Center in his hometown. Erland listened with interest when Karl mentioned that as a teenager, before moving to Europe, he had read books and novels in French, Russian, German, and English. Karl recollected how avidly and full of passion he read at the time, but he was not able to fully understand the genius of Shakespeare.

"Now in my later years, when I can more fully understand Shakespeare, I have unfortunately lost my passion, and there is no spark left!"

CHAPTER 37

Erland laughed out loud at this and thought it the best thing he had ever heard. He took Karl's hand and shook it vigorously as he thanked him repeatedly. He reached for the phone and called a friend (Karl guessed it was Ingmar Bergman) and related Karl's anecdote with much delight. Then he said, "Okay, I will write. I must say you have staged your paintings wonderfully!"

When Karl visited him again in September 2007, his Parkinson's disease was far advanced. Karl presented him with the catalog of his exhibition at the Nordic Heritage Museum in Seattle. At Christmas 2009, when Karl came home after four months in the hospital and a successful treatment for high-risk lymphoma, he sent Josephson a New Year's greeting card. Josephson responded with a copy of his recently published book with a personal dedication to Karl. "Thank you for sending me the art books that helped me escape into a fantasy world of beautiful shapes and colors. For a moment I forgot my horrible disease. We are both fighting long-term illnesses!" Josephson died three years later in 2012 at the age of eighty-nine years.

KARL MOMEN AT
MONTE CARLO BIENNALE, 1991

Chapter 38

INTERNATIONAL RECOGNITION

Karl was invited to participate in three successive Monte Carlo Biennale exhibitions in 1989, 1991, and 1993. The 1991 event was the largest and most important sculpture show in Europe and included the work of forty invited artists. The opening reception for the artists was held at the Monte Carlo Casino and Banquet Hall. Unfortunately, because of an important meeting with Utah Governor Norman Bangerter in Salt Lake City, Karl could not attend the grand opening banquet and missed out on the publicity interviews with all the TV and newspaper journalists. Karl was only able to attend the show a week after the opening since he had another prior commitment. He was obliged to attend a special luncheon in his honor, hosted by New York art dealer Marisa del Re, who was showing his work at her gallery at the time.

After the luncheon, Marisa and Karl traveled independently to the Monte Carlo Biennale. She invited Karl to join her at the opening reception of the Monte Carlo golf tournament. She said she wanted to compensate him for missing the biennale opening reception and that she had arranged a surprise for him. On the morning of July 27, Marisa's daughter-in-law joined Karl for breakfast at the Meridian Beach Hotel. After breakfast, she conducted him through the park and the casino to show him where his two sculptures had been placed. *Metropolis* was on the south side of the Hotel de Paris, and *Fafners Path* was in front of the Cafe de Paris.

They then drove up the hill to the Monte Carlo Golf Club. When they reached the club situated on a high plateau above the city, he noticed there was a large party of people around a long buffet table. Marisa introduced Karl to a lady friend and mentioned with a smile that if he was tired of speaking French or English he should feel free to speak Farsi to this lady since she was French Iranian. It turned out that she was the owner of the most famous catering company in the Cote d'Azure. While they were chatting about the situation in Iran, Karl spotted Princess Caroline coming toward their table. Marisa introduced Karl to the Princess and jokingly said, "Here is my lost artist Mr. Karl Momen. The Governor of Utah did not allow him to bring his *Tree* sculpture to our show!" Everyone in the party laughed at this comment. The Princess took a seat with them and questioned Karl about his sculpture in the desert. "Why did you choose to build it there?" she asked.

"I would have loved to have built it here, but Monte Carlo does not have an arid salt desert," he replied. Marisa took a Biennale catalog from her portfolio and showed the Princess a picture of Karl's sculpture *Metropolis.* Caroline said that she would look at it on her way to Hotel de Paris.

"I like the patina on your sculpture," she said as she took her leave of Karl's party and made her way toward the golf course.

After the princess's departure, Marisa and Karl walked over to the hors de oeuvre table. Marisa's daughter-in-law said that it was a pity that they did not get a photo of Karl with Princess Caroline. Marisa said that it was too late and that she could have a photo taken with her and Karl instead. She took a call on her cell phone and then she announced that they should all meet at Karl's sculpture in two hours since a photojournalist of *Nice Matinee* would like to do a story on Karl and his work. The article was published with a photograph of Marisa and Karl standing behind *Metropolis.*

Karl was remarkably prolific throughout his life; however, he had difficulty in parting with his paintings and sculptures to collectors or their agents. He preferred to reserve his works for museum exhibitions. This opportunity arose shortly after he completed the *Tree of Utah.* Karl had formed a strong and lasting relationship with Neil Hadlock, whose foundry Wasatch Bronze had cast all Karl's bronze pieces. Karl considered his work of equal standard to the finest foundries he could find in Europe. Neil had made a point of introducing Karl to the major artists in the state. On a visit to Brigham Young University Museum of Art, Neil introduced Karl to James Mason, the founding director of this new museum that had recently opened on the campus. Mason was impressed by Karl's exhibition in Berlin and invited him to exhibit at the museum. Karl said that this would be a great honor for him, and an agreement was quickly reached on the exhibition details. Mason asked Karl if he could organize a sponsorship, and Karl said he would look into it.

Karl brought this opportunity to the attention of Heins Heuer, the cultural manage of Lufthansa who discussed the request with his boss in Frankfort. Again, agreement was reached, and the airline agreed to sponsor the shipping cost of the artworks and the publication of a catalog for the exhibition. Karl ended up paying for the advertising poster for his exhibition. In return, Mason commissioned Karl to create a sculpture for the museum's sculpture garden. Consequently, the *Temple of Mercury* was cast by Wasatch Bronze and installed near the museum's main entrance. The exhibition opened in 1995.

After successful shows of Karl's *Shakespeare and Wagner Suite* at the refurbished San Francisco Opera House and a showing of a collection of his works at the Marissa del Re Gallery in New York, the next important development was a traveling exhibition of Karl's works to several US museums organized by International Art and Artists (IAA), a curatorial company based in Washington, D.C. David Furchgott, director of IAA, immediately saw the potential for a traveling exhibition of Karl's paintings. Karl was able to secure sponsorship for this exhibition from Barbro Osher, president of the Barbro Osher Pro Suecia Foundation in San Francisco. Barbro had been a longstanding friend and admirer of Karl's work. The exhibition entitled Nexus traveled to the following museums between June 2004 and July 2006: The Swedish-American Museum, Chicago, Illinois; Hillstrom Museum of Art, St. Peter, Minnesota; Nordic Heritage Museum, Seattle, Washington; Krasl Art Center, St. Joseph, Michigan. Individualized catalogs were produced for each venue. Karl paid to have the color catalogs printed by Wallin and Dahlholm in Sweden and to have them shipped to each venue. This exhibition was well received by audiences at each museum, with positive local media reports in each city.

A few days after the opening of his exhibition at the Nordic Heritage Museum in Seattle, Karl was invited to have lunch with Allan Osberg, the chairman of the board. At lunch Asgard told Karl that their curators were impressed with Karl's Wagner

KARL MOMEN AT TECH MUSEUM

Suite and that they would like to acquire all ten paintings for the museum's permanent collection. After some negotiation around the fact that there would be no agent or gallery fees involved, the men settled for a flat price of $300,000 for the suite of ten paintings. After lunch, Karl returned to the museum with Osberg and was handed a check for the full amount. The museum was later rebuilt at a cost of $450 million as the New Nordic Heritage Museum and opened to the public in April 2018, with Karl's ten Wagner Suite paintings prominently displayed in the hall leading to the main gallery.

During the course of the Nexus exhibition's tour, another significant exhibition of Karl's work opened at the Tech Museum of Innovation in San Jose in California. Situated in Silicon Valley, the heart of digital transformation in the United States, the term refers to the large number of silicon chip innovators and manufacturers in the region. The area is now home to many of the world's largest high tech corporations, including the headquarters of thirty-nine businesses in the Fortune 1000 and thousands of startup companies. The Tech Museum of Innovation is dedicated to celebrating and promoting new ways of thinking in a dynamic world of technocratic digital achievement. Karl's architectonic vision was embraced by the museum as complementary to the high tech, innovative spirit of the museum. Karl produced three new paintings for this collection, each exemplifying the high tech aesthetic of the museum and its alignment with Silicon Valley. His large bronze "Metropolis" sculpture was displayed at the entrance of the museum. Meredith Taylor, director of the museum, interpreted this work as symbolizing "unity and community."[13]

Then, at the advanced age of eighty-four years, when most artists have hung up their palettes and packed away their paintbrushes, Karl was invited to participate in the West Palm Beach International Art Fair in January 2018. Paul Fisher, a celebrity art promoter based in Florida had become aware of Karl and his work and had selected him for an exclusive retrospective showing at the fair. The fair opened for five days, and Karl was honored to attain the highest sales record of all the exhibitors at the fair. Significantly, he donated all proceeds from the sale of his work to his Tree of Utah Momen Foundation in preparation for the construction of a museum and interpretive center at the site of the *Tree of Utah.*

Metropolis, 1990

Chapter 39

AN HONORARY RETROSPECTIVE EXHIBITION AND THE EFFECTS OF A DEADLY DISEASE

In his childhood, Karl had heard it said that "diseases don't knock on the door—they just come in!" Karl's mother was convinced that a disease would strike when least expected. It did not matter how healthily one lived or one's station in life. Karl's father was a fatalist and not much concerned with his health. He lived to be 104 years of age without ever having had an illness that Karl could remember. Karl did not recollect him even coming down with a cold. He was always active and a hard worker. Two days before he died, he said that he wasn't feeling well, and the doctor wrote him a prescription. The old man instructed Karl's bother not to buy the medicine since it would be of no use. That evening he did not eat, and at midnight, he asked Karl's mother to send for Karl's brothers and sisters.

Karl's father talked to Karl's brothers and sisters for about an hour, prayed, and passed away peacefully. In his prayer he gave thanks to the Lord and to those around him. Karl was in Stuttgart at the time and received news of his father's passing in a letter from his brother two weeks later. Karl's mother lived to ninety-seven years of age without any serious illnesses, but in the last two years of her life, she had become senile.

In April 1943, during the Russian occupation of their hometown, there was a typhoid epidemic. A rumor went around that the typhoid outbreak had started in the refugee camps outside their city where some of the survivors of German concentration camps in Eastern Europe were temporarily housed. It was here that the former prisoners received their first medical attention before they were transported to India and then on to the United States and Canada. Karl and his three-year-old sister were the first to contract the disease, and then Mahmud, his eighteen-year-old brother, caught it. Karl's older brother Mohammad nursed them both over the critical stages of the disease. He was twenty-three years old at the time and the best-educated member of their family. He worked as the youngest deputy director of the province's finance department. Mohammad stood six feet two inches tall and had the good looks of a film star. He was also the best-dressed young man in the city. People often spoke of his kindness and genteel attitude toward everybody he met. He nursed Karl and his sister at their bedside and ensured that they received the best care available. It was during the worst period of World War II when medicines were scarce and there were food shortages. An effective antibiotic for typhoid had not been invented yet. Karl's sister and brother recovered, but then Mohammad contracted the dreadful disease and died after a two-week illness. Not only family and friends, but also all the local people in their part of the city mourned his death. Close to a thousand people were at his funeral, many of whom had not known him personally but knew him by his reputation. Karl's mother was totally distraught at his death. She screamed and tore out her hair at his deathbed. With tragic pleading, she plaintively wailed, "Why did you take away my flower?"

Karl did not understand his mother's anguish at the time, but when he saw again photographs of this handsome young man who had been cut down in the prime of his life, he could understand her grief. Mohammad was the nicest person Karl had ever known in his young life. He was always patient and treated Karl to ice cream and pastries on outings in Mashhad. He even saw to it that Karl was dressed well. At that time, Karl did not know what loving somebody meant, but he knew that this brother was his favorite person, and he missed him long after he was gone. Karl left his parental home in Mashhad when he was nineteen years old.

With the advantage of long-lived parents and with what he regarded as the great mercy of Providence, Karl had been blessed with relatively good health for seventy-five years of his life, except for the occasional checkups for neck and back pain caused by bending over his drawing table and standing in front of his easel for long hours at a time. He believed he had been helped by the fact that he had enjoyed swimming since he was nine years old. By the time he turned eighteen years of age, he was awarded a silver medal in the national one-hundred-meter freestyle event.

In 1952, the National Iranian Olympic Team decided to add swimming to their program. Mr. Bambaychi was the swimming team's coach and the sports teacher for all the boys' high schools in Mashhad. In May of that year, the head of the Iranian swimming team came to Mashhad to supervise the selection and qualification of contestants for the Iranian swimming team for the next Olympic games in Helsinki. Unfortunately, Karl was a few seconds too slow to qualify for the one-hundred-meter freestyle event. He considered this the worst defeat of his life. He continued with swimming throughout his life, doing between four and six thousand meters a week, with the exception of those times when he was traveling and access to a pool was limited. For the previous thirty years, he had spent spring and summer in Stockholm and the winters in California. After he sold his house in Sausalito, and later his condominium in Washington, D.C., he rented a suite at the Embassy Suites in San Rafael in California. In 2009 he purchased a townhouse in West Palm Beach, Florida.

Karl had been taking his vacations every year or two in Hawaii for the previous thirty years. He took these vacations as a health cure, and he would spend his time walking on the beach, swimming in the ocean, and reading the latest chart-topping best sellers. He usually spent his time at the Hawaiian Hilton Village at the end of Waikiki Beach, which was not as crowded as the other hotels in the area.

His regular daily vacation program began with breakfast and the newspaper. From 10:00 a.m. to noon, he would go for a walk on the beach while listening to classical music with his favorite radio host. At noon he would typically have a chicken salad at the Outrigger Beach Bar. After lunch, he would read a book in the shade of his favorite palm tree, far from the pool and bar. At exactly 2:00 p.m., he would plunge into the ocean for an hour of swimming and then go back to his room for a shower. He would watch the news on TV and catch an episode of *The Simpsons* with Bart Simpson, who Karl considered to be the most revolting character of all time! The evenings would find him on the street between the Ala Moana Mall and Diamond Head, eating dinner usually at a buffet restaurant. Back at the hotel he would watch the news and perhaps a movie on TV before retiring with a book. Although this routine might appear boring to most, Karl found it rejuvenating. After each trip he was ready to work uninterruptedly for months on end and was able to endure the busy travel schedule of his exhibition program.

Over the previous thirty years, he had often enjoyed the company of relatives, friends, and colleagues on these vacations. They would arrange their vacation dates to coincide with his and meet on the island. During their stay in Hawaii, he would adapt himself to their schedule. He found it pleasant to stroll and sightsee with them. They would have dinner at some of the best restaurants. Waikiki's Hays Grill was one such restaurant. For the previous twenty years, he had never eaten dinner on his own in a restaurant. Lunch was a different matter. It was his experience that most hotel guests who were on their own would have a book or newspaper as company and eat their menu items as nutritional supplements, not giving much attention to taste. They were either reading or looking at business papers and talking on their cell phones, usually in restaurants that had never made it to the top rankings.

It was March 2008, and, as was his habit, Karl traveled to Hawaii and checked in at the Hilton as usual. The first week was occupied with his normal routine, but he had invited his niece Marjan, an art therapist and artist who was working in Maui, to spend the weekend with him. She was one of his best friends and his trusted confidant. She was beautiful and always upbeat. Karl had reserved an upgraded suite for her at his hotel. After his regular swim and shower, he went to the lobby to await Marjan's arrival. Upon meeting her, he helped her check in, and they had a drink, followed by dinner. The two had a lot to talk about and enjoyed observing people in their immediate vicinity.

As a pleasant diversion, Karl accompanied Marjan on her shopping excursion to the various fashion stores the following morning. She also showed him her sketches and the photos of her latest painting. In the afternoon, he had his swim and joined Marjan for dinner again. To his surprise, he felt tired after dinner. After excusing himself, he retired early to his room. He awoke at about 2:00 a.m. feeling cold. In fact, he was shivering and shaking uncontrollably. He had a habit of turning off the air conditioning before going to bed. When he looked at the thermostat and saw that it read seventy-five degrees Fahrenheit, he thought it must be wrong. He put extra blankets on the bed. After an hour of shivering uncontrollably under this pile of blankets, he fell asleep. Some hours later, he awoke totally saturated with perspiration. The bed sheet, comforter, and pillow were all soaked. He called room service to change his bedding, and he eventually managed to fall asleep again.

The next morning everything was back to normal, as if nothing had happened during the night, and Karl joined Marjan for brunch. Later they took a catamaran ride and went on a walk along the beach. That afternoon he had his usual swim and enjoyed a good dinner. On Sunday afternoon, he took leave of Marjan and she returned to Maui. Karl had all but forgotten the terrible night he'd had, but a few days later, on the night before his return to San Francisco, the same terrible night sweat returned, and he had to have his bedding changed again. A week after his return to the Embassy Suites, he had another of these episodes. The following morning he called a physician he knew and was able to make an appointment for later the same day. After a thorough examination and blood test, the physician concluded that there was nothing wrong with Karl and that he was just suffering from jet lag. Later that summer, back in Stockholm, Karl experienced the same distressing symptoms. His regular house doctor examined him and conducted more tests. Again, the diagnosis came back that there was nothing wrong. However, these terrible episodes reoccurred a few more times before Christmas of that year and again in February of the following year in San Francisco. Again, doctors examined Karl, and again, they could find nothing wrong. He had recurring attacks in April in Florida and in May in the Middle East. On each occasion, the hotel's room service was called to change the bedding in his room.

Karl traveled to Florida in mid-March and returned to Stockholm in mid-May. He spent two weeks in Tehran before flying back to Sweden on June 11. Throughout this period he continued to work, swim, and travel. The attacks continued, but he began to accept them as part of his life. However, in June 2009, after he had been back in Stockholm for two weeks, the fever attacks increased in frequency to every second night. It was mid-summer holidays and his doctor was away, so on July 11, he went to the City Acute Emergency room. When he asked if he should have a blood test or an x-ray, the doctor said that Karl had bronchitis and he prescribed an antibiotic. After ten days there had been no change to his nightly fever attacks. He returned to the emergency room, and another doctor said that he had developed asthma. The new doctor said that he was certain of this and that no blood test was necessary. When Karl went to have the prescription filled, the pharmacist said that he thought he should get a second opinion about his diagnosis before taking the asthma medicine. During those three weeks, Karl lost twenty-eight pounds.

Eventually he contacted Dr. Ingrid Berg, the head nurse in the Grevture Lakar Mottagning Hospital, who had been a friend of his for over forty years. She called Dr. Lagerkrantze from his vacation and sent Karl to a lab for a blood test. The results came back the next day—negative. But he still had a temperature of over one hundred degrees! Dr. Lagerkrantz spent over an hour on the phone with the emergency room at Karolinska Institute Hospital and then had Karl admitted.

In the Karolinska ER, the doctors took a battery of tests and x-rays. Karl was placed on a drip, because his body had insufficient immune defenses. The next morning it was heart angiography and lung x-rays. By the afternoon, they had determined that he had a tumor on his kidney. He was moved to the urology and kidney department of the hospital. The biopsy results came back three days later, and Karl was grateful that it was not cancerous. He was under constant watch twenty-four hours a day. By the fifth day in the urology department, the doctors were sure that it was the kidney that was at fault and that the tumor was not cancerous. But they had also discovered some unexplained dots in his lungs. He was tested for tuberculosis and the results came back two days later—also negative. Then it was decided that he should be examined under their nuclear isotope diagnostic machine, which they referred to as "PET." After these tests, the head of the urology department came to see Karl. She was a most reassuring woman and a great comfort to Karl during these dark days.

CHAPTER 39

"We know what is wrong with you. We are sending you to our hematology department. Dr. Per Bernell, the head of that department, will explain everything to you."

Karl was moved to a single room in the hematology department. He knew that single rooms were reserved for the more chronic cases. The head of the department explained to Karl that they were first going to give him an intravenous drug to boost his immune defenses. He was also told that Dr. Bernell would visit him the following day to explain his condition to him. The next morning at about ten o'clock, a tall gentleman with gray hair entered the room, accompanied by four other doctors, the head nurse, and another nurse. Dr. Bernell was handed a clipboard with a diagram on it. He sat at the end of Karl's bed and asked how he was doing. Straining to reply, Karl said, "I am still alive."

Bernell smiled and said, "It looks to me that this is the first time you have been seriously ill. And I also know that you are the architect who designed our pathology building." Then the doctor explained that Karl had been diagnosed with "highly malignant lymphoma." It was curable but would take time and would depend on the patient's physical condition. Karl hastily told the assembled group, "I was in the best physical condition until three weeks ago. I have been swimming all my life and doing four thousand meters a week—all until I was admitted to hospital!" The group laughed.

"I am glad for that, but you are going to be here for a while. We are sure that you are going to come through this," reassured Dr. Bernell.

After the group left his room, Karl called his friend Dr. Djavidi on his cell phone and told him that he had been examined by PET and that the diagnose was highly malignant lymphoma. Dr. Djavidi said that he would look up this disease since it was relatively new. He had retired ten years previously and was not familiar with all the latest developments. Karl was placed on a drip with new intravenous drugs for two days. When he asked the doctor "What is highly malignant lymphoma?" She replied,

"It is difficult to explain, but PET has discovered a lymphoma composite in your lungs and belly. We're going to get rid of it. You have a strong psyche and body, and this is going to help you."

Karl spent forty-four days in the hospital and another four months at home recuperating with home care. Throughout this time, he received chemotherapy. Over the period of his illness he had over four hundred punctures from syringes and drips to his arm and leg veins. He also lost his hair and nails. However, after this ordeal, Karl recovered, and he was grateful that he had come through this terrible disease and its torturous treatment.

Prior to his admission to the hospital in Sweden, he had spent three months in the US arranging the customs clearing and shipping of his paintings from his studios in San Francisco and West Palm Beach for his biggest show yet at the Royal Academy of Arts in Stockholm.

It had been just five days after his return to Sweden that he was forced to seek medical attention at the City Acute Emergency Room. It was also here that he was eventually admitted to the Karolinksa Hospital at the insistence of Dr. Lagerkrantz. It was also here that he witnessed firsthand the professional efficiency and kindness that the doctors treated their patients with. Every morning, the head of the department and all the doctors had a closed-door conference to discuss the progress of each of their patients over the past twenty-four hours. The hospital staff constantly checked on the progress of each of their patients, both night and day.

While lying in bed in his hospital room, nurse visits were frequent and constant, and this care continued when he was receiving treatment and recuperating at his home. He received daily visits to check on his progress and administer his medications throughout his recovery. The hospital staff was so attentive that he found himself wondering if these doctors and nurses had any private lives!

Karl's cousin, a urology surgeon in Bethesda Maryland, called him every Saturday during his ten-month recovery to find out how he was doing. After his illness had been cured, his cousin informed him that the Karolinska Institute Hospital was one of the ten best hospitals in the world and was tops in diagnostics. He told Karl that if he were to have had the same medical treatment in the United States, it would have cost him approximately two-and-a-half million US dollars. Karl had no health insurance in the US, despite the fact that he was an American citizen. He mused, "It is no accident that Swedish and other Scandinavian health care services are among the best in the world, even though every Swede complains!"

To his regret, he realized that he too had complained in the past, but now he knew that he had escaped the claws of a deadly disease, and he felt blessed to have received the finest medical attention he could possibly have hoped for.

It was during this critical period of Karl's life while he was being treated at the Karolinska hospital for his serious illness that the retrospective exhibition of his work opened at the Swedish Royal Academy of Art in Stockholm. The exhibition comprised sixty-eight paintings and twelve sculptures. Herman du Toit, curator of Karl's 1995 exhibition at the Brigham Young University Museum of Art, opened the exhibition. Karl had great respect for Olle Granath, the Permanent Secretary of the Royal Academy of Fine Arts, the director of the Academy at the time. Karl felt humbled by the great honor to have a retrospective exhibition of his work at this prestigious venue. Granath spoke at the opening and praised Karl for his work and the tenacity with which he had remained true to his artistic vision throughout his long career.

Karl had come to know Granath late in his life, but their friendship grew quickly. Karl valued the wealth of experience that Granath had accumulated over his lifetime. Karl respected his advice, and they often had long discussions over lunch about his art and its place in contemporary art. The exhibition was well received and attended. The bright and definitive geometric compositions resonated in the Academy's modernist all-white galleries.

Several years later, after Granath had retired from active service at the Royal Academy, he invited Karl to participate in a special group exhibition at the Villa San Michele on the Isle of Capri. Granath continued to administer in the cultural program at the Villa. The Villa was donated to the Swedish state by Axel Munthe in 1948 to promote Sweden's cultural links with Italy and to provide a home for visiting Swedish artists, scientists, composers, authors, journalists, and university students with an interest in Italian and classical culture and humanistic research. Karl felt deeply honored by this invitation and was glad to participate.

Dream Island Suite: Winter, 2008

Chapter 40

A ONE-MAN ARMY WITH LIFELONG FRIENDSHIPS

Even before Karl turned thirteen years of age he enjoyed the freedom of choosing his high school, and although he lived in his parental home, he was financially independent as a result of his income from his painting. He was free to buy his own clothing and went to the movies as often as he liked. Like any other teenager, he lived at home and had lunch and dinner with his family, but he also had his own small studio at home. He never asked his father for pocket money or needed his parents' approval for his expenditures. He also never told them how much money he was earning from the sale of his portraits and from painting movie billboards for the theaters.

Karl never kept a record of his daily expenses or a diary of his comings and goings like his cousins did. He dealt with bazaar merchants, wealthy citizens, and imams as he painted their portraits and religious commissions. He negotiated with the movie owner who commissioned him to paint ten-foot-high billboards for his theaters. These people all respected Karl and treated him no differently from their other clients and customers. His work was no better and no worse than many of the other artists they bought from. Rather, he had a different touch that the others could not offer, thanks to his broader exposure to the Russian avant-garde styles through his association with Edris, or "Popov" as he was known.

He attended numerous public gatherings, religious ceremonies, and political meetings. He even assisted the shops in selling his paintings. As a youth he spent his free time playing billiards and chess at the Vox Soviet Cultural Center with his cousins and school friends. He did what most teenagers did in his neighborhood at that time. However, he had become independent and made all his own decisions about his education, work, and lifestyle without anyone's assistance. His father had total confidence in him. When his father was Karl's age, he was already helping his father run his Persian shawl workshop.

Karl's unfortunate life-long trust in sealing a deal with a simple handshake had cost him both financially and emotionally. In his entire life he had only needed the help of lawyers on two occasions: Once when a person he trusted had agreed with a handshake to take care of his bills while he was traveling in other countries. They had not signed an agreement, and the man betrayed his trust. The second time was when Karl trusted a ReMax Real Estate broker's lawyer in Santa Rosa to draft a promissory note that was not honored by a prospective buyer of his house. The broker's lawyer had omitted the most important paragraph that should have said that the deal would be canceled if the note was not paid. The buyer had bad credit and soon declared bankruptcy. Karl lost the entire down payment of several hundred thousand dollars that was supposed to have been paid back to him. However, this did not stop the broker and the ReMax lawyer from receiving their commissions and fees! Unfortunately for Karl, he had on several occasions trusted his opponent's lawyers. If he had been younger, he would certainly have consulted an advisor before trusting such unscrupulous people.

Karl was only employed for four consecutive years from 1961 to 1965. After that comparatively short period, he ran his own architect's office. He was self-employed, working as an architect and also as an artist. He had never been a member of any artist's community or a member of any board. He had never given exclusive rights for the sale of his work to any agent or gallery. In other words, he had been a lone wolf in the jungle of the art world.

Karl had always made all the decisions with regard to his projects himself, without having to consult with anyone—with all the risks and consequences that come with this often dangerous territory. He always dealt single-handedly with museums, arts councils, galleries, publishers, insurance agents, transport companies, and his finances. He worked hard, putting in lots of time and traveling many thousands of miles to convene with governors, ministers, ambassadors, mayors, museum and opera directors, and heads of governmental agencies. He received sponsorships and grants from such corporations and foundations as the Barbro Osher Pro Suecia Foundation and the National Endowment for the Arts for his exhibitions and catalogs. Karl had a long established friendship with Barbro Osher, and he valued her patronage of his exhibitions. Some of his travels and the transportation of his artworks were sponsored by Lufthansa and American Airlines. He had the publication of his *Homage to Shakespeare and Wagner* book and his serigraphs and posters of Wagner's Ring Cycle for the San Francisco Opera funded by American Airlines and Livia Insurance Company. These sponsorships were made possible through his own personal efforts since he never employed an agent or representative.

Working independently had its rewards and its drawbacks. It was labor intensive and time consuming, but he always had prompt results. People either accepted his proposals or declined them. He prided himself in the way he always represented himself in a proper and honest manner. On the occasion of his retrospective exhibition at the Royal Academy in Stockholm, Olle Granath, the general director of Swedish Museums was asked,

"Who arranged this show for Karl Momen?" His reply was, "Karl Momen arranges Karl Momen's shows—he is a one-man army!"

In the end, Karl Momen succeeded by doing everything his own way, the defining trait that characterized his career.

Although Karl worked independently and made his own decisions—for better or worse—throughout his life, he developed life-long friendships with a few select individuals. He remained a confirmed bachelor throughout his life and was financially independent, but his friendships sustained him through some of the most difficult challenges of his life. He often turned to these friends for advice and support as his career evolved. Carl Gustav Yrwing, a Stockholm art dealer who maintained a villa in Italy became a dear friend of Karl. Over the years he was instrumental in placing many of Karl's works in private and corporate collections. He came to Karl's aid during Karl's retrospective exhibition at the Royal Academy when he was hospitalized for his disease. Yrwing also introduced Karl to the Swedish publisher Christer Wallin of Walin & Dahlhom and helped Karl with his participation in his San Michele show on Capri.

Perhaps Karl's most important long-term friendship was with Inga-Lill Ståhl, the former financial director of ABBA, the Swedish music group. Ståhl had been a personal friend that he could confide in over the years. Karl had known her for over fifty years, and she had often provided advice and moral support when he needed it most.

The most significant financial sponsorships Karl received were from his Swedish friend Barbro Osher of the Barbro Osher Pro Suecia Foundation in San Francisco. She was introduced to him by his neighbor in Stockholm.

ARCHITECTURAL RENDERING OF PROPOSED VISITOR CENTER BY XR3D STUDIOS

Chapter 41

THE TREE OF UTAH VISITOR CENTER

After the thirtieth anniversary of the *Tree of Utah* passed without notice, it became painfully obvious to Karl that the state of Utah and its arts agencies had no idea of the true value of the sculpture, of its poignant spiritual message, or of its place in the international art world. No attempts had been made since its dedication to apprise locals of its significance in the absence of visitor access from the adjacent highway. Consequently, state officials turned a blind eye to its existence and were content to allow the structure to fade in people's memories, notwithstanding the fact that Google reported that in 2017 more photographs of the *Tree* were uploaded than of any other artwork in the United States and that articles about the *Tree* frequently appeared in overseas art and architecture periodicals.

The *Tree* intrigues millions of motorists annually as they pass the sculpture on their road trips from Salt Lake City to Wendover and points further west, and for motorists traveling from California to Utah ski resorts. It was not unusual to see chartered buses with parties of Asian tourists on the highway adjacent to the *Tree*. They came especially to view this remarkable Utah landmark although there was no access to the structure and no interpretive material provided by the state's arts agencies.

In response to the inability of the state apparatus to rectify this situation, Karl decided that he would establish a museum and interpretive center at the site of the *Tree* that would afford visitors the opportunity to learn more about it, its symbolism, and what inspired it. Visitors could also learn about its unique construction and the Bauhaus and other avant-garde art movements that inspired it, along with the ecology of the Bonneville Salt Flats on which it is located. Karl immediately went to work and drew up

CHAPTER 41

the plans for a striking but modest facility that would be situated adjacent to the *Tree*. This new museum would exemplify the Bauhaus style as a compliment to the *Tree*. The museum would feature an enclosed, air-conditioned observation deck where visitors could have an uninterrupted view of the vast expanse of the Bonneville Salt Flats. It would be self-sufficient, utilizing an array of concealed solar panels on its roof for electric power. Visitor rest-stop facilities would also be provided since it would be the first significant view area that motorists would encounter along this long and featureless highway when traveling from points west to Salt Lake City.

Karl consulted with Herman du Toit, curator, biographer, and Karl's long-time friend, and it was agreed that in the absence of state support they would register a nonprofit foundation to raise funds to finance the construction of a museum and interpretive center at the site of the *Tree*. Funds would also have to be raised for the necessary road works to allow motorists access to the facility. Although Carlos Braceras, the director of Utah's Department of Transport, was supportive of the project, no state funds would be allocated for the road works, and all costs related to the building of off ramps and a pedestrian bridge would have to be raised by Karl.

Consequently, the Tree of Utah Momen Foundation Inc. was registered with the State of Utah Department of Commerce on December 9, 2016, through the law offices of Lewis and Hansen, with Karl as president and Du Toit as executive director. According to the Foundation's Articles of Incorporation, the purpose of the Foundation is to support the maintenance and preservation of the *Tree of Utah*, owned by the state of Utah, and to fund and maintain the construction of a museum and interpretive center at the site as an educational resource for the people of Utah about the history, ecology, and the future of the Great Salt Lake, and to provide information about the architectural history of the *Tree* and the Constructivist and Bauhaus movements that inform it. Information will also be provided about the unique techniques that were used in its construction.

Du Toit arranged a special meeting at the state capitol for Karl with representatives of the governor's office on January 18, 2017, to apprise state officials of this development and to seek permission to proceed with fundraising for the construction of the museum through the newly established nonprofit foundation. The meeting was held in the governor's boardroom under the chairmanship of Michael Mower, the deputy chief of staff to Governor Gary Herbert. In addition to Karl and Du Toit, also in attendance were Jill Remington Love, director of the Department of Heritage and Arts of Utah and her deputy Brian Somers. Eric Tholen, director of the state's Department of Administrative Services arrived late to the meeting due to a prior commitment.

After a brief presentation by Du Toit, recapping recent developments regarding the establishment of the Foundation, all agreed that the Foundation would proceed with fundraising activities on behalf of the project, and Michael Mower confirmed that the state would have no objection to the building of a museum and interpretive center at the site of the *Tree of Utah*. However, the state would not participate financially in this project. He reported that Carlos Braceras, director of Utah's Department of Transportation, had communicated that the cost of the road works at the site would require an input of approximately two million dollars to that department.

Both Karl and Du Toit were pleased with having crossed this important bureaucratic hurdle. Du Toit informed all present at the meeting that the *Tree* was of significant unrealized educational value and that it had the potential to provide visitors to the state, Utah residents, and the statewide K–12 school community an opportunity to learn not only about the *Tree*'s construction but also about geometric abstraction and the important architectural styles that have defined modern architecture during the twentieth and twenty-first centuries, including the influence of the Bauhaus, Le Corbusier's International Style, and Constructivism—all of which informed the design and construction of the *Tree of Utah*. It would also house displays and interpretive media concerning the history and future of the Great Salt Lake and the Bonneville Salt Flats. The visitor center would provide an income stream for its maintenance from the sale of souvenirs and vending machine refreshments as a rest stop for the millions of motorists that drive by this remote location on the Interstate 80 highway every year. Tooele County would also benefit from its share of the sales tax on the visitor center's sales.

The visitor center would give visitors an opportunity to learn about the remarkable prestressed concrete casting techniques that were used in its construction, including the twenty-four enormous underground concrete piles that were driven ninety feet into the desert to support the sculpture and its gigantic concrete spheres—the largest ever constructed by this method at the time. Du Toit arranged for Karl to meet with various heads of the state's arts and museums agencies and other interested parties to inform them of these developments. After a week of such meetings, Karl flew back to Palm Beach, Florida, and Du Toit started work on a comprehensive biography of Karl that would capture and reflect the career and life experiences of this unique and multifaceted artist and his work.

Chapter 42

A BELATED TRIBUTE

After its dedication and donation to the state of Utah, Karl Momen expected that the *Tree of Utah* would garner some interest from locals and particularly from those concerned with aesthetic interventions in the barren parts of this arid region. However, apart from a few local news reports and some voices raised in consternation at the audacity of Karl Momen for adding such an inscrutable and unexpected embellishment in this desolate location, the state apparatus and its arts organizations were conspicuously silent. The silence lasted over thirty years.

It was not until Herman du Toit, the curator of Karl's exhibition at the Brigham Young University Museum of Art in the summer of 1995, and more recently the executive director of the Tree of Utah Momen Foundation, approached state officials with regard to the building of a visitor and interpretive center at the site of the *Tree* that awareness was aroused. People in authority began to realize the magnitude and character of Karl's magnanimous artistic contribution to the state three decades previously. Karl had secured pledges of sponsorship for the construction of a visitor and interpretive center at the site of the *Tree*, predicated upon the construction of road access to the *Tree* from the adjacent Interstate 80 highway. The proposed visitor center would contain exhibits and displays of video and graphic interpretive material to inform visitors of the aesthetic history and cultural value of the *Tree* as a unique manifestation of Constructivist/Bauhaus architecture and of its function as an emblem of human aspiration in this remote location.

The center would also inform visitors about the history, ecology, and future of the Great Salt Lake and the Bonneville Salt Flats that were in close proximity to the *Tree*. Karl had previously drawn up architectural plans for the proposed visitor center, but his proposal had fallen on deaf ears at the Department of Construction and Facilities Management (DCFM). This department had been assigned stewardship over the *Tree* by the state. However, the *Tree* fell outside the professional purview and expertise of this department that was charged primarily with the construction and maintenance of state buildings. The DFCM had never before been given curatorial custodianship of a public sculpture. This would normally have been the responsibility of the state's arts and museum agencies. However, these agencies had turned a blind eye to the *Tree*. However, they can be forgiven for abrogating their responsibility for providing interpretive information and curatorial care of such a significant acquisition in the state's public art collection. Much of their inaction could be attributed to the lack of public access to the *Tree*. It would be irresponsible to direct tourists to the *Tree* if there was no way to visit the site or even stop along the adjacent federal highway to view the *Tree* since this would constitute a traffic violation. Attempting to access the *Tree* with off-road vehicles across the desert would be equally hazardous due to the marshy terrain at certain times of the year.

With state approval, Karl had established the Tree of Utah Momen Foundation in 2017 as a charitable non-profit foundation. The foundation's express purpose was to raise funds for the construction of the proposed visitor center at the site of the *Tree*. Karl had received pledges of support and sponsorships to cover the cost of construction of the visitor center. All his donors required was road access to the site and approval of a building permit.

Early in 2019, Herman du Toit took it upon himself as executive director of the foundation to visit with state and parastatal officials in order to gain perspective on the issue and to garner support for the project. His first meeting was with Paul Monson, the president of the Utah Chapter of the Institute of Classical Art and Architecture. Monson was an architect who appreciated the aesthetic and architectural value of the *Tree* and was intrigued with the prospect of the visitor center, but his organization could do little to help. He referred Du Toit to Kirk Huffacre, the executive director of Preserve Utah (the former Utah Heritage Foundation). Huffacre was equally enthused by the idea of the visitor center and was surprised that no recognition had been given to Karl over the years for his magnanimous creation and donation of such a valuable architectural and aesthetic resource to the state. He said he would support and promote the project within his organization's sphere of influence wherever he could. He recommended that Du Toit also visit with Crystal Young-Otterstrom, the executive director of the Utah Cultural Alliance. Du Toit found Young-Otterstrom enthusiastic and extremely supportive of the visitor center project. She expressed her willingness to advocate for the visitor center with the state legislature. At this point, Du Toit realized that he would have to get the state legislature involved with the project in the event of an appropriation bill having to be approved for the funding of the roadworks at the site.

Du Toit next met with the Shawn Milne, the Tooele County commissioner. The *Tree of Utah* was situated in Tooele County, and he would need to ensure that Milne was apprised of any construction plans in his area of jurisdiction and gain his approval. Du Toit then met with his local House Representative Norman Thurston, who was most impressed with the plans for a visitor center but was even more concerned with the fact that Karl had never been recognized for the contribution he had made to the state. He suggested that Du Toit visit with Rep. Merrill Nelson, the house of representatives member for Tooele County, with a view to having Karl awarded an honorary citation on the floor of the House during the forthcoming legislative session. Du Toit found Rep. Nelson to be enthused with the idea of a visitor center at the site of the *Tree.* Rep. Nelson was also surprised that no note had been taken of Karl's contributions by the state government. He suggested that the interpretive displays at the center include an overview of the history, ecology, and future of the Great Salt Lake and the nearby Bonneville Salt Flats. Du Toit and Karl had already discussed this as a desirable function of the center, and Du Toit agreed to ensure that these interpretive displays became part of the attraction of the visitor center.

Rep. Nelson arranged for the award of an honorary citation to Karl as a long overdue accolade that he was happy to sponsor in the House of Representatives. He also commended Du Toit for bringing this matter to the attention of the House. So after more than three decades, Utah Government had eventually been alerted to the magnanimous role that Karl and the *Tree of Utah* had played in raising awareness of the state of Utah overseas and of the value and cultural legacy of the *Tree* for the state.

On February 7, 2019, Karl was invited to appear on the floor of the House of Representatives in person, and the honorary citation was read and awarded before the full House by Representative Nelson.

Utah House of Representatives

Official Citation honoring

Karl Momen

In recognition of his unique artistic contribution to the state of Utah, the Utah House of Representatives commends Karl Momen.

Mr. Momen's creation, Metaphor: The Tree of Utah, an 87-foot sculpture stands as a monument beside Interstate-80 at mile marker 27 in Tooele County. It was during a cross-country road trip in 2003 that Mr. Momen was struck by the beauty of the Bonneville Salt Flats and was inspired by the arid splendor of the area. Karl there envisioned a sculpture that would symbolize "the God above the universe" in Shiller's Ode to Joy, which is inscribed on a plaque at the base of the sculpture. Momen's Tree of Life rises as a tree blossoming in the desert, rising heavenward from its barren surroundings. After working several years on the sculpture and self-financing the project, Mr. Momen generously donated his work to the State of Utah. It has since become an internationally recognized expression of modernist architecture in the Bauhaus tradition and as an iconic symbol of the State of Utah for many in Europe and the Far East.

Mr. Momen continues his generosity to the State of Utah as he is poised to invest $2.5 million of out-of-state donated funds in the Tree of Utah Momen Foundation to construct a visitor center at the Tree of Utah site. This facility will service the over 2.2 million travelers who travel past the sculpture each year, providing the opportunity to learn about the profound spiritual and aesthetic significance of the Tree of Utah as well as the history, ecology, and future of the Bonneville Salt Flats area that houses the art.

For Mr. Momen's personal, financial, and artistic contributions to enhance our great state of Utah, we honor him today, February 7, 2019 with this citation.

Speaker Brad Wilson

Representative Merrill Nelson

HOUSE OF REPRESENTATIVES · STATE OF UTAH

Chapter 43

THE LONELY PATH

Tell me, Muse, the story of that resourceful man who was driven to wander far and wide after he had sacked the holy citadel of Troy. He saw the cities of many people and he learned their ways. He suffered great anguish on the high seas in his struggles to preserve his life and bring comrades home. But he failed to save those comrades, in spite of all his efforts. It was their own transgression that brought them to their doom, for in their folly they devoured the oxen of the Sun-god, and he saw to it that they would never return. Tell us this story, goddess daughter of Zeus, beginning at whatever point you will.[14]

So begins the tragic tale of Odysseus, the ancient hero, who was struck with misfortune and spent twenty years trying to make it back to Ithaca, his homeland. Like the hero of Homer's *Odyssey,* Karl would also eventually return to the origin of his travels—not the geographical location of his homeland, Iran, but rather the metaphysical locus of his artistic talent. Little did the ambitious art student at the Kunst Academy in Stuttgart realize that it would be the stories, myths, and folklore he had heard at his father's knee that would eventually become the fountainhead of his artistic talent; that the world of dramatic narrative and mythological symbolism would underpin his artistic odyssey and later inform the iconography of his most notable artworks.

Karl would eventually recognize the one unique source of inspiration that had remained a sustaining influence in his life throughout all the years of his journeying—just as Odysseus had been sustained through his perilous travels by his love of Penelope. Karl's love of music, drama, and the theater had schooled him in the very fabric of human experience—a powerful

CHAPTER 43

and fecund counterpoint that would serve to enliven and animate the otherwise passionless geometric abstractions of his modernist aesthetic. Consequently, his artwork rises above the soullessness of pure formalism. In spite of its abstraction, his art engages us through its significant form and also through the constant tension that is evoked between the cool rationally conceived compositions and the dynamic colors and textures that enliven familiar shapes with the passion of a warm and humane spirit. Karl is ever cognizant of the viewers of his artworks as sentient beings. Through his unyielding passion he was able to motivate his deliberately conceived and carefully considered compositions. It was through his abiding love of the theater and of fine music that he would eventually discover the sounding board of his artistic vision. According to James Mason, former dean of the College of Fine and Performing Arts at Brigham Young University:

"Momen is the artist/painter as actor. Within the self-imposed rigor and internal order of his indefatigable style, there is an inherent and persuasive intonation that rises first to gesture and then becomes at once interpretation and confession. The dynamic compositional elements of his paintings ebb and flow as their changing relationships reflect the timeless flux and transformative power of Shakespeare's masterful characterization of the human condition."[15]

In his Homage to William Shakespeare and Richard Wagner Suites, Karl was able to synthesize his passion for operatic and dramatic literature with his love for the musical equivalent of these forms, which he found in the emotional fervor of Wagner's musical dramas. This alignment went beyond a congruence of subject matter. In the same publication, musicologist James Mason made a similar observation:

"Wagner held his works together with recurring concise themes or 'leitmotifs' that were varied and developed throughout his music. Momen uses geometric elements such as spheres, cubes, and cones in a similar way for their symbolic and unifying value."[16]

Karl had not only discovered a new iconography of formal elements, but he had also discovered what he needed to say. His was a language of passion, touched by an ancient reverence for the world of mysticism that transformed stolid forms into universal signifiers of the human condition.

This artwork is also devotional. The indomitable spirit that motivated and gave strength to Karl during his darkest hours is infectious. One cannot help but be touched by the subtle gradations of color that rise to vibrant hues and luxurious textures as they celebrate the essential nature of a dynamic and vibrant universe, a greater reality of which his work affirms that we are all a part of.

Although not an adherent of Islam, Karl had grown up in Mashhad, Iran, a city known as "The Holy City" in the midst of devout Muslim believers. His family did not participate in religious observances, and, consequently, he had been allowed to form his own religious views. Although seminal religious doctrines had found acceptance in his life, he had become intimately acquainted with the powerful institutional role religion played in society. His distrust of formal religion was coupled with his skepticism of Middle Eastern politics. He came to see the state as an overbearing and fickle force that had a life of its own, capable of robbing individuals of their agency and destroying their essential creativity, as in Galileo's case. He regarded the world of technology as closely associated with the institutional hegemony of formal religion and state government. It often acted as the handmaiden of the state's most dehumanizing interdiction of its citizens. In the end, Karl upheld the sanctity of his own individual creative actions, sanctioned by an inspired and unsullied universe that he saw as a Divine phenomenon worthy of veneration and as the handiwork of our Creator God.

Karl's sense of reverence for God's creations and his veneration of a Divine Creator found expression in his most significant work—the *Tree of Utah*. This eight-seven-foot high concrete structure was constructed at enormous personal expense by Karl and completed in 1986. It is situated in the desolate Great Western Desert in Utah. At the dedication ceremony of this unique structure, hundreds of people gathered to hear outgoing Utah Governor, Norm Bangerter, accept the *Tree* from its maker on behalf of the people of Utah. Karl was struck by the stark beauty of the Bonneville Salt Flats and was inspired by the arid splendor of the area. He had envisioned a sculpture that would pay tribute to "the God above the Universe" as expressed in Schiller's "Ode to Joy," the text of which is inscribed on a plaque at the base of the sculpture.

Notwithstanding the cultural conservatism of the state and the reticence of the local art community to come to terms with such an extraordinary manifestation of a single artist's vision and resourcefulness, the *Tree of Utah* has become a permanent feature on this region's cultural horizon. The only other artwork of these proportions to impinge upon the Utah landscape was Robert Smithson's *Spiral Jetty*. The poignant spiritual symbolism of the work was also lost on its potential viewership, who were denied physical access to the site and to interpretive material.

Karl was never corrupted by his negative experiences of governments and formal religion. He was always cognizant of a meta-reality that he could access through the world of myth and imagination. He was first introduced to the magic of fables at his father's knee. Later in life he would rediscover that same awe in the opera and in the literature that he loved. He never lost his capacity for wonder.

Little did the Iranian boy in a far-off land realize that it would be the pure colors and geometric motifs of the rugs, woven and hand dyed at his ancestral home, that would be the precedent for his assertive use of scintillating color and bold abstract forms. Nor did he imagine that his work would one day grace the walls of the world's finest galleries and art centers. As a result of his migration between the Old and New Worlds, he had achieved a unique synthesis of cosmopolitan influences. These influences ranged from his earliest childhood memories of the neoclassical paintings in his family's homes in Iran, to the seminal experience of studying under the influence of some of Europe's most significant masters of the modernist movement of his day.

Karl had become the lone avatar of his own unique vision. Although fully schooled in the sophisticated art of his day, he doggedly continued in his own way. Just like Odysseus of old, Karl was shrewd and wily, but also generous and noble spirited. Although he never married, he was eternally wed to his quest for an art of origin—to the search for an art that would give palpable form to his transcendent view of the world and to his Utopian ideal. He had learned to hold the things of his own unique origination dear since this would be all that would ultimately differentiate his art from that of others.

In 2004, at seventy years of age, Karl embarked on a significant new direction in his painting. His love-hate relationship with the world of technology led him to the Tech Museum of Innovation in San Jose, California, where he had been invited to mount an exhibition of paintings and sculptures. He was enthused and intrigued by the opportunity to mount an exhibition in a museum dedicated to man's use of technology and in a venue that celebrated the dramatic advances in the world of high tech and digital electronics. All his life he had pitted his art against the incursion of technology in the domain of human thought and action. Now he was being invited into the lair of the beast! The ancient Greeks had an aphorism that best described his newfound situation: *that which a man fears most will surely come to him!* Nevertheless, Karl accepted the invitation and mounted a successful exhibition in May 2005.

Although partially retrospective, Momen also included several new works that had an uncanny correspondence with the leitmotifs found in the world of digital technology. It was as if his alter ego, that part of his psyche that had always rejected the deterministic constraints of the world of technology, had found new life in celebrating the shapes and forms that had evolved within this modern industry.

In his painting *Cyber Superlative,* completed in 2003, he embraced the iconography of this new field with allusions to electronic components, such as printed

Cyber Superlative VI, 2003

circuit boards and electron paths, cast against a cosmic background of orbs and spheres held in a state of dynamic equilibrium. Art and science had found an unlikely alignment in this new work. One may well ask how these two conflicting paradigms could coexist? Both are ways in which we try to explain the world around us. Art and science make their advances in tandem—in response to the spirit of genius that inspires innovation. Theories in physics and mathematics are often described as "elegant" or even "beautiful" in response to their intrinsic formal or aesthetic qualities. On the other hand, we have also come to rely on images and metaphors to explain the more arcane principles of our rapidly advancing scientific theories. The marriage between art and science is as old as the pyramids and as immediate as the designer cases of our cellphones.

Then, as if in response to this strange attraction and in answer to a more radical questioning of his relationship with geometric abstraction, Karl's art took another profound turn. In a new series of paintings entitled Organic Suite, Karl confronted the issue of geometric abstraction through a new iconography. These new paintings were a departure from his main body of work. For the first time,

Karl had forsaken the use of hard geometric edges that defined his earlier compositions. Instead he started using softer, more organic profiles to his forms.

In his *Organic Suite* Momen used elegant tree-like limbs that have no geometric edges, as in his earlier works. These simple forms are timeless symbols of the natural world, rendered with the consummate assurance of decades of experience and with the ideas that suffuse this genre. These new works evince the universal processes of life and growth set within the traditional flat compositional space of his paintings. The inclusion of an orb that is more reminiscent of an organic form than a planetary sphere is evidence of a new appreciation for the elemental character of natural things. This development in Momen's style had come late in his life and was in direct response to his accumulated understanding of the nexus between the world of technology and the greater organic universe. This suite of unique works was shown at an exhibition at Galleri Cupido in Stockholm early in 2006. This exhibition marked a radical breakthrough for Momen. He had attained a new understanding of how his conceptual worldview could be expressed through the language of formalism in a postmodern world, and in so doing, he had aspired to the next plateau in his quest for the Utopian ideal that was part of his odyssey as an artist.

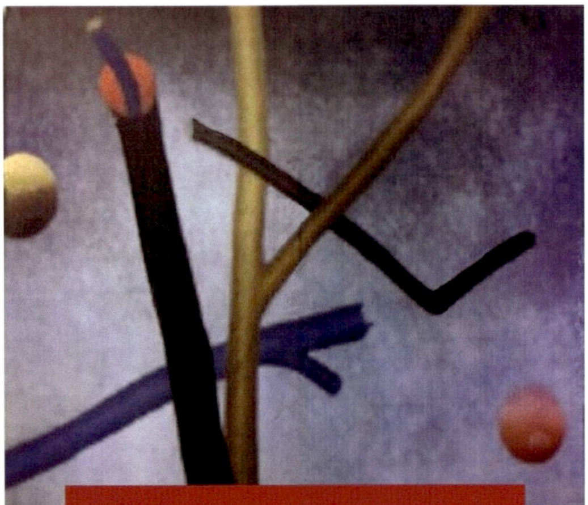

***Organic Suite*, 2004**

In the work *Life Form with Purple Planet,* completed in 2004, we see for the first time tubular organic limbs that have been flattened out against the picture plane in very shallow space. One of the forms escapes beyond the upper edge of the format as similar forms on either side reach upward as metaphors of Momen's characteristic Utopian striving toward the new, the unknown, and perhaps the unknowable. The inclusion of a subtly tinted sphere stabilizes and balances the construction of the image in an impeccably conceived composition. The sphere also acts as a counterpoise to the limbs rising simply and elegantly from the base of the painting. In similar works in this suite, these organic limbs have central cores that are reminiscent of fiber optic tubing —perhaps a reference to Momen's excursion into the world of high technology. The faint shadow cast by the central limb in this painting creates an interesting tension between the receding background of the image and the painted surface of the work, reminding us once again that we are engaged in an image evoked by paint on a flat surface.

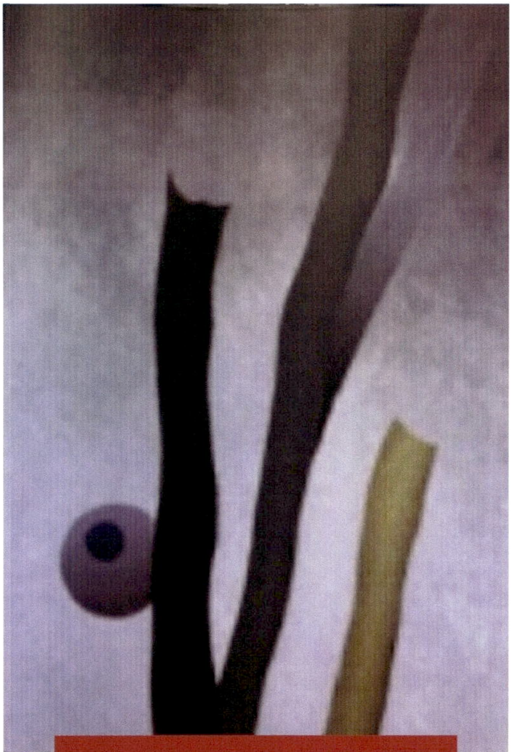

Life Form with Purple Planet, 2004

Another work simply titled *Organic Suite,* from the same series, is divided into two longitudinal panels in the form of a diptych. Here an array of treelike limbs are also rendered against a subtly modulated background that serves to project the central dark limb of the arrangement dramatically into the viewer's space as it looms forward, revealing its scarlet interior and a central core. The limbs are also subtly modeled as credible forms in space, unlike former elements that were often presented as flat geometric shapes. This remarkable development of style reflects a more mature understanding of the nature/technology dichotomy and speaks volumes about Momen's realization of corporeal structure within his vocabulary of abstract form.

Throughout his career, Momen had eschewed the many progressive art movements of his day and chosen instead to follow the impulse of his own Constructivist/Bauhaus vision. He has traveled the lonely path of his own personal destiny. Also, like Odysseus of old, he had been compelled to forsake his fellow travelers along the way. Many artists of his day had been passionately concerned with emulating and become part of new movements that were superficially enticing, gaining their popularity through self-promotion and the insatiable attention of news media that yearned for any aberration of the status quo. Some had fallen prey to the mesmerizing call of the sirens along their paths and had found themselves drawn onto the rocks of destruction. Others had prostituted their talents in order to benefit from the short-lived allure of seductive art movements that had little value other than the gloss and popular appeal of their novelty. Like Odysseus's crewmen, they had been lost, and "it was their own transgression that brought them to their doom, for in their folly they had devoured the oxen of the Sun-god."[17]

Epilogue

THE PERSISTENCE OF THE CONSTRUCTIVIST IDEAL

Karl Momen's worldview, and consequently the conceptual framework of his art, were formed by his alignment with one of the most radical and influential art movements in the history of modern art. Art historians loosely refer to the movement that played such a significant role in the formative years of his education, and continued to influence his art throughout his career, as Constructivism. This movement was originally comprised of four distinct groups: the Russian Constructivists and Suprematists, the Dutch De Stijl, and German Bauhaus groups, all of which shared the same broad conceptual goals.

Much of what we call "modern art" developed from a radically new way of looking at art and art-making that had its beginnings in the avant-garde art world of Eastern Europe during the early part of the twentieth century. This movement rejected the tenets of Romanticism, Impressionism, and even Post-Impressionism that had emerged at the time. Its proponents advocated radical new art forms that would have the capacity to speak on a universal level to all people. Attempts to give cohesion to the movement's manifestations at various times and in its various forms resulted in such titles as Constructivism, Constructionism, International Constructivism, Geometric Abstraction, Structuralism, and Constructive Realism. The genesis of the movement is attributed to the pioneering work of the Russian artist Vladimir Tatlin and his compatriots Naum Gabo (1890–1977), Antoine Pevsner (1884–1962), Kasimir Malevich, Aleksandr Rodchenko, and El Lissitzky during the early years of the twentieth century.

The cohesion of the movement in central Europe was dealt a blow when some of its chief exponents were forced to flee with the rise of the Nazi party in Germany. Many of the artists and designers who were central to the Constructivist movement were affiliated to the Bauhaus, Germany's most important and advanced art and design school. The school was forcibly closed by the Nazis in 1933, and the departure of Antoine Pevsner, Walter Gropius (1883–1969), Piet Mondrian (1872–1944), and Oskar Schlemmer (1888–1943) among others, effectively exported the principles of Constructivism to Paris, London, and the United States.

With the collapse of the USSR and the lifting of restrictions, new research has revealed the pervasive influence that Constructivism had on the art of the twentieth century in establishing the mindset of later art movements that we conveniently refer to today as "modernism." The publication of Soviet research in England during the 1980s and 90s by researchers Anatoli Strigalev, Selim O. Khan-Magomedov, Anatole Senkevitch, Jaroslav Andel, and other Russian scholars has contributed much to our understanding of the powerful ideas that permeated the short-lived avant-garde movement in Easter Europe at the beginning of the twentieth century.[18] English researchers Christina Lodder at the University of St. Andrews and Stephen Bann at the University of Kent have also contributed significant work in developing western scholarship in this area.[19]

Responding to the criticism that more recent art historians have leveled at the movement and its artists, Irving Sandler, noted American art critic and writer, explained the conceptual orientation of the artists of Karl Momen's generation who were inspired by the Constructivist vision:

"Constructive artists today are motivated by their psychic needs. Assumptions that their work is anti-personal are simplistic. But it is not self-expressive, at least when compared to Expressionist art. Nor is it emotive, but that does not make it unfeeling. A square can be as felt as a brushstroke. Constructive art today—as it did in the past—stands opposed to Expressionism and Romanticism, because it is often based on references external to itself. Indeed most constructive artists have often established connections to other fields of human knowledge. They yearn to root themselves in something larger than the subjective itself, something more serious perhaps. They desire to escape the condition that Donald Barthelme wrote about in his novel *Snow White*. 'There is not enough seriousness in what we do,' Kevin said. 'Everyone wanders around having his own individual perceptions. These, like balls of different colors and shapes and sizes, roll around on the green billiard table of consciousness . . .' "[20]

Constructivism differed radically from the traditional art forms that preceded it.

The movement was manifest in art works that were *built* or constructed, rather than cast or carved. Constructivists often used "hard edge" or geometric designs and never thought of their work as merely representational or pictorial. They rejected the conventional art of their day that tended to be painterly, narrative, and highly representational. They often relied on sheer technical virtuosity to render images and objects of great verisimilitude but were void of any real social relevance. Rather, the Constructivists worked to communicate their ideas about art and their hopes for a better society in a coherent manner through nonobjective art making. They developed a philosophy that would be found to be in harmony with the principles of the new Gestalt psychology that were just beginning to be articulated, and with the new formalism that English art critic Clive Bell had proposed, which aligned with his notion of "significant form."

The Realist Manifesto of August 5, 1920, that was signed by Naum Gabo and his brother Antoine Pevsner, confirmed that Constructivism was anti-aesthetic, anti-mimetic, anti-romantic, and anti-nostalgic. Ironically, it was against this foil of rigor and high-minded ambition that the essential humanity of these artists is revealed. George Rickey, a long-time scholar of Constructivist art concurs:

"With their slow evolution, their steadfastness, their independence coupled with self-effacement, one surprising quality persists—the irrepressible humanity of these supposedly lackluster artists."[21]

The manifesto gives valuable insights into the context within which these revolutionary ideas about art and art making were first manifest. It also provides an indication of the potency and radical nature of the new forms that were advocated by the Constructivists. These ideas would find a renewable life long after Stalin and Hitler thought they had eradicated the avant-garde, and they would reverberate throughout the art schools and galleries of the west. This was also the milieu within which Karl Momen formed his own artistic sensibilities during the 1950s and 60s—some while after the Constructivist philosophy had been decontextualized from its original sociopolitical roots.

The meaning of Constructivism lies beyond the mechanistic designs or the formalistic properties of its artworks. Constructivist works can best be appreciated through an understanding of their makers' epistemological perspectives. Of all the movements of the past one hundred years, Constructivism emerges as a singular example of high-minded artistic ambition and conceptual coherence that continues to influence the art of the modern and postmodern era. Constructivism initiated what could easily be considered the principle artistic accomplishment of the past one hundred years: non-representational art. Prior to the advent of Constructivism, purely abstract designs remained the province of decorative art.

Motivated by their social consciousness, Constructivists conceived of integrating art with architecture, engineering, industrial, and interior design, as well as typography—in the belief that art should serve people in utilitarian, everyday ways. Rather than an art movement, Constructivism is a philosophy that uses art forms to express its understanding of the essential nature of things. Mark Daniel Cohen, a New York-based art critic and sculptor writing for *Sculpture* magazine at the beginning of the twenty-first century, defined Constructivism as

"The deployment of geometric structures in purely abstract arrangements intended to reveal the hidden principles of organization inherent in the nature of space itself. In essence, there is a tradition of sculpture that is metaphysical in its objective that is turned toward the revelation of the basic structure of objective reality."[22]

The elusive nature of Constructivism as a movement can be attributed in part to the difficult task of defining a clear line of influence that extends from one leading artist to another due to their individuality and their independence of each other. But it is also due to the difficulty that postmodern art historians have had in coming to terms with the notion of an "objective reality." George Rickey explained the geometric abstraction of Constructivism as "a precise and logical ordering of thoughts about space arising from the human experience of it."[23] From this statement, we may infer that Rickey, and the Constructivists, see "human experience" as a universal phenomenon.

It is in the area of universalism that postmodern art critics have had the most difficulty with Constructivism. The founders of the Constructivist movement believed that their art revealed absolute and universal truths about human nature, society, and the elemental forces that govern the cosmos. They also believed that their art was a sign or indicator to a universal Utopian society in which collectivist and rational ideals would coexist in perfect harmony in the creations of perfect men and women. Although these social and spiritual dogmas have given postmodern art critics justifiable cause for skepticism, Irving Sandler again comes to the defense of the Constructivists:

"The pioneers of constructive art asked too much of their art on behalf of their visions. But this is no reason to turn our backs on their humanitarianism, on their sense of social responsibility, their concern with the social uses of art, their esteem of reason and order, and their optimistic belief in a better future."[24]

This kind of optimistic idealism runs counter to the tenor of a modern society that suffers in large part from loss of belief and seeks meaning in the interactions of phenomena that are often seen as arbitrary and hermeneutic—an epistemology that is remarkably similar to the dialectic materialism of a former age. According to Ada Louise Huxtable, the incorrigible skepticism of our age, our failings, are part of a much larger theme. She claims that our shortcoming can be attributed to

"... the failure of a moral vision and the breakdown of ideals of a society in transition. What we have lost is what sociologists and psychologists call our 'belief systems'—those commonly held convictions that guide our acts and aspirations . . . we believed devoutly in social justice, of the perfectibility of man and his world, in the good life for all. The Bauhaus taught that the machine would put beauty and utility within the reach of everyone. Le Corbusier's 'machine to live in' and 'radiant cities' would reform human habitation. We believed that the world could be housed and fed; that we could bring order to our cities; that misery and hunger are not eternal verities . . . We also believed that everyone had a right to beauty, that aesthetic values equaled moral values. What was useful was beautiful and good, and what was good was good for all of us . . . The arts, used properly, could bring both pleasure and practical benefits to society . . . this was the century that equated art, technology, and virtue and concluded that the better life, and the better world, were finally within our grasp."[25]

Constructive art reinforces our belief in the worth of reason and rational process, and that is one of its satisfactions. George Rickey contrasts the attributes of the Constructivist mindset with

"... those traditional qualities toward which [postmodern critics] are now strictly, sometimes belligerently, neutral. They don't care for taste, harmony, unity, composition, pleasure-giving, technical virtuosity, or connoisseurship."[26]

However, in spite of its detractors, Constructivism continues to inform fundamental concepts of art appreciation and art-making throughout the western world and particularly in the way that art is still taught in college art programs through courses in design and "foundation studies." The movement's influence is clearly evident in developments such as geometric abstraction, hard-edge painting, post-painterly abstraction, and systemic and modular art in the forms of minimalist art as well as in the preponderance of architectonic elements and production-based aesthetics that permeate the art of the modern era.

Constructivist influences are clearly evident in the work of post World War II era artists in Britain, such as Victor Passmore, Anthony Caro, Robert Adams, and Bridget Riley. During the same period in America, Constructivist principles found expression in the work of Al Held, Frank Stella, Ellsworth Kelly, Alexander Calder, Donald Judd, Sol LeWitt, Dorothea Rockburn, and Joaquin Torres-Garcia to name but a few. At the beginning of the twenty-first century, the Constructivist impulse continues in the work of a host of artists as diverse as Jesus Da Silva and Graham Porter. Perhaps the most interesting contemporary developments can be seen in the field of architecture where the aesthetics of French philosopher Jaques Derida has revealed the postmodern face of Constructivism in the architectural designs of Daniel Libeskind and Zaha Hadid.

The scholarship of the twenty-first century consistently reinforces the extent to which the underlying philosophy of classical Constructivism was instrumental in establishing the nonobjective mindset that continues with us into the twenty-first century. Works of a Constructivist character are still being produced and exhibited all over the globe. It is also the impulse that most significantly informed the worldview and consequently the artistic sensibilities of Karl Momen. Although Constructivist art has been confronted at various stages of its development by opposing trends and antithetical movements, a glance at the work of artists over recent decades shows how frequently Constructivist thought emerges. However, we should not approach new Constructivist art with preconceived notions of what we think such art should signify in terms of its historical manifestations, but rather from our present day experience of it.

KARL MOMEN AT CUPIDO

Appendix

ENCOUNTERS WITH ACTORS, ARTISTS, AND CELEBRITIES

Karl's many travels often resulted in chance encounters with world-famous celebrities. In 1960, Karl was a student in Stuttgart when on one particular occasion he decided to have lunch downtown on his own at the Ketterer restaurant. Seated at the restaurant, he soon noticed a uniformed American G.I. at an adjacent table. The American noticed that they were both dining on their own, so he moved over to join Karl. It soon became apparent to Karl that he somehow "knew" this stranger. He realized that he was sitting across the table from Elvis Presley.

Presley had been drafted into the U.S. army at this time and was stationed in Stuttgart. As fate would have it, their paths had crossed. Karl could speak very little English at the time. However, Presley was extremely amiable and, in his broken German, asked Karl if he liked his music.

Karl's reply was abrupt, "No!"

Presley took this response in good humor, and after they shook hands, they continued their conversation about less contentious matters. The American performer must have appreciated Karl's forthright candor since he had several bottles of whiskey and a few cartons of cigarettes delivered to Karl's apartment later that day.

Fifty years later, on a warm but rainy day in June 2010, Karl was at his winter home in West Palm Beach, Florida, when he had a profound reversal of opinion about Elvis Presley's music. He had spent the day in the city, shopping for a new computer, and returned home in the evening. He looked through his mail and turned on the TV to watch the seven o'clock German news on the ZDF channel. After ten minutes, he switched to the Mezzo music channel, and finding nothing of interest, began surfing the movie channels. On TCM he caught a glimpse of Elvis Presley and first thought it was a rerun of a fifties movie; however, he then saw that Presley was wearing a show costume. There were several Hollywood celebrities present: Cary Grant, Sammy Davis Jr., and George Hamilton, among others. He continued watching and soon found that the program was a live broadcast of an evening concert held in Las Vegas. He had never seen Elvis performing live and had seen only one of his films when he was cast opposite the late Julia Probes, the ballroom dancer. After noticing how relaxed Presley was, he realized how gently he performed and how appreciative he was of his audience. This was contrary to the stereotypical image of Presley as a loud rock-and-roll singer. For the first time, Karl actually enjoyed listening to his performance. These songs were totally unknown to Karl in the fifties and sixties. Here Karl found something new that he liked. After two of his more romantic songs, Presley walked from left to right on the stage and bowed to the audience. He smiled sincerely and allowed girls and even elderly ladies to reach out to him. After the second number, he allowed at least fifty women to kiss him—many crying with happiness.

Karl remembered Presley's smile and his politeness when he told Presley to his face that he did not like his music. At that time, Karl was but a poor and arrogant architecture student taking out his frustrations on a world-famous star. He could now see how rude and insensitive it had been of him to share a table with Presley and to tell him that he did not like his music. How surprised he was when Presley took Karl's hand as they parted and told him, "You are an honest man!"

Now, years later, as Karl watched Presley's performance, he realized how generous he was to his audience, and Karl felt ashamed. In that moment, he offered a silent prayer that God would bless Presley's soul and remember him for the gentle and generous King that he was.

By the end of 1964, when Karl was working for himself, after being awarded several architectural commissions, his status changed from being an employee to being the owner of his own business. He was also his own secretary, engineer, and draftsman. He found that he could spend more quality time with his clients than other large consulting companies were able to spend with their clients. It now became necessary for him to socialize and entertain his clients. He would need to invite his clients to lunches at expensive restaurants or to dinners at out-of-town restaurants with live music and entertainment. Karl found that Berns Restaurant and Salon fit the bill admirably as one of Stockholm's most prestigious restaurants. The building's art nouveau architecture and interior design leave a lasting impression with its

APPENDIX

large mirrors, chandeliers, upholstery, and magnificent wooden décor. The restaurant opened in 1864 and soon became famous for its world-class performers and cabaret artists.

Another restaurant that Karl frequented with his guests was the Röda Rummet Bar and Restaurant on Barnhusgatan. It was a common watering hole for the cultural elite, with regulars such as August Strindberg, the Swedish playwright; painter Verner von Heidenstam, the Swedish Nobel Prize laureate in literature; and Carl Larsson, the famous painter and interior designer. Lenin was also among the regulars from 1906 to 1907 when he fled Russia to Stockholm. Here he met with the leaders of the Swedish Social Democratic party.

Berns Restaurant was the most well-known cabaret venue in Stockholm and had become particularly popular after the end of WWII with performances by some of the most famous international celebrities of the day, including Maurice Chevalier, Josephine Baker, Marlene Dietrich, Frank Sinatra, Dean Martin, and Sammy Davis Jr. Pütsep International traditionally held its fall dinner for its entire staff at the restaurant after the summer vacation.

After a few months of membership at the exclusive Gamlingen Key Club, Sten Holmquist, the owner, introduced Karl to several of these personalities, including Eartha Kitt and Shirley Bassey. With Karl's annual club membership came weekly classical and jazz concert tickets. These tickets were often difficult to get, and he was privileged to be favored in this manner. Jazz had become increasingly popular among the Scandinavians and the British. Karl thought they were the most jazz-obsessed nations in Europe at the time! After his concert attendances, Karl would retire to Gamlingen in hope of seeing some of the jazz artists who had performed that evening. By his own admission, he had become a music-addicted architect!

One Saturday evening, after a Duke Ellington concert, Karl invited his friend Bozorgnia to accompany him to Gamlingen in the hope of meeting the Duke. To their mutual satisfaction, Holmqvist wasted no time in introducing both men to Ellington who had indeed arrived at the club. Soon they were seated at his table along with Jony Hodges, his main saxophonist. After ordering drinks, Bozorgnia mentioned that it was Iran's national holiday the following day and he extended an invitation to Ellington to join in the celebration at the embassy. Ellington graciously accepted, and the following evening, Bozorgnia and Karl picked up Ellington in a chauffeur-driven embassy limousine and accompanied him to the Iranian Embassy where the ambassador welcomed them. Various other ambassadors and Swedish ministerial officials were present, and it was an enjoyable evening.

After this event, Karl became a regular at Gamlingen's jazz receptions. He particularly enjoyed listening to Nina

Simone, who frequently performed at the club until Sten Holmquist opened a bigger club on Grevturegatan a quarter-mile from Stureplan. The new club had a bigger dance floor and orchestra. The club also sported a roulette wheel and blackjack tables. It was situated in the most fashionable part of Stockholm, with many fine hotels in the vicinity. Karl found the new club convenient since it was not only within walking distance of his apartment and office, but it was also conveniently situated to the Royal Opera House, Concert Hall, Royal Dramatic Theater, and the top restaurants and fashion boutiques in the city. Holmquist always maintained a large table at-the-ready at his club to greet, wine, and dine the many celebrities who frequented his establishment, and Karl had the opportunity to meet many of these interesting personalities.

It was at one of Karl's lunches with Chris Folker at Berns Restaurant that he found himself in the company of Chris Seaton, another architect he had previously met at his colleague Tanaka's home. When the conversation turned to Folker's technical problems of accommodating the orchestra, as well as performers and patrons on the dance floor, Karl mentioned that he had previously designed a moving dance floor elevator at another venue. Chris looked at Karl in amazement and exclaimed,

"That is perfect!"

During the following week, Karl attended opera and concert performances with his friends. They soon met in the cellar underneath Berns restaurant where Chris showed Karl the scope of the project, and the two architects began to earnestly design the new elevator stage with its equipment. They worked all summer, and the new stage was ready at the beginning of September. Evening performances began with performers on the raised stage that could rise four feet above floor level, and then when the stage was lowered, it became level with the floor so dancing could proceed to the appreciative applause of the guests.

Early in October, a week before the grand opening, Folker informed Karl and Chris Seaton that Marlene Dietrich had expressed a desire to inspect the new stage and that they should be on hand for her visit. Dressed in their best English tweeds for the occasion, Karl and Seaton met Dietrich and enthusiastically showed her the workings of the new stage. She even rode the stage up and down to test its operation. She expressed her pleasure and appreciation to both men for their inventiveness. Dietrich would become a regular performer at the club until the end of her career. When she was satisfied with her inspection, Folker invited the party to enjoy a leisurely lunch at his Chinese restaurant.

During the two-hour lunch, Karl engaged Dietrich in conversation in German—her home language. The actress was intrigued to hear that in 1954, as a young man in Mashhad, Karl had painted a billboard advertising her film "Golden

Earrings" in which she starred with Ray Millard. Later, when Karl conducted Dietrich to the lobby of her hotel adjacent to the restaurant, she was even more impressed to learn that Karl had worked with her fellow countryman Max Ernst and had contributed significantly to the architectural design of Helga Heinkel's new mansion in Kilesberg when he was a student of Herman Reise in Stuttgart. Karl considered it an honor to be photographed in Dietrich's company as the many celebrity news photographers thronged around them.

In mid-1964, Chris Folker became managing director of the Angeles Hotel, a new and prestigious six-hundred-room establishment on Humlegarden opposite the Royal Library. Karl began referring his new Middle Eastern clients to Folker with the result that the Angeles Hotel became the preferred destination for Iranians and for visitors from the Emirates of the Persian Gulf. Karl became a member of two of the top "key" clubs in the city on the recommendation of the Iranian cultural Attaché who Karl knew as a childhood neighbor. It was the same diplomat who had introduced Karl to Sten Holmquist, the owner of the Gamlingen and Bolagte jazz club.

During this period, Karl established friendships with several well-known actors. Among these was Lars Amble, an actor, director, and producer at the Royal Dramatic Theater. Amble also owned and directed the Maxim Comedy Theater in Stockholm. He and his wife, Gunborg, lived in an apartment adjacent to Humlegården, near the Royal Library, and close to Karl's home. Often, on a summer's evening as Karl was making his way home, he would join the couple at the Storehov Bar for a glass of wine. Amble became Karl's close friend and respected confidant from 1965 to 2015.

On one occasion, Amble mentioned to Karl that he was going to be very busy, because Jerry Lewis was going to be in town to make a new movie. The film was to be called *The Day the Clown Cried.* Jerry Lewis directed and starred in this 1972 movie that was never released. In the movie, a circus clown is imprisoned by the Nazis and goes with Jewish children to their deaths in a concentration camp. Lars, who was blond, six feet two, and Arian looking, was going to play the SS commander of the death camp. Karl was introduced to Jerry Lewis at Amble's home, and Lewis visited Karl at his home in Stockholm on several occasions while he was working on the movie. Karl was impressed with his cultural knowledge and the depth of his intellectual inquiry. Lewis was impressed with Karl's book collection and his fifteenth-century Persian miniatures. Lewis was particularly interested in Iranian history and the ancient Iranian tradition of reciting Persian poetry. Karl was amazed that Lewis could recite many verses by Omar Khayyam from memory. Lewis was also taken with Karl's Shakespeare theater record collection.

Lewis invited Karl onto the set of the movie several times to see how the production was progressing. Karl thought that this would be one of Lewis's best movies. Unfortunately, Lewis decided not to release the movie.

Karl often frequented antique stores while he worked in Stockholm. Herbert Geisenburger owned the Orima Antique Store and became a firm friend of Karl. Geisenburger specialized in Russian icons, a particular interest of Karl's. They would often have lunch at the popular Beckhasten restaurant with two of Geisenburger's friends, George Rauch and Martin Weil. Rauch was also an antique dealer, and Weil was a producer of fine woven fabrics. Karl called them the "three musketeers" since all three had immigrated to Sweden—from Berlin, Hamburg, and Vienna respectively—during the 1930s. Karl enjoyed listening to three different German dialects on these occasions. Football was the most frequent topic of conversation at these impromptu meetings, and they would have endless discussions about which European city they thought was the best for watching the game.

Karl had bumped into Erland Josephson (1923–2012), the famous Swedish actor and author, at Orima Antique Store a few times, and the men soon discovered that they shared a common interest in Russian icons. But it wasn't until Karl met Josephson at one of the three musketeers' lunches that Karl got to know him personally. Josephson would write the introduction for his Shakespeare exhibition catalog.

As a teenager, Karl had become addicted to movies when he worked part time as a projectionist. However, there were no concert halls in his hometown of Mashhad at the time. He became equally addicted to concerts, operas, and the theater after he attended his first concert at the Liederhalle Concert Hall in Stuttgart in 1958. Attendance at these weekly performances became his weekly entertainment on Sundays and Wednesdays after work. Karl had a weekly subscription to the opera house until 1979 when he moved to San Francisco. By the mid-1960s, Karl had become an international globetrotter. He would often embark on long trips to the US by TWA, and later, when American Airlines took over, he became a member of the "Admiral's Club." American Airlines would later sponsor his *Homage to Shakespeare and Wagner* book, as well as his poster for the grand reopening of the San Francisco Opera House after an earthquake retrofit in 1999.

During long hours of international air travel, Karl had occasion to meet numerous celebrities, which included actors, directors, politicians, and businessmen. Karl was always an affable first-class traveler. He would introduce himself to his seating companions, wishing them a pleasant flight. He would then allow his neighbor to take the initiative. Most conversations began with their first onboard drink and a friendly toast of "Cheers!"

He once received some invaluable advice from a gentleman he met at breakfast in Selfridge's hotel in London. While Karl was reading the morning paper, he noticed a steward approach a couple at a neighboring table. The steward courteously informed the woman, "There is a phone call for you at the front desk, madam," whereupon the lady rose and left the table. She returned five minutes later, whispered in her husband's ear, gave him a polite kiss, and walked out of the breakfast room. The gentleman turned his head toward Karl's table and asked,

"Are you married?"

"Unfortunately, not!" replied Karl.

Then, with a knowing smile, the now deserted husband replied, "You should be grateful for that!"

The man then mentioned that it had taken him a lot of time and effort to obtain two tickets for a Royal Albert Theatre performance of *The Constant Wife* by Somerset Maugham and showed Karl the two tickets.

"I will give one to my secretary and you can have the other. The play features Ingrid Berman and Eric Porter if you are interested."

Karl had to restrain himself from shouting aloud in sheer excitement. "Of course! I am Swedish!" he exclaimed and hurriedly took out his wallet from his jacket.

The man smiled and mentioned that he was glad that the ticket would go to one who would appreciate it. He rose to go to his room and returned with the program and the ticket in an envelope. He asked the waiter to bring him coffee, and when Karl offered to pay for the ticket the man replied,

"Please take the ticket, but promise me that you will pretend that you don't know anything about our meeting when you sit beside one of the most beautiful women in London!"

After breakfast, Karl asked the clerk at the hotel reception desk if there had been a review of *The Constant Wife* at the Royal Albert Theater. The clerk handed him a copy of the *Guardian* newspaper, and Karl read the glowing review of Ingrid Berman's performance. That afternoon, he bought a bouquet of flowers from the hotel florist and penned a note to Ms. Bergman in Swedish introducing himself as a Swedish architect who, as a teenager, had painted a billboard of Berman's movie for the Ferdowsi Theater in Mashhad in 1948. When Karl arrived at the theater, he was immediately conducted to his designated seat in the exclusive section of the theater. Karl reflected that the gentleman who had given him the ticket must have been of high social status and well known to the theater staff. At the first intermission, an attendant approached Karl, asked him to wait a few minutes, and then conducted him to a special meeting with Ms. Berman! She had a few well-wishers around her, but when she saw Karl, she greeted him warmly. She asked if he was enjoying the performance. She thanked him for the beautiful flowers and said that an architect and an artist must have selected them. Then, speaking Swedish, she asked Karl how long he had been in Sweden and if he liked working there. He replied that he missed Stockholm in the springtime.

Bergman was very inquiring of Karl and asked at which hotel he was staying. When she asked if Karl had a photograph of the movie billboard he had painted for her film, he replied that unfortunately he did not. She said she would have loved to see it with Persian lettering. Before taking her leave for the next performance, she invited Karl to lunch at the Ritz Carlton Hotel the following afternoon. She asked Karl if he could bring a photograph of the last hospital he had designed. The following day as they were conducted to their table, Bergman introduced Karl to the director of the hotel restaurant. Karl showed her photographs of his hospital design and his paintings. Bergman was interested to know about the goings on in Iran and about the Shah. She ordered a simple meal with Evian water. Afterward, Karl conducted her to her limousine, where her driver opened the door and Karl took his leave of her. She thanked Karl profusely for showing her pictures of his hospitals and art works. She wished Karl good luck, and they shook hands before the actress stepped into the vehicle.

In the fall of 1977, while waiting in the Rome airport lounge for a late flight back to Stockholm, Karl found himself seated at the side of Helena Döse, a well-known Swedish soprano in the Vienna Opera. She was married to an Austrian musician. Karl began a conversation by complimenting her on her role as second dame at the Don Giovani Opera the previous year in Stockholm. She blushed and thanked him for the compliment. Karl told her that he had a reserved seat at the opera every Thursday night for several years and that he had seen and heard her perform in various roles over the years. By way of introduction, he explained to Döse that he was an architect working on a project in the Persian Gulf and that he was a frequent flier in the Middle East. After a two-hour wait, their boarding was finally announced, and they made their way toward the aircraft. Karl asked if Döse would honor him by having lunch with him at the Opera Källare Restaurant in Stockholm the following day. She accepted the invitation and said if Karl did not mind, she would bring a friend with her. They agreed to meet at one o'clock when the restaurant was not so crowded.

Karl was waiting at the restaurant at the appointed time when Döse arrived with a lady friend that Karl recognized as a frequent opera attender. He guided the ladies to a table, and they ordered lunch and drinks. In their conversation, Döse

APPENDIX

mentioned she would be back in September to sing Eva in *Die Magister Singer von Nuremberg*, and then she announced that Karl and their guest would each be receiving an opera ticket as her guests. After a long lunch with stimulating conversation, Karl walked Döse to the stage entrance where they took leave of each other.

A few months later in October, there was a flurry of publicity about the forthcoming production of *Die Magister Singer von Nuremberg*. Just a few days before the grand opening, Döse called Karl to tell him that she had two tickets for the grand opening for him. Karl picked up the tickets and asked his accountant, retired Captain Rungren, to join him at the premier event. He was seated in the middle of the second row of the theater. It was one of the best Wagner productions, directed by Götz Friedrich, that Karl had ever attended. Helena Döse delivered an excellent performance, and Eric Seden, who sang the part of Beckmesser in his rich baritone voice, gave a superb performance. The stage set was one of the best that Karl had ever seen of this play. After the last encore, Helena held a large bouquet of yellow roses in her arm with the congratulatory card that Karl had included. This moment was captured in the official video that recorded this famous performance. The next day Helena called Karl to thank him for the wonderful flowers. Karl and Helena met several more times thereafter.

There were few direct flights between Stockholm and San Francisco, so Karl would take the opportunity to make a stop in New York where he would stay a few days. During this time, he would visit museums during the day and attend concerts, the theater, or operas in the evenings.

On Thanksgiving night in 1979, Karl landed by TWA at JFK Airport and took a taxi to the Hotel Algonquin near Times Square. This was smaller and not a well-known hotel where artists and performers often chose to stay. The hotel had arranged a complementary dinner for all guests for the occasion that night. Coming down from his room to the dinner, Karl met Peter Ustinov in the elevator. Karl recognized him immediately and introduced himself exclaiming, "Sir, you have not changed much since I painted you in 1957!"

Ustinov asked almost spontaneously, "Could I have a copy of that?"

Karl explained that it was painted for a billboard for a movie in Mashhad, Iran. Ustinov looked at Karl in disbelief.

"You must be joking!" he said as the elevator reached their floor. Karl explained that he was only thirteen years old when he painted the picture and that he was now a Swedish architect.

"You must tell me all about it!" Ustinov said enthusiastically.

At the table, Karl told him about the portrait of Stalin that he had painted for the Vox Cultural Center in Mashhad after the Red Army had occupied Iran during WW II. When Karl mentioned Herand Mangasarian, the owner of the movie theater in Mashhad, Ustinov exclaimed in amazement, "I met Mr. Herand Mangasarian in London during a London premier!"

Karl proceeded to show him pictures of his paintings for *The Hunchback of Notre Dame* with Gina Lollobrigida in a red blouse, and his oil painting of Vatsnetsov's *Aljonuska and Ivanuska.*

After dinner, the men shook hands and Ustinov wished Karl a happy Thanksgiving. He mentioned that he'd had a delightful dinner with Karl and that it brought back many delightful memories for him. During the dinner, Ustinov gave Karl some preview information of his play on Beethoven's Tenth Symphony. Some days later, after reading the review in the *New York Times*, Karl sent Ustinov a congratulatory note and a copy of his 1978 Lützow Plats exhibition catalog.

On a spring day in 1985, while managing the construction of the *Tree of Utah*, Karl received a telephone call in his hotel room from Neil Headlock, a local artist who had become a personal friend. Hadlock owned Wasatch Bronze, a foundry in Lehi, where Karl had many of his sculptures cast. He asked if he could meet Karl for lunch. They agreed to meet at Herb's Hamburger where one could get the best burgers in Salt Lake City. Karl often had lunch there with his artist friends Neil Hadlock, Dennis Smith, and Gary Smith—Karl called them the "three musketeers." Their homes and studios were beside each other in Alpine, Utah, about twenty miles west of Salt Lake City, in a secluded community on a river with their own pond. An elderly Frank Riggs also joined them on occasion. Karl had gotten to know these gentlemen over the previous three years that he had lived in Salt Lake City. They also knew his contractor Don Reimann and his sons. Karl knew that like most people in the western states, they preferred beef to alternative foods.

Neil met Karl at Herb's, and over lunch he mentioned, "As you know, I'm helping Robert Redford with his new Sundance Cultural Center, so if you're interested, we can go to Sundance after we've visited the foundry to see how your Valhalla sculpture is progressing. I could introduce you to Bob and his architect."

Karl agreed. They traveled to the foundry, and after checking on the half-finished cast, they drove on to Sundance, a twenty-minute drive. When they reached the resort, they saw that there was still a lot of snow on the surrounding ski slopes. Neil pulled in next to one of the unfinished buildings and turned off the car. He said that he would usually go up to Redford's home but that he had arranged to meet him at that particular building. A young man at the entrance told Neil that Redford was on his way. Karl viewed the incomplete building while Neil spoke with the young man.

Redford arrived fifteen minutes later with a man who was obviously an architect since he had a roll of drawings under his arm. Redford said to Karl, "So you must be the sculptor?"

Karl replied, "Yes. Hello," and shook Redford's hand.

Neil walked over to introduce the two, but Redford answered that they had already met. "Perhaps you would like to look over my architect's plans?"

Karl immediately responded, "I am a hospital architect and I'm afraid I would not be much help."

Speaking to his architect, Redford said, "Karl is an architect, so perhaps you could show him what you've been doing?"

The architect agreed that his work was different from hospital design. Redford laughed and said, "We actors have no such limitations."

After an hour of looking around, Neil drove Karl back to Salt Lake City. Later in September, Neil Hadlock called Karl to tell him that he had an invitation for them to attend the Sundance Art Festival on Saturday, September 28, 1985. Karl accepted, and they arrived in the afternoon on the appointed day. They had missed the opening ceremony but were in time to see a short modern dance performance. Over fifty artists' booths were set up on a rather soggy field. Paintings were displayed on easels out in the open. There were also numerous sculptures on pedestals and wooden boxes.

As Karl walked around, he found Gary Smith with his colorful new paintings. Neil Hadlock also displayed some of his sculptures. Governor Norman Bangerter was there with his wife. Karl noticed Carol Nixon, the director of the Utah Arts Council, Carol Makita, anchor for KSL TV, Elaine Jarvik, the journalist for the *Deseret News*, and his friend Professor Mattis and his wife, Naomi. Numerous other journalists, officials, and artists were milling around. It seemed he already knew many of the people in the crowd. While strolling around, he bumped into Dennis Smith.

"Have you said 'hello' to Robert Redford?" Dennis asked. Karl replied that they had met briefly, so he walked Karl over to where Redford was standing surrounded by a group of actors. Karl recognized Paul Newman, George Hamilton, Dennis Weaver, Sydney Polack, Stefanie Powers, and one actor he knew personally as Cameron Mitchell. Karl had met him a few times at Frank Harris's home in Los Olivos near Santa Barbara in California. Karl shook hands with Redford and Cameron Mitchel. Dennis asked Redford if he had ever met Karl before.

"Yes, I've met Karl, and he's going to be Utah's Christo!" Redford turned to greet

Governor Bangerter. Sydney Polack, who had been talking to Paul Newman, looked across at Karl and asked,

"Are you related to Picasso?" Everyone within earshot turned to look in Karl's direction. Newman turned to Sydney and said, "You should do a Picasso with him. He's Picasso in person!" Karl was somehow not embarrassed, and he wasn't pleased with the attention either.

With a smile on his face, Karl replied, "My art is enough for me, and besides, I cannot act!"

Cameron Mitchell laughed out loud and said, "Don't be worried Karl. Sydney can make any monkey play a genius." He immediately gave Karl a hug. "I hope you don't take it personally?"

Then they all burst out laughing. Karl knew Cameron Mitchell because of his commissioning Cameron to photograph the construction progress on the *Tree of Utah.*

Over the laughter Karl said, "Fortunately, I am neither a monkey nor an actor. Hollywood is already overcrowded with the former."

Newman, who had also been laughing, came over to Karl and shook his hand.

"Karl, you are very quick! You should write sketches for TV."

Karl told Newman that he had seen his *Long Hot Summer, Cat on Hot Tin Roof,* and *Rocky Graziano* dozens of times and hoped to see them many more times. Karl invited him to come to the dedication of the *Tree of Utah,* and the assembled group continued their good-humored banter late into the night.

ENDNOTES

1 Tom Holert. *Political Whirlpools and Deserts: Michelangelo Antonioni, Robert Smithson and Michael Snow*, 1982.

2 Author's interview with Karl Momen, 2006.

3 Interview with the artist September 2010.

4 Ibid.

5 Johansson, Stig, essay in Momen. *Exhibition Catalogue*, published by Marisa del Re Gallery, New York, 1991.

6 Interview with Karl Momen at his studio in Sausalito, CA. August 15, 2000.

7 Ibid.

8 Ibid.

9 Karl Momen, *Homage to William Shakespeare and Richard Wagner*, San Francisco, CA: Homage to the Classics Foundation, 1998.

10 Ibid., 25.

11 Karl Momen, *Homage to William Shakespeare and Richard Wagner*. San Francisco, California: Homage to the Classics Foundation, 1998, 7.

12 Ibid., 29.

13 *Of Innovation*, Momen catalog, 2005, 6.

14 Homer, *The Odyssey: Revised Prose Translation*, D.C.H. Rieu (translator). London: Penguin Books, 1991, 5.

15 James Mason, *Homage to Shakespeare and Richard Wagner*, San Francisco, California: Homage to the Classics Foundation, 1998, 7.

16 Ibid.

17 Homer, *The Odyssey: Revised Prose Translation*, D.C.H. Rieu (translator). London: Penguin Books, 1991, 5.

18 See articles by these writers in Richard Andrews ed., *Art into Life: Russian Constructionism 1914–1932*. New York: Rizzoli International Press, 1990.

19 See Lodder, Christina, *Russian Constructivism*. New Haven Connecticut: Yale University Press, 1983, and Stephen Bann ed., *The Tradition of Constructionism*. New York: Viking Press, 1974.

ENDNOTES

20 Barthelme, Donald, Snow White. New York: Athenaeum, 1977, 29. Quoted by Irving Sandler in *Concepts in Construction: 1910–1980*. Exhibition catalog of traveling exhibition organized by Independent Curators Incorporated, New York, 1982, 20.

21 Rickey, George, *Constructivism: Origins and Evolution*. New York: George Braziller, 1995, x.

22 Cohen, Mark Daniel, *Constructivism: The Penetration of Nature's Structure* Sculpture (Jan/Feb. 2000), 33.

23 Rickey, George, *Constructivism: Origins and Evolution*. New York: George Braziller, 1995, x.

24 Sandler, Irving, *Concepts in Construction: 1910-1980*. Exhibition catalog of traveling exhibition organized by Independent Curators Incorporated, New York, 1982, 18.

25 Huxtable, Louise, *Is Modern Architecture Dead?* in *The New Review of Books*, July 16, 1981, 17–18, quoted by Irving Sandler in *Concepts in Construction: 1910–1980*. Exhibition catalog of traveling exhibition organized by Independent Curators Incorporated, New York, 1982, 18.

26 Rickey, George, *Constructivism: Origins and Evolution*. New York: George Braziller, 1995, x.

INDEX

INDEX

INDEX

ABOUT THE AUTHOR

Herman du Toit was awarded postgraduate degrees in art history, studio sculpture, and sociology of education from the former University of Natal, in South Africa, where he served as the director of the School of Fine Art at the Durban University of Technology. After immigrating to the United States, he was awarded a J. Paul Getty Fellowship for his PhD study at Brigham Young University of art museum interpretive practices at some of America's leading art museums. He served as head of audience education and development at the Brigham Young University Museum of Art before establishing his own curatorial consultancy.

He is the author of numerous books and articles on the visual arts and serves as the executive director of several not-for-profit foundations. In his spare time, he likes to produce fine art prints in his photogravure studio in Provo, Utah. His prints, drawings, and sculptures are held in private collections in South Africa, England, and the United States. He and his wife Sandy are the parents of four married children and have sixteen grandchildren.